Voice and Eye in Faulkner's Fiction

HUGH M. RUPPERSBURG

Voice and Eye in Faulkner's Fiction

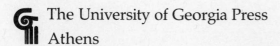 The University of Georgia Press
Athens

Copyright © 1983 by the University of Georgia Press
Athens, Georgia 30602

All rights reserved

Set in 10 on 12 Palatino
Printed in the United States of America

Library of Congress Cataloging in Publication Data

Ruppersburg, Hugh M.
Voice and eye in Faulkner's fiction.

Bibliography: p.
Includes index.
1. Faulkner, William, 1897–1962—Criticism and
interpretation. 2. Faulkner, William, 1897–1962—
Style.
I. Title.
PS3511.A86Z9652   813'.52   82-7092
ISBN 0-8203-0627-4   AACR2

For P.S.R.

In most books, the *I*, or first person, is omitted; in this it will be retained; that, in respect to egotism, is the main difference. We commonly do not remember that it is, after all, always the first person that is speaking. I should not talk so much about myself if there were anybody else whom I knew as well.

—Henry David Thoreau to his readers in *Walden*.

A Poet is the most unpoetical of anything in existence . . . he has no Identity.

—John Keats to his brothers.

I didn't say it. . . . The character said it.

—William Faulkner to Meta Carpenter.

Contents

Acknowledgments

I would like to acknowledge a number of people who were of assistance during the preparation of this study. I am especially indebted to André Bleikasten, University of Strasbourg, France, for the suggestions, advice, and criticism which helped shape and hone my methods. James Colvert, Carl Ficken, Edward Krickel, Warren Leamon, John MacNicholas, James B. Meriwether, Joel Myerson, Noel Polk, and Robert H. West read early drafts of various chapters and made many useful comments which found their way in one form or another into this book. Professor Meriwether read an entire early draft and made numerous valuable suggestions. Charles East, of the University of Georgia Press, gave advice and encouragement from the moment I offered him the manuscript. The University of Georgia Department of English provided me with typists, xeroxing, and a summer research grant. Gratitude also goes to my research assistants, Susan McLain and John Davis, to Lynn Whittaker for her thorough proofreading, and for various favors to A. T. Ferguson, Cleo Hudson, Robert Ballentine, Christoff Hudson, George B. Martin, Ken Attaway, Roy Brady, Max Childers, Butch and Kay Bydalek, Charles and Sue Smith, Renee and Tom Hudson, Margaret Caruthers Ruppersburg, Hugh Ruppersburg, Gussie Caruthers, Michael Ruppersburg, Garland Watkins, and the University of Georgia Libraries.

Finally, I wish to express my deepest gratitude to Patricia Smith Ruppersburg, my wife. Despite pregnancy, the early months of motherhood, and the demands of her own business, she provided moral, emotional, and financial support; criticized, offered suggestions, proofread, and did far more than her share of parenting so that I might bring this work to a finish.

H.M.R.

Voice and Eye in Faulkner's Fiction

Introduction

William Faulkner's avowal that he wanted "to be, as a private individual, abolished and voided from history, leaving it markless, no refuse save the printed books" reflected a lifelong compulsion for anonymity which extended from his personal life into his fiction. Observing a doctrine of authorial impersonality, Faulkner effaced himself completely from his fiction, stripping from his novels and stories all evidence of their author's identity.[1] He typically answered questions about his work in a way which suggested that he regarded the characters he had created and the lives he had chronicled as totally separate from himself. Time after time, no matter how deft or persistent the questioner, he evaded discussing what he meant to do in his books, what he was trying to say. Though he was frequently quite willing to discuss politics, southern history, and the literature of other writers, rarely did he associate his personal opinions with the meaning of his novels.

As a writer and artist, Faulkner established with his fiction the kind of relationship which a painter enjoys with the finished canvas. The nature of the painter's medium prevents him from "speaking" directly to his audience. The painting itself—its totality as a finished work of art—must "speak" for him, manifesting his view of the world through visual imagery independent of its creator. Faulkner never spoke *in* his fiction. He spoke *through* it. A similar analogy applies to the dramatist, who creates an imitation of life, an artistic illusion which exists independently on the stage. Drama depends inherently on the dramatist's impersonality. If he makes one of his characters a mere mouthpiece for his own opinions, he runs the risk of destroying the dramatic illusion. Shakespeare's plays are great, John Keats believed, because of their impersonality. They bear no trace of their creator's character. In his own doctrine of impersonality—"negative capability"—Keats created a poetry pure unto itself, free of the artist's personality, utterly reflective of the world at hand.[2]

Faulkner's novels imitate life, creating and maintaining an illusion founded in reality. Rather than providing a forum for the discussion of ideas and observations about human nature, however, they reflect and refract the world through the eyes of its inhabitants. In the absence of the artist's personality, structural elements become especially important. They determine the shape of the novel's content, the manner of its presentation, and the reader's response to it. In 1939 Conrad Aiken was one of the first to perceive this critical principle when he observed that Faulkner's concern with the novel as *form* placed him above his contemporaries: "What Mr. Faulkner is after, in a sense, is a *continuum*. He wants a medium without stops or pauses, a medium which is always *of the moment*, and of which the passage from moment to moment is as fluid and undetectable as is the life itself which he is purporting to give."[3] Aiken illuminates several central aspects in Faulkner's concept of the novel, primary among them the axiom that novelistic structure may parallel the shape and meaning of the world which the novel represents. Form and idea can be equivalent. Structure can become theme.

Until recently, narrative structure and its influence on characterization, plot, and meaning have not concerned Faulkner criticism in a major way. Some critics have focused on character and theme with little regard to structure, confident that the fiction's surface leads straight into its depths. Faulkner's frequent use of characters who also serve as narrators has encouraged this tendency. The fiction speaks through its characters, who express many different philosophies and attitudes. Their perceptions and experiences—the microcosmic embodiment of all human experience—hold the keys to the meaning of Faulkner's achievement. He repeatedly stressed this fundamental principle of his writing: "I'm just a writer. Not a literary man. . . . I write about people"; "A writer is trying to create believable people in credible moving situations in the most moving way he can"; "If the writer concentrates on what he does need to be interested in, which is the truth and the human heart, he won't have much time left for anything else."[4] He simultaneously deemphasized style: "the theme, the story, invents its own style"; style is a result "of a need, of a necessity"; "style is incidental."[5]

Moreover, the surface texture of his fiction—rural settings, occasional violence, bucolic individuals, frequently unsophisticated and unselfconscious narrators—might combine with the emphasis on characters to convince unwitting readers that Faulkner attached little importance to form, or even that he lacked the skill to make it a central element. He did clearly intend to keep narrative structure unobtrusive, using it to focus attention away from itself towards character and event. The writer creates his story, he said, "through methods, through style, because . . . he is simply trying to tell it in some way that it will seem troubling or true enough or beautiful or tragic enough to whoever reads it."[6] E. M. Forster expressed similar sentiments in *Aspects of the Novel*: "The novelist who betrays too much interest in his own method can never be more than interesting: he has given up the creation of character and summoned us to help analyse his own mind, and a heavy drop in the emotional thermometer results."[7] Faulkner never bothered his readers with his own personality. And he employed structure merely as one of several means to an end, never as an end itself. Yet readers who allow the unobtrusive nature of narrative structure to lull them into accepting its unimportance delude themselves. Its unobtrusiveness is the measure of how well Faulkner manipulates it. And the careful reader is well advised to heed how narrative structure works, for it lies at the very core of Faulkner's fictional method, of his conception of the novel as an artistic medium.

Against the rather profound restrictions of his desire for literary anonymity, Faulkner had to wrestle with the strength of his own personal vision as an artist. Beginning with *The Sound and the Fury*, structure became a means by which he could translate personal vision into fiction. His greatest writing seethes with emotion, the intensely felt experience of a moment, the vivid apprehension of life and its contradictions, of death, time, and knowledge. Fragmented, refined, transformed, and reconstituted, Faulkner's vision settles in the texture of his landscapes, in the talk, behavior, experience, and perceptions of his characters, in the unfolding of their stories. His unceasing efforts to pack every last particle of intensity and meaning into his fiction made him one of the great structural innovators in the history of the novel.

Like most innovators, Faulkner has often been misunderstood. Like Melville and Joyce, he frequently utilized narrative techniques which flagrantly violated traditional literary conventions. As an art form, of course, the novel is a fluid, changing medium which the novelist has the prerogative to define and redefine as he sees fit. In *The Sound and the Fury*, again in *As I Lay Dying*, again in each succeeding novel, Faulkner sought to make such a redefinition. The reader who expects him to write in the manner of Henry James, for instance, or according to the strictures of Percy Lubbock, will likely mistake innovation for sloppiness, deliberation for carelessness.[8] If Faulkner's fiction is ever to be properly understood and appreciated, readers must dispense with the standards of other writers and of critics, at least at first, and grant his work its own artistic integrity, evaluating it solely on the basis of the standards which it sets forth for itself. Only when his stories and novels can be considered in light of those standards will Faulkner's significance as an artist and his place among other writers of the century begin to come clear.

Faulkner conceived of fiction as an *organic* form: his novels and stories rely upon a deep, inherent relationship among structure, language, theme, plot, and character. All narrative elements interdepend. Though the fictional surface may emphasize character (where Faulkner ultimately wants the reader's attention centered), in structural terms character is merely one element coeval with a number of others. Thus, the novels usually function not as sequential, chronologically ordered narratives but rather as organically complete wholes. In some of the novels narrative structure directly symbolizes one or more of the main themes. The four-part structure of *The Sound and the Fury* (the first two parts in particular) rather obviously reflects the theme of fragmented and fragmenting time. *Light in August* and *The Hamlet* explore the nature of society and the folk imagination through characters who speak in various ways for the community. *Requiem for a Nun* depicts the influence of history on present-day individuals by juxtaposing prose narratives (chronicling the progress of human and natural history) alongside dramatic scenes specifically illustrating Temple Drake's dilemma. The multilayered structure of *Absalom, Absalom!* depicts a similar theme. While form implies progress toward a discovery of the real Sutpen, in fact the narrative moves away from the real, towards the mythical. In such instances the reader must recognize narrative structure both as a method of organizing subject matter and as the symbolization of theme, an expression and reflection of meaning.

The reader likewise must assume an important role in characterization. Faulkner never enters to evaluate the inhabitants of his fiction. Narrators, on the other hand, describe them at length, but what they say is not always trustworthy, especially if they are characters themselves. Rarely omniscient, they often can do little more than speculate about the thoughts and behavior of other human beings. This method of characterization clearly differs from that in Henry Fielding's *Tom Jones*, where Fielding, the *apparent* narrator, often described his characters first and then confirmed his characterizations by illustrating their behavior in various situations. In *The Sound and the Fury*, however, Quentin, Benjy, and Jason describe themselves and each other from three different perspectives, none of which can be considered equivalent to Faulkner's. The reader, relying upon his own intelligence, experience, and common sense, must evaluate their behavior, attitudes, language, moral judgments, and thought patterns according to his own standards and those which the novel establishes. Irony aids the reader's judgment of characters who stand in seeming independence of their author. As the reader involves himself, voluntarily or not, in the characterization process, in the novel's working as a whole, he simultaneously engages in the explication of one of Faulkner's major themes—human nature. The reader's active and willing participation in the narrative process lies at the core of Faulkner's method.

In the past decade, full-length studies by John Irwin, Donald Kartiganer, Arthur Kinney, and Joseph Reed have examined various aspects of Faulkner's narrative structure.[9] Each of these has, to differing extents, helped to unravel the intricacies of Faulkner's narrative form. Yet no full-length study has focused exclusively on that thoroughly basic structural component traditionally known as point of view. The six chapter-essays which follow undertake to fill that gap. Influencing every element of Faulkner's fiction, from characterization and plot to language and meaning, point of view is a critically important aspect of narrative form. Faulkner employs it in a way more complex, more convoluted and involuted, than any other successful novelist of the English language. Readers who fail to recognize its importance may seriously misunderstand his art, and his artistry.

This study is primarily descriptive in nature. The first chapter discusses generally the nature of Faulkner's point of view. Succeeding chapters consider four representative novels, two well known and two relatively neglected: *Light in August, Pylon, Absalom, Absalom!,* and *Requiem for a Nun.* Although the selection is arbitrary, reflecting my own personal interests, the novels chosen employ in widely varying fashions the essential characteristics in Faulkner's use of narrative perspective. To consider in detail more than these four novels would quickly lead to redundancy. *The Sound and the Fury* and *As I Lay Dying,* which may seem to some readers the most structurally unusual of Faulkner's works, are not examined individually. Their narrative structures have probably received more critical attention than any of the other novels. Predominantly character-narrated, they come under discussion in the first chapter, and in the analyses of *Light in August* and *Absalom.* Such episodic novels as *The Wild Palms, Go Down, Moses,* and *The Hamlet* are similarly treated. *Soldiers' Pay* and *Mosquitoes,* the earliest and most imperfect of Faulkner's novels, are not examined at all; this is not a study of how point of view evolved, but of how it *works* in four novels which matter. Nor have I cast my observations in any of the various critical modes currently in fashion, preferring to allow my subject to determine the form which I follow. These limitations have proved necessary to a full exploration of the subject at hand.

By so restricting the works discussed, I have been able to explore four significant novels in a thorough, perhaps exhaustive fashion. My aim has been to achieve not a comprehensive analysis of the fiction in general but a specific comprehensive discussion of point of view, of the elements that constitute the essential structural methods which Faulkner applied in his writing. Very simply, understanding these methods is fundamental to understanding Faulkner's fiction and art.

Chapter One
Narrative Perspective: Voice and Eye

Soldiers' Pay, Mosquitoes, and *Sartoris* (the truncated *Flags in the Dust*) suggested early in Faulkner's career the importance which individual human beings would come to assume in his fiction. If the first two novels are noteworthy for nothing else, they can be lauded for their variety of characters. In *Mosquitoes* especially, a diverse crew of passengers while away their cruise on the *Nausikaa* with effete, desultory conversations about art, men and women, and human nature. Undoubtedly a bad book, not at all like the much better ones which followed, this second novel gave Faulkner an opportunity to experiment with ideas which soon formed the fabric of his greatest fiction. It also displayed, in such figures as Dawson Fairchild, the Semitic man, Eva Wiseman, Mr. Taliaferro, and others, Faulkner's interest at the time in using characters to debate, and embody, the concerns which he wanted to explore through the writing of literature. Of course, *Mosquitoes* is fundamentally flawed by its preoccupation with *ideas* rather than with action, with life—a fact which Faulkner must have recognized. Asked at the University of Virginia whether he agreed with Malcolm Cowley that the book is a "very bad early novel," Faulkner responded, "In that case I'll agree with Mr. Cowley because I was still learning the craft, but . . . if I could write that over, I probably wouldn't write it at all. . . . it's not a—not an important book in my list."[1] *Mosquitoes* marked a dead end for Faulkner. It was the sort of novel which D. H. Lawrence or Aldous Huxley could handle so much better than he, a novel he must have found sterile and lifeless even as he wrote it. No surprise then that he abandoned or began to modify radically most of its structural methods soon after finishing it.

In *Flags in the Dust*, even more so in *The Sound and the Fury*, characters cease talking about ideas and begin living. Though occasionally such individuals as Old Will Falls, Dilsey, and Lena Grove *seem* to represent certain basic human qualities—instinct, closeness to the soil, religious faith, perseverance—Faulkner had wholly rejected the notion of personifying ideas in his characters. Rarely do his characters

7

turn out to be as simple, or ideal, or imperfect as at first they might appear. Dilsey, admirable though she seems, proves more complex than the endurance and piety which sustain her during her servitude to the Compsons. Lena, uneducated and hardly concerned with intellectual matters, is considerably more than a bovine Southern farm-girl. Faulkner's characters symbolize nothing. Instead, what happens to them—their behavior, emotions, thoughts, perceptions, and experiences; their complexity as human beings; the ways in which others perceive them—constitutes the prevailing metaphor through which Faulkner explores and illustrates theme. Out of the metaphor of individual perception blossom his innovations in point of view, one of the most important and distinctive elements in his writing.

Nowhere do these innovations announce themselves with a greater clamor than in the opening sentences of *The Sound and the Fury*. They must have proven unusually shocking to the relatively few readers who first encountered the book in 1929, for they herald a major change in the character of the modern novel, an important expansion of its powers as a literary form. One might speculate as well over the shock which Faulkner himself experienced as he wrote them:

> Through the fence, between the curling flower spaces, I could see them hitting. They were coming toward where the flag was and I went along the fence. Luster was hunting in the grass by the flower tree. They took the flag out, and they were hitting. Then they put the flag back and they went to the table, and he hit and the other hit. Then they went on, and I went along the fence.[2]

Exactly what is happening here? Who is the speaker? Why does he describe apparently meaningless actions with such journalistic matter-of-factness? Who is Luster? Who are the two men? What are they hitting? The words themselves provide no answer. With no preparation, no introduction to character, situation, or setting, the reader finds himself suddenly immersed in the consciousness of another human being. And what a human being! No author or narrator intrudes to explain him. The reader has only the speaking character's perspective for guidance. He must see and experience exactly and only as the character sees and experiences.

Therein lies the essence of Faulkner's point of view, the reader's immersion in, and merger with, the consciousness of literary characters. Point of view grew increasingly complex and varied in the novels which succeeded *The Sound and the Fury*. Faulkner soon added to the viewpoints of single individuals the perspectives of an entire community and discovered a major interest in the interaction of the two. He also began using external narrators to intrude into his characters' minds, uncovering their subjective lives from a critically objective perspective. These various narrative patterns, separately and in combination, permitted him to reconcile his compulsion for authorial impersonality with a conviction underlying all his work—that individual experience embodies basic truths of the human condition. Faulkner remains always unseen. Characters speak only for themselves. They may serve as narrators. Or an uninvolved, external narrator may observe and describe them, penetrating their conscious and unconscious minds, channeling their perceptions to the reader. Because characters are fallible human beings, their observations and experiences do not always reflect reality. Truth is called constantly into question. One person's view of events may differ considerably from another's, and one, or both, or most often neither may prove correct. Because characters' perceptions form the source of so much of the narrative, point of view strongly influences narrative structure—the order in which events are described. Point of view almost exclusively dictates the structure of *Absalom, Absalom!*, as it does also in the first section of *The Sound and the Fury*, where Benjy's fragmented mentality rambles with seeming abandon among different periods of his life. Bonding theme, character, situation, setting, and structure, point of view plays a crucial role in Faulkner's concept of the novel. Michael Millgate appropriately emphasizes its importance: "The problem of point of view embraces, after all, some of the most crucial questions of literary technique: from whose angle and in whose voice is the story told? Where does authority lie in the novel, and whom, as readers, should we trust? Where does the author himself stand, and how do we *know* where he stands?"[3] To Millgate's questions can be added: What potential impact can point of view have on a novel's themes? For what purpose does narrative viewpoint cast doubt upon every character's credibility? What do novels written in this way *mean*?

Traditionally, point of view has denoted the perspective of a story's narration. When a character tells the story, referring to himself as "I," the narration is *first* person. When no readily identifiable individual relates the story, there is no use of the first-person singular pronoun, and characters are referred to by name and with "he" or "she" pronouns, the narrative is *third* person. The adjectives *omniscient* and *semi-omniscient* denote the limits of the third-person narrator's knowledge. In their widely used textbook *Modern Rhetoric*, Cleanth Brooks and Robert Penn Warren define point of view as "a physical point from which the specified or implied observer looks at the thing described"; narrative is produced by "a person who bears some relation to the action, either as observer or participant, and whose intelligence serves the reader as a kind of guide to the action."[4] Brooks and Warren include in this definition the importance of whether a character does the narrating and the extent of his knowledge and reliability. Other critics, foremost among them Wayne C. Booth in *The Rhetoric of Fiction*, similarly consider the inherent complexities of point of view.[5]

Because point of view is often understood to mean little more than "voice" and "perspective"—who speaks, and how much he knows— related structural elements may be overlooked. The narrator is the most critical component in point of view, but the first- and third-person categories create difficulties in discussing his existence. First person at least establishes the narrator as a character who bears some relation to the events he describes. Third person, however, suggests not a character or human personality but, according to Brooks and Warren, "a kind of disembodied intelligence before whom the events are played out."[6] Such a definition precludes the third-person narrator's existence, at least in the sense of a person who narrates. Every narrative has a narrator—there can be no narrative without one. The printed words on the page explicitly verify his existence. Faulkner's third-person narratives often appear to be produced by a very concrete, discernible personality—a human personality, with frequently human limitations. But it is dangerous, and incorrect, to ascribe the characteristics of this personality to Faulkner. As the ultimate narrative source, Faulkner is the author, the omniscient creator of fiction who knows all because he produces all. In *Light in August* and *Absalom, Absalom!*, however, the third-person narrator often possesses only limited knowledge; he can frequently do little more than guess what a character might have believed, employing such words as *maybe* and *perhaps* to reflect his apparent uncertainty. Whether participating character or uninvolved observer, the narrator remains always distinct from his creator. Gérard Genette, a French narrative theoretician and interpreter of Proust, thus argues for a quite different means of distinguishing narrators: "The novelist's choice, unlike the narrator's, is . . . between two narrative postures . . . : to have the story told by one of its 'characters,' or to have it told by a narrator outside of the story. . . . every narrating is, by definition, to all intents and purposes presented in the first person. . . . The real question is whether or not the narrator can use the first person to designate *one of his characters*."[7] Of course, if the narrator remains uninvolved and does not use the first-person pronoun, then his physical identity becomes less important, though never negligible. The first- and third-person categories really have no meaning. In their place, *character narrator* and *external* (uninvolved) *narrator* will serve more accurately.

One of the inherent fallacies resulting from the first- and third-person terminology, as Genette has noted, is the idea that first-person narrative, implicitly subjective, can somehow be inferior to the more impersonal, dramatic objectivity of third-person narrative.[8] Such a notion assumes that a narrating character cannot speak of himself with conscious irony, or that the author cannot place the narrator in an ironic context which casts doubt on all that he says. In fact, character narration can project a wholly objective characterization, an immediate and vivid evocation of human personality. Moreover, fiction and drama are two substantially different genres. Drama lacks the barrier which the fictional narrator interposes between reader and story. A dramatist labors inescapably under the Aristotelian fact that he portrays an "imitation of an action," either serious or comic. An audience views his play directly, watching actors perform it on the stage before them. They see what characters do, listen to what they say, and do not need to be told about it by a third party. The reader of fiction, on the other hand, always receives the narrator's description through the medium of the printed word: he never *sees* the action; he only *reads* about it. Genette explains this fundamental difference, pointing out that "in contrast to dramatic representation, no narrative can 'show' or 'imitate' the story it tells. All it can do is tell it in a manner which is detailed, precise, 'alive' and in that way give more or less the *illusion of mimesis*—which is the only narrative mimesis, for this single and sufficient reason: that narrative, oral or written, is a fact of language, and language signifies without imitating."[9] Drama and fiction share much in common, but the assumption that fiction imitates life in the same manner as drama may lull the reader into a false sense of confidence in what characters do and say, especially when they are narrators.

Yet Faulkner's point of view and the particular brand of fiction which he wrote create an illusion which on the surface does seem "dramatic." And just such an illusion lures the reader's attention away from the author's personality, towards fictional characters and events. "Dramatic" fiction presents its characters as real and independent individuals, and it invites the reader to judge them accordingly. The external narrator passes little judgment on them himself. He relates events to the reader exactly as they happen. He consistently describes and reports from an objective, reliable vantage point, unless he indicates an uncertainty or partial knowledge of his topic, in which case he always identifies speculation. The reader learns of other events through character testimony. Stephen Dedalus, in Joyce's *A Portrait of the Artist as a Young Man*, aspired to write this type of fiction. The writer's sensations, he explains, cease to be of importance; instead, "the centre of emotional gravity is equidistant from the artist himself and from others. The narrative is no longer purely personal. The personality of the artist passes into the narration itself. . . . The dramatic form is reached when the vitality which has flowed and eddied round each person fills every person with such vital force that he or she assumes a proper and intangible esthetic life."[10] Though the writer may create the *illusion* of objective drama, his subjective influence appears everywhere—in diction, characterization, tone, structure, theme—in all the elements which compose a narrative. In a sense, such fiction confers on the reader the same requirements which the dramatist imposes upon his audience. Without the narrator's judgmental commentary, the reader, like the audience at a play, must weigh the words and actions of characters, recognize fabrications, contradictions, and ulterior motives, and reach his own conclusions. If the writer has done his job well, he will elicit from his reader the responses he desires.

Point of view creates in Faulkner's fiction a complex dynamic relationship among author, narrator, character, event, and reader. Its influence is everywhere felt. In the case of an external narrator, readers must consider his attitudes towards his characters and how deeply he intrudes into their consciousnesses. Is his knowledge complete or limited? Is he restricted only to their present-time lives or can he delve into their pasts? What is his attitude towards them? Does he seem emotionally detached or sympathetic? A narrating character's personality and his role in the story strongly affect the content and credibility of his narrative. Did he merely hear about it? Did he witness it? Or did he play a part in it? How reliable are his sources? To whom, if anyone, does he talk, and for what reasons? What does his manner of speaking, his language, reveal about him? How does his version of events compare with the versions of other narrating characters? Encompassing several crucial structural elements, each exerting a major influence, point of view embraces considerably more than one simple expression can define. The following terms and their definitions are intended to reflect the major aspects of point of view. They have been specifically tailored to the characteristics of Faulkner's writing.

Narrative: the story; more generally, the fabric of fiction. Narrative denotes the content of novels and stories, as well as of some essays and nonfiction works (Faulkner's "Mississippi," for example; Thoreau's *Walden;* Hemingway's *Green Hills of Africa;* Joan Didion's *Slouching Towards Bethlehem;* Norman Mailer's *The Executioner's Song).* More specifically, narrative means the story which the narrator tells, although he is an inherent part of the narrative.

Author: the artist, the creator of narrative. He remains always separate and apart, though he may choose to identify with the narrator's voice (a choice which Faulkner never makes). As a physical being, the author cannot belong to art; he can only produce it. Faulkner virtually never places his own words and opinions in a narrator's mouth. Equating any author with his narrator is hazardous. In *Tom Jones,* for instance, Fielding pointedly identifies himself as the narrator in the first chapter's opening lines. Yet a careful examination reveals this narrator—a pompous, verbose, pretentious personality—to be a satirical self-parody, a source of much humor, and demonstrably different from the actual writer of the novel. When the author does not suggest such a relationship, other factors may still encourage the reader to look for it. The narrator may be a sympathetic character who speaks with such force and authority that he tempts the reader to identify his voice with the author's. Nick Carraway in Fitzgerald's *The Great Gatsby,* Gulley Jimson of Joyce Cary's *The Horse's Mouth,* Jacob Horner of John Barth's *The End of the Road,* and Stingo in William Styron's *Sophie's Choice* are interesting, in some ways admirable figures. But to grant them authorial power denies them their full province as characters, negates the function of irony, leads to shallow readings and complete misinterpretations. Faulkner's narrators are always fallible, and his meaning often hinges on their fallibility.

On several occasions Faulkner illustrated in curious fashion how completely he applied this concept of authorial impersonality. In *Mosquitoes,* the girl Jenny describes a man whom she once met, a "little kind of black man . . . kind of shabby dressed . . . such a funny kind of man." She remembers his name with some difficulty—Faulkner. Twenty years later, in a passage intended for *Intruder in the Dust,* Gavin Stevens describes a certain book to his nephew: "a novel of about twenty years ago by another Mississippian, a mild retiring little man from over yonder at Oxford, in which a fictitious Canadian said to a fictitious, self-lacerated Southerner in a dormitory room in a not too authentic Harvard: 'I who regard you will have also sprung from the loins of African kings.'"[11] The "retiring little man" is obviously Faulkner; the book, *Absalom, Absalom!* In both instances Faulkner was clearly writing tongue in cheek, but he also felt sufficiently removed from the narrative to make himself a minor character. In his semi-fictional, semi-autobiographical essay "Mississippi," he modeled the primary character on himself. Yet factual discrepancies between the character's experiences and Faulkner's draw a clear distinction between the two. The essay's character is fictional and literary; Faulkner, of course, was real.[12]

In another instance Faulkner characterized, in a letter to Malcolm Cowley, the external narrator which he had created for the Compson Appendix: "the purpose of this genealogy is to give a sort of bloodless bibliophile's point of view. I was a sort of Garter King-at-Arms, heatless, not very moved, cleaning up 'Compson' before going on to the next 'C-o' or 'C-r.'"[13] This explanation dramatically enunciates Faulkner's attitude towards the independence of author and narrator, towards the writing of fiction: he purposefully creates a specific personality through which to channel his story. This created personality in the Compson Appendix directly determines the form of the story's telling: the clinical succession of entries on each family member; the "heatless," impersonal tone of a disinterested genealogist. Describing the Appendix narrator as third person is simply inaccurate, just as it is inaccurate for *Light in August*, *The Hamlet*, or *A Fable*—told by external narrators who, though unidentifiable as characters, have nonetheless discernible personalities.

Of course, the author can never detach himself completely. He must feel sufficiently motivated to be able to write the story in the first place. As an artist, in fact, he is not detached at all. He chooses setting, characters, tone, language, themes, plot, and structure. In form and substance his fiction mirrors his life and personality. He alone is responsible for its existence.

Perspective: the character and narrator viewpoints through which the story is told. If the perspective belongs to a character, he may narrate himself or be the focus of an external narrator's attention. If it belongs to an external narrator, events and characters are objectively described from a solely external perspective. More often than not, narration in Faulkner's fiction involves a combination of internal and external perspectives which simultaneously complement as well as contradict one another.

Narrator: the fictional source of narrative. He may or may not be a character; he may or may not reveal his presence. If an external narrator, he narrates the entire work. If a character, he may narrate only a small part. External narrators are most important for their description of character, scene, and event, for their evocation of tone. On the other hand, the reliability of narrating characters, their potential involvement in the story, become integral concerns of the narrative. Character narrators may also occasionally appear to serve as external narrators by describing objectively events in which they were only indirectly involved. The narrating character in "A Rose for Emily" plays no active role, but his opinions of Emily Grierson directly reflect his community's attitudes, which happen to be one of the story's main interests. In Thomas Wolfe's *Look Homeward, Angel*, the narrator appears to be external, but on three occasions he refers to himself with the pronoun *I*, establishing himself as a character, however uninvolved. In fact, Eugene Gant may very well be the narrator who produces the narrative, telling his own life story.[14] Usually, however, the narrator's identity as a character is more obvious, and his credibility becomes a critical issue. The possibility that the scholar-narrator of Nabokov's *Pale Fire* has murdered the writer whose poem he explicates jeopardizes the truth of all he says. So does the possible mental instability of the governess in Henry James's *The Turn of the Screw*. The narrator's role as a character inevitably creates an ironic potential which reflects upon him as well as his narrative. Regardless of how uninvolved and objective he might seem, this potential cannot be ignored, and his words cannot be accepted without question. In Faulkner's novels, moreover, character narrators often address listeners—other characters—whose identities and relationships to the narrator become important. When the Reporter harangues his editor in *Pylon*, Byron Bunch explains his behavior to Hightower in *Light in August*, and Reverend Sutterfield in *A Fable* tells the runner about a stolen horse back in Mississippi, their motives for talking to their listeners become a significant issue in the novel as a whole.

Focal character: an individual whose thoughts, emotions, and perceptions the narrator employs to tell the story. In much of *Sanctuary* Horace Benbow is a focal character, like Joe Christmas in chapters 5–12 of *Light in August*, Quentin Compson throughout *Absalom, Absalom!*, and Ike McCaslin in four chapters of *Go Down, Moses*. Focal characters usually play a major role in the narrative, but they may also be relatively minor, even anonymous figures whose perspective represents a larger body of opinion, such as a church congregation, a mob, or an entire community. As one of the characteristic elements in Faulkner's fiction, focal perspectives constitute a major source of his narrative realism. They allow the narrator to report objectively and precisely a character's subjective response to his environment. When a character is not sufficiently articulate to tell his own story, the narrator uses his focal perspective to speak *for* him, revealing his inner thoughts and feelings. Such narrative emphasizes the focal individual's identity as a *character*, preventing the reader from too readily identifying with his perspective, transforming him into an object of logical scrutiny. Typically, Faulkner uses several different focal perspectives in combination, though one usually predominates. Most events in *Pylon* are described through the Reporter's perspective, but the perspectives of Hagood, Jiggs, and several minor characters also occasionally reinforce or replace it. Focal-character narration accounts for much of the structural variety in Faulkner's fiction, and more often than not it appears along with character narration. Though characters narrate the first three sections of *The Sound and the Fury*, an external narrator relates the fourth section from Dilsey's perspective. *Light in August, The Hamlet, Intruder in the Dust, A Fable,* and *The Mansion* employ a more balanced combination, creating a wavelike fluctuation between the subjective views of speaking characters and the external narrator's objective intrusions into a focal individual's mind.

Audience: the person or persons whom the narrator addresses. An external narrator usually addresses the reader, to whom he pays little attention and whose identity has little or no bearing on the narrative. (A notable exception is "The Jail" in *Requiem for a Nun*, where the narrator directly beckons the reader to participate in the story). Nor do the character narrators in *The Sound and the Fury* and *As I Lay Dying* acknowledge the presence of their audience. In fact, they share less a relationship with the reader than do most external narrators. But in *Sanctuary, Light in August,* and the novels which followed, narrating characters invariably address an audience—a single listener or a group of listeners. Narration becomes a form of conversation, a dynamic social interchange between individuals which implicitly belongs to the content of the narrative. The listener's identity, his knowledge of the subject, and his relationship to the speaker all may affect the credibility and form of what the speaker says. In *Absalom, Absalom!,* the reader learns that Quentin has talked at great length to Shreve, a Canadian, to educate him about southern history and custom so that he will not misunderstand or ridicule the story of Thomas Sutpen. Quentin's compulsion to explain Sutpen to his roommate, and to himself, proves as thematically significant as Sutpen himself. Rosa Coldfield, on the other hand, tells her story to Quentin because she wants a favorable version of her role in the Sutpen saga preserved for posterity. Accordingly, she characterizes Sutpen as a "demon" and herself as his innocent victim. In *The Wild Palms* the tall convict wants both to entertain his fellow inmates and to explain the reasons for his month-long absence from Parchman Penitentiary. Character narrators in the Snopes novels also desire to entertain and educate their listeners by talking about the latest exploits of the Snopeses. They thus may exaggerate or distort or suppress information to create humor or suspense or to win their audience's sympathy.

Distance: the degree of separation between narrator and story, between reader and narrative. Distance concerns how much knowledge the external narrator reveals, determining how deeply he intrudes into the focal character's perspective. He may do nothing more than report the focal individual's words and physical actions. Or he may enter the focal character's consciousness and relate his thoughts. He may go even further, merging with the focal character's subconscious mind and memory, explaining what the focal character himself may be totally unaware of. The important narrative forms which these variations in distance characterize are specifically considered in the chapter on *Light in August*.

Distance also concerns the nature of the external narrator's emotional involvement, revealed through the tension or excitement of his narrative, through irony, or through outright expressions of sympathy and distaste (rare in Faulkner's fiction). Because the external narrator does not participate in the narrative action, emotional involvement, ulterior motives, and personality flaws do not compromise his reliability. Though he may also range back and forth in time and space, his knowledge of events in the narrative's present time usually seems more certain. When he discusses the past-time experiences of focal characters, he often speculates, as if he is unsure of the facts. Throughout most of *Absalom, Absalom!*, in fact, the external narrator restricts himself almost entirely to what the present-time narrators have learned about the past. If he knows the truth, he never bothers to reveal it.

What narrating characters know, and reveal, affects other kinds of distance, primarily spatial, temporal, and personal. Characters are naturally limited by their spatial and temporal relationship to the story, by the typical human strengths and weaknesses of their personalities. Did they witness or take part in the story? Did they merely hear about it from someone else? How long ago did it occur? The more temporally and spatially removed a character is from his subject, the less likely he is to report accurately. And when a character talks about events which he did not witness or participate in, when he relies on second- and thirdhand evidence, the credibility of his narrative suffers considerably. A narrating character also wields little control over his emotional involvement. Witness, for instance, Gavin Stevens's futile attempts to remain objective about Linda Snopes in *The Town* and *The Mansion*. Obviously, the distance established between the external narrator and his narrative relates directly to the function of irony. When the narrator distances himself completely, doing nothing more than reporting event and dialogue, irony serves as a means of characterization. The reader then confronts in an immediate way the inevitable contradictions of life and human nature, the complications and dilemmas of an individual's social involvement. Irony also illuminates the effect of a narrating character's personality and his role in the narrative.

Distance may change radically from scene to scene and story to story according to the various narrative elements involved. In retrospective narratives, the narrator's temporal separation from his subject may endow him with objectivity: the maturity and experience which Bayard Sartoris in *The Unvanquished* and Lucius Priest in *The Reivers* have gained over the years enables them to describe crucial childhood events with relatively detached perspicacity. Yet time may also dull the memory of reminiscing speakers, warping their stories—the case with Rosa Coldfield in *Absalom, Absalom!* On the opposite extreme, a narrating character may tell a story in which he played no part, which in fact he may have heard of only from other characters who themselves played no part. Such spatial separation obviously damages the narrative's credibility. A narrator's emotional involvement in a subject from which he is temporally or spatially distanced, like Quentin with the Sutpen story and Ike McCaslin with the fourth section of "The Bear," compounds the potential for inaccuracy, doubt, and mystery.

One final kind of distance stems from a fundamental Faulknerian theme, the basic failure of understanding which isolates every individual. Language and the human mind are too finite. The individual usually can understand his own motives and desires only partially, if at all; understanding the motivations of other human beings simply lies beyond his ability. Inevitably, Faulkner's fiction uncovers and leaves unexplained certain ambiguities of human character. No matter how many perspectives, external or character, describe a person, in the end the essence of him remains unknown. This theme is perhaps nowhere more eloquently illustrated than in the figure of Joe Christmas. Numerous characters, along with the entire Jefferson community, try to fathom him, but they never succeed. Because of their failure, in death as in life he remains unexplained—the ultimate example of isolation in Faulkner's fiction.

Distance in Faulkner's novels thus places an inescapable burden on his reader. Very often the "facts" never come clear, and the reader must ferret them out as best he can. By omitting all information or explanations other than those which characters possess, Faulkner draws the reader in, compelling him to view events from the same vantage point as characters, in a sense establishing him as a "second narrator" who must gather facts, evaluate opinion, and order the story into lucid, comprehensible form. "The ripples of *narrative consciousness*," according to Arthur Kinney, "thus spread out through the various scenes of Faulkner's novels to embrace our sense of the work *as a whole*, our *structural consciousness*, and, beyond that, to a sense of the significance of the accumulation of incidents and images as we put them together, what we may term our *constitutive consciousness*."[15] Reaffirming the mystery of human character and event, distance more than lures the reader into the narrative process. In many of the novels, distance itself—between individuals (*Light in August*, the Snopes trilogy), generations (*Flags in the Dust, The Unvanquished, Absalom, Absalom!*), and different modes of experience (*The Sound and the Fury, As I Lay Dying*)—becomes a theme of profound significance.

Reader: the author's audience. Inherently part of the narrative process, the reader stands at the opposite end of the spectrum from the author, who writes to communicate, in some way, for whatever reason, with the reader. The reader must actively engage in the narrative process. Passive acquiescence guarantees both his own failure as well as the artist's.

Narrative structure: all the elements traditionally subsumed beneath the umbrella term "point of view." More generally, narrative structure designates the overall pattern of the novel's construction—as a series of episodes, a sequential account of related events, or a chronologically discontinuous narrative. In Faulkner's novels, character perspectives —individual perceptions of events—determine narrative structure more often than the chronological order of the events being described.

Faulkner's fiction varies in structure as richly as in character, theme, imagery, and symbolism. Faulkner never seemed content with one structural pattern. In each novel he employed a unique set of narrative elements, a different framework of structural relationships. One need only compare *The Sound and the Fury, Absalom, Absalom!, Go*

Down, Moses, Requiem for a Nun, and *The Reivers* to confirm this fact. Often, it seems, a novel's subject dictated to an extent its form. *Light in August*, for example, displays its concern with the nature of community through anonymous character perspectives representative of community response, its variety of characters, and the italicized community voice in chapter 13. *Go Down, Moses* exemplifies economic exploitation and racism through a series of superficially unrelated chapters which illustrate how these forces have affected marriage, black-white relations, Ike's attitude towards his heritage, and the course of southern history. *Intruder in the Dust* depicts Chick Mallison's education in human nature and community racism through his own perspective. Despite this fundamental diversity, however, two basic structural patterns—which employ external narrators, narrating characters, and focal individuals in varying relationships—appear with some consistency throughout Faulkner's fiction.

The first pattern involves character narration, with or without the frame of a presiding external narrator. Neither *The Sound and the Fury* nor *As I Lay Dying* openly uses an external narrator (except in the fourth section of the Compson novel). Their narration does not seem conscious; that is, characters do not consciously address other individuals or the reader. They merely speak, or think, in a disembodied voice not at all reflective of how they really talk: Benjy, a mongoloid idiot, cannot talk at all, and Quentin apparently produces his narrative after his suicide (or immediately before, or at the moment of—at any rate, he does not physically speak it, because he is dead).[16] Ilse Dusoir Lind's definition of symbolist drama, whose tenets Faulkner adopted to an extent early in his career, aptly characterizes the narration of these two novels: "The symbolist dream play—and symbolist drama generally—was determinedly antirealistic. Its goal was to induce in the viewer a special state of mind, an attitude of profound, enraptured contemplation, in which the viewer had a sense that ultimate meanings were being or were about to be glimpsed."[17] The result is a Faulknerian stream of consciousness, which differs considerably from that of Joyce. In the stream-of-consciousness narratives in the first six chapters of *Ulysses*, a focal character, Stephen Dedalus or Leopold Bloom, thinks often quite randomly about a wide variety of subjects—usually whatever he happens to be doing or seeing at the moment. Among his thoughts are interspersed the framing comments of an external narrator, who informs the reader where the character is or what he is doing, thus placing each of his thoughts in a specific context. Joyce conveys the reality of thought and perception by imposing no unnatural order on the content of his characters' minds and by focusing on the typical events of a typical day in Dublin, Ireland. Faulkner's characters—Benjy, Quentin, Anse Bundren, and Dewey Dell, for example—have a narrower range of interests. Their perspectives center on a person or a series of related events—Caddy Compson or the death of Addie Bundren. The external narrator seems to play no role at all. Their thoughts merely exist, on the page, in a kind of narratorial vacuum. Joycean stream of consciousness functions in a real world, in a realistic narrative context, while the narratives in *The Sound and the Fury* and *As I Lay Dying* exist apart from reality. That Faulkner's stream-of-consciousness narrators do not consciously "speak" their stories implies the presence of an external narrator, who treats them as focal characters and reports their thoughts, saying for them what they never would, or even could, say for themselves.

Though both *The Sound and the Fury* and *As I Lay Dying* employ similar types of character narration, they do differ significantly. The three character narratives of the Compson novel concern events revolving around Caddy. The minds of Benjy and Quentin wander among memories and events which occurred over a period of as many as thirty years. Jason, unlike his brothers locked into the present rather than the past, howls in obsessive agony over how Caddy's daughter has stolen "his" money. For these narrators Caddy serves as a catalyst who prompts them into remembering their own lives and thinking about themselves in relation to her. In three different ways she embodies the very essence of what their lives mean. Thus, their narratives benefit from the diffusion of their thoughts. *As I Lay Dying*, on the other hand, focuses specifically on the events surrounding Addie Bundren's death and burial. It employs fifteen as opposed to three narrating characters. Their interests, with a few significant exceptions, concern the narrative's present time. They also seem more aware of the external world than the Compson narrators. Several of them—Cora Tull, Doc Peabody, and Samson, for example—reflect a social dimension essentially absent in *The Sound and the Fury*. Yet neither the Bundren nor the Compson novel characterizes the narrative structure which Faulkner employed during the remainder of his career. They also contain the only authentic "interior monologues" he ever wrote: even Miss Rosa's monologue in chapter 5 of *Absalom, Absalom!* differs from them substantially. After *As I Lay Dying* Faulkner always provided his narrating characters a realistic social motive for talking, and with listeners.

Narrative Perspective: Voice and Eye

Retrospective character narrative, a more traditional form, occurs in *The Unvanquished* and *The Reivers*, where Bayard Sartoris and Lucius Priest relate events from their past lives. In both novels the narrating character functions much like an external narrator, treating himself as a separate individual except for his use of the pronoun *I*. Retrospective narrative establishes an implied comparison between the narrator in the present and his character in the past—how events he describes have shaped the person he has become. Both Bayard Sartoris and Lucius Priest seem interested in illustrating a lesson which they have learned. The "Odor of Verbena" episode depicts Bayard's rejection of violence for more civilized methods of dealing with adversaries. In *The Reivers*, the relationship of the opening sentence—"GRANDFATHER SAID:"—to the rest of the novel clearly establishes that Lucius Priest relates his childhood trip to Memphis in order to teach his listener, his own grandson, a lesson about the responsibilities of maturity and adulthood. In fact, the grandson is the narrator (though he speaks outright only the first two words), recording his grandfather's story exactly as it was told him, implying that he too finds the lesson worth passing on. When a retrospective narrator relates events from his childhood, the limitations of his juvenile perspective inevitably contrast with the experience of his mature vantage point. Often humor results, as in *The Reivers*, "Uncle Willy," and "That Will Be Fine" (a hilarious and neglected work). Yet the juvenile perspective may also heighten mystery, suspense, and terror. Quentin's apparent indifference to Nancy's terror in "That Evening Sun" allows him to observe events in a relatively objective manner; his innocence prevents him from rationalizing her fear away (as his father does), emphasizing it dramatically to the reader. The mature perspective from which he narrates enables him to recognize his own childhood innocence, and to empathize (as he could not as a child) with Nancy.

The Reivers might also be described as a directed narrative, directed by the narrator towards his listener—the typical Faulknerian character narrative. Although the directed nature of *The Reivers* narrative serves mainly to justify its general form as an exemplum, in other novels the hearer-teller relationship of directed narration becomes a fundamental influence on the narrative content. It also symbolizes social interaction and provides an important source of community characterization. The listener's identity directly affects what the narrator tells him and may also govern his reliability if the listener gives him some reason for withholding information. The narrator usually addresses a listener for the purpose of entertaining or educating him, or to explain his own role in the story.

The Town and portions of The Mansion utilize a somewhat different form of character narration. Speakers such as Charles Mallison, Gavin Stevens, and V. K. Ratliff discuss numerous events from past and present, many of which they learned of only from other characters. Though these narrators often speak retrospectively, they show much more concern with the rise of the Snopes clan than with themselves. Because their lives become so deeply intermeshed with the Snopeses', however, they reveal much about themselves in the course of their narrations. Actually, they address the reader rather than each other, as if recording the story for posterity, but what they reveal in their narratives is clearly based on their conversations with each other. They describe episodes, suggest theories, analyze personalities, disagree with and correct each other. In earlier novels such as Light in August and Absalom, Absalom!, Faulkner illustrated the gathering of information through focal characters, community perspectives, and external narration. In the last two Snopes novels, however, the narrating characters specifically concern themselves with explaining how they have acquired information, and they seem amused with what they characterize as Jefferson's obsession with the Snopeses (an obsession which they clearly exhibit). In The Town Charles Mallison shows special interest in his Uncle Gavin's relationship with Eula Varner; he bases his account on personal observation and the hearsay of relatives and townspeople. His narrative holds considerable ironic potential. Like the other narrators, he believes he can discuss the Snopeses objectively. Stevens, Ratliff, and Mallison present themselves more as disinterested, wryly amused community analysts than as the deeply involved characters which they invariably are. Time and again events reveal their utter unobjectivity. In fact, their lack of self-awareness merely deepens their involvement. Charles, like Ratliff, often seems aware of the inherent irony in his narrations; his sense of humor clearly emerges in his account of Gavin's "conflict" with De Spain over Eula. Gavin, on the other hand, the most educated and civic-minded of the major narrators, seems the most deluded about the motives underlying his behavior, especially his behavior towards Eula and her daughter Linda. Though he professes amusement at the Snopeses, he really lacks a sense of humor. In the end, however, even the wily Ratliff succumbs to self-deception. At the conclusion of The Mansion, he and Stevens talk themselves into helping Linda secure

Mink Snopes's release from prison, implicitly setting in motion the events which conclude in Flem Snopes's murder.

A last form of character narrative bears special mention. As a character prepares to address a listener, the external narrator takes over, focusing upon his perspective to tell the story for him. In such an instance, the character goes ahead and talks to his listener, but the novel does not record his words, presenting instead the external narrator's version of them. This narrative structure occurs in portions of *Pylon*, *Absalom, Absalom!*, *Requiem for a Nun*, and the "Notes on a Horse Thief" section of *A Fable*. In *The Wild Palms*, the tall convict tells his fellow inmates about his adventures in the Mississippi River flood. But the narrative does not relay his words. Instead, the external narrator speaks for him, producing his own account focused exclusively on the convict's perspective. He even pauses occasionally to describe the convict talking to the other prisoners, as if to remind the reader whose story is being told. The reasons for such narrative vary. Most important, it provides structural variety and allows the external narrator to supplant relatively inarticulate characters in the narrative process.

Directed narration in the "Old Man" chapters of *The Wild Palms* and in other novels incorporates elements of the second major structural pattern in Faulkner's fiction, framed narrative. An external narrator "frames" the story from his own perspective—introducing characters and settings, providing transition between scenes, and offering occasional comments on the action. Framed narrative almost always appears in combination with character narrative. Focal character perspectives occur prominently. The external narrator's noncommittal, objective viewpoint contrasts with the biased, subjective views of characters. Though he may show sympathy, he usually does not evaluate a narrating character's reliability. He also rarely tells the story himself, relying instead on character perceptions. Nor does he insure that the story is told correctly; he merely frames, organizes, and presents it exactly as characters perceive it.

Framed Faulknerian narratives bear a number of typical characteristics. First, the external narrator rarely possesses complete knowledge of the focal character, especially of his past life, and he usually indicates the limits of his knowledge in one way or another. Second, though he occasionally may note mistakes and inaccuracies in a focal character's perspective, more often he remains objective, reporting without evaluating. Focal perceptions are *always* unreliable, to some extent, simply because in Faulkner's world human knowledge is by nature flawed and limited. As with character narrative, the reader must anticipate and recognize flaws in the focal individual's knowledge and personality. Third, on rare occasions narrating characters appear to describe another person from his perspective, establishing him as a kind of *pseudo*-focal character. Yet the perspectives of such characters are invariably unreliable. Characters lack the abilities of a true external narrator, and they inevitably rely upon fabricated, imagined information to create their pseudo-focal perspectives. An especially noteworthy example occurs in chapter 7 of *Absalom, Absalom!*, where Mr. Compson describes Sutpen's murder from the focal perspective of Wash Jones. Having never met Jones, who himself died hours after Sutpen, Mr. Compson has no way of knowing what Jones thought or felt. Using a few bits of evidence, he almost entirely fabricates his imaginative, vivid account. Gavin Stevens similarly explains Joe Christmas in *Light in August* and Lucas Beauchamp in *Intruder*, but in both novels he substitutes his own fallible understanding of human nature for facts. Genuine focal characters differ substantially from the pseudo-focal perspectives which appear occasionally in character narratives.

A minor variation of framed narrative characterizes the Compson Appendix and the prose sections of *Requiem for a Nun*. In both the narrator relates most of the story himself, employing focal perspectives only slightly and character narrators not at all. In another variation, *Intruder in the Dust* relies almost exclusively on Chick Mallison's focal perspective, making little use of character narration.

Framed narrative allows the presentation of a multiplicity of perspectives, a panoramic survey of contrasting human attitudes and experiences. It also enables internal character narratives to be "layered," passed among various members of a community, as in the Snopes trilogy, or passed down through time. In *Absalom*, Quentin tells his roommate in 1910 a story which Thomas Sutpen first told General Compson in 1835. Five characters pass the tale along, changing and embellishing it as they go, with the external narrator framing the entire process. Though layered narrative may shroud all the facts of an event in doubt, the conflicting versions of reality which it presents nevertheless possess their own inherent validity and meaning. As the characteristic structure in much of Faulkner's fiction, framed narrative carries an immense potential for *depth*, for relativistic three-dimensionality in time and space, in characterization, meaning (especially in the themes of time and human knowledge), and the examination of the human community. It is a major reason for the artistry of such novels as *Light in August*, *The Hamlet*, *Go Down*, *Moses*, and *A Fable*.

Faulkner's desire to give preeminence to his characters helped lead him towards the narrative structures underlying his mature stories and novels. Contrasting external and internal perspectives afford numerous views of character. External narrators characterize through descriptions of physical appearance and behavior. Narrating characters, on the other hand, present themselves solely from their own perspectives. They may consciously seek to make a good impression, or they may be wholly unaware of how they project their personalities—the case in both *The Sound and the Fury* and *As I Lay Dying*. Because the external narrator remains uninvolved, the reader must reach his own conclusions about such characters, as if they are strangers whom he has met for the first time on the street and whose talk, gestures, dress, behavior, and general demeanor influence the opinion which he forms of them. His resulting opinions may vary considerably from the image the character wishes to project. Jason Compson, for instance, thinks of himself as a suffering martyr, struggling against the ineptitude of all around him, beleaguered by a complaining mother, mongoloid brother, and delinquent niece. Yet the reader perceives him quite differently.[18] Doc Hines, Mr. Compson, Jewel Bundren, and Lucius Priest evoke their own personalities in a similar way. Focal perspectives likewise do not require the narrator's intrusion. He presents a character's view of himself accurately and usually without comment. In this manner readers become acquainted with Ike McCaslin, Harry Wilbourne, and Mink Snopes. More often, however, focal perspective and character narration work together to evoke the personalities of such characters as Joe Christmas, the Reporter, V. K. Ratliff, and many others.

Individuals may also be characterized through the reactions which they prompt in those around them. Ratliff speaks his own mind when he talks about Eula Varner or Flem Snopes. Other characters, primarily Mallison and Stevens, may disagree with him, and they explain why. The reader must consider their opinions in light of their personalities, their roles in the story, and the evidence which they rely upon. Jason holds such a distorted concept of human nature that any opinion he expresses is gravely suspect. Gavin Stevens talks in a more humane, amiable, rational way. Still, he often expresses suspicious opinions, though his beguiling personality may wrongly convince the reader of his credibility. The ironic context of such narratives as the title story of *Go Down, Moses, Intruder,* and *The Town* provides a counterforce against his personable nature and uncovers his flaws. Eventually, out of the biased views of various characters, there emerges a fuller, more rounded, more accurate view than any one character alone can give.

In a few significant instances, Faulkner depicts an individual from the exterior, solely through the eyes of those around him, without the benefit of his own focal perspective. Flem Snopes, center of interest in three novels, never serves as a focal character; his own view of himself never appears. Characters who discuss him frequently fail to perceive his humanity, often ascribing bizarre and unlikely motives to his behavior. Much of what they "know" about him is pure conjecture and hearsay (including his presumed impotence). Sooner or later, the total absence of his perspective must cause the reader to wonder whether Flem can be all that other characters suggest. Stevens and Ratliff, in their obsession with the Snopes "invasion" of their community, reduce him to an abstraction. The discerning reader must finally provide a compensating view of Flem's character—one founded on the necessity of his humanity and which imbues him, at the end of *The Mansion*, with pathos. Faulkner himself never established characters as bloodless symbols, bereft of humanity. In the end, however, there may simply be no satisfactory view at all. The reader can only guess and wonder—as he must do with Joe Christmas, Thomas Sutpen, and Flem Snopes.

Most of Faulkner's novels characterize through a combination of exterior characterization, physical description, and character perspective. In the absence of the narrator's subjective evaluations, the ultimate burden falls upon the reader, again drawn in by the narrative's refusal to work conventionally. Faulkner challenges him to respond, tempts him to reach simplistic conclusions, then provides ample evidence to crush them. To meet the complexities and contradictions of the modern world, he created a corresponding fictional world, utterly lacking in formulaic or facile solutions to the problems and dilemmas which face its inhabitants.

Narrative structure's organic relationship with characterization, form, theme, and setting weighs inherently on the meaning of the novels and stories. Conrad Aiken's praise for Faulkner's concern with the novel as form bears repetition.[19] Meaning resides in the shape of fiction, in the manner of its telling as well as its content. Indeed, such

elements as perspective, narrator, and distance hold no meaning unless considered as part of a larger structure. Warren Beck observes
that "it is not possible to comprehend Faulkner's point of view from
separate quotations but only from implications in his novels as wholes
and from the positions of his various characters in relation to those
implied themes."[20] The structural patterns which predominate dictate
certain laws fundamental to the interpretation of Faulkner's writing.

Narrative structure reflects meaning. It also becomes meaning. Unreliable narrating characters, narrative perspectives which leave all
"facts" in doubt, which indeed deny the possibility of ever discerning
the reality of an individual or event—these define truth as illusory
and unknowable, perhaps even as an ideal and perfect knowledge
which simply does not exist. Because the narrative structure of such
novels as *Light in August* and *Absalom, Absalom!* never reveals the
truth, the reader shares the frustration of characters who seek truth.
Faulkner's people live in an environment of ever-shifting values, of
moral, ethical, aesthetic, and theological relativism which offers no
"stillpoint of the turning world" for guidance. Given the failure of the
ideal, the absence of external solutions to internal human problems,
the novels repeatedly throw the weight of responsibility and suffering
back upon the individual, who must deal as best he can with his
world's imperfection. Yet self-reliance is no ideal either. Numerous
characters struggle for self-knowledge, but they never achieve it.
Some, like Quentin and Christmas, die because of their failure. Others, McCaslin, Gavin Stevens, and the Reporter, for instance, ruin
their lives and often the lives of others because they are too confident
of what they know. A few—Byron Bunch and Temple Drake (in *Requiem*)—continue to struggle, realizing that though the ideal might lie
ever beyond them, the struggle itself, the process of motion and
change (Faulkner's definition of life), is necessary to growth and
fulfillment.

Narrative structure also emphasizes the primacy of individual perception—not as an ideal means of confronting the world but simply
as the *only* means. Human imperfections flaw human perspectives.
But they also reveal the quality of the human mind, of life in a social
environment. Faulkner's thorough reliance upon character perspectives bespeaks his conviction that the world bears significance only as
it impinges upon the life of the individual human being. It can be
known, and felt, only as the individual knows and feels it. It has importance, meaning, significance, only as the individual sees fit to ascribe such values to it. Hence, though what the tall convict, Harry

Wilbourne, Gavin Stevens, and Boon Hogganbeck believe—about themselves, other people, the situations in which they become involved—may be demonstrably wrong *in the reader's mind*, and perhaps even in Faulkner's, their perspectives are nonetheless meaningful and valid. They cannot be rejected merely because of their imperfections. When Rosa Coldfield, General Compson, and Shreve McCannon posit three substantially different interpretations of Thomas Sutpen, in the process uncovering three vividly divergent opinions of time, life, and human nature, Faulkner does not intend that any one of them should be ignored. The novel's meaning resides in each of them. Each, in its own way, has importance. Because of the relativism of meaning in Faulkner's world, no one character can ever be totally right in what he believes, but he cannot be totally wrong either.

Like James Joyce, Faulkner wrote novels which place a considerable burden on the reader, perhaps too great a burden for many contemporary readers to bear. Like Joyce, Faulkner essentially redefined the reader's role. But those who can meet the challenges of his fiction find ample recompense for their effort. Even readers who misunderstand Faulkner can still enjoy him (his definition of what his novels *mean* would probably allow ample latitude for misunderstanding). T. S. Eliot defined the literary critic's duty as "the elucidation of works of art and the correction of taste."[21] In Faulkner's fiction, perhaps more than any other element, narrative structure requires elucidation. By coming to terms with narrative structure, the critic can meet the challenges of Faulkner's achievement and become the ultimate reader, pointing the way, through criticism and teaching, for other readers to follow.

Chapter Two
Light in August

"I have just finished reading the galley of LIGHT IN AUGUST," Faulkner wrote Ben Wasson in 1932. "I don't see anything wrong with it. I want it to stand as it is. This one is a novel: not an anecdote; that's why it seems top heavy, perhaps."[1] In many ways Faulkner's fifth major novel takes a significant evolutionary stride beyond the innovations of *The Sound and the Fury* and *As I Lay Dying* and the relative orthodoxy of *Flags in the Dust* and *Sanctuary*. For the first time in his career Faulkner traces the growth and development of a single human character over a period of thirty years. And discounting the failure of *Mosquitoes*, for the first time he explores the common experience of a group of individuals radically different from one another in identity and background. The narrative structure of *Light in August*, a fusion of traditional and innovative techniques, permits the exploration of a number of varied themes: the meaning of individual experience; the nature of community and the individual's place in the community; isolation; obsessiveness; the growth of and need for identity; the past's influence upon the present; the interrelatedness of all human lives and events; the prison of environment and the myth of free will.

Faulkner's earlier novels evinced a particular concern with the family: the Sartorises, Benbows, Goodwins, Compsons, Bundrens, and others. They often focused on relationships among family members and their varying individual perspectives on the world. But when he began work on *Light in August* late in the summer of 1931, Faulkner expanded this concern to encompass the individual's relationship with the community, that cohesive group of individuals living together voluntarily under a common set of laws and customs. In *Light in August* Faulkner for the first time defines the individual not only from the individual's viewpoint but from the ways other people—members of the community—see him too. In *Flags in the Dust* Jefferson provided the general background against which Faulkner portrayed the Sartoris and Benbow clans. In *The Sound and the Fury* and *Sanctuary*, the community, though always in the background, does not play a major role; moreover, these novels explore the specific experience of the individual—his confrontation with evil, for example, or with his own psychic decay. Through fifteen character narrators, *As I Lay Dying* continues the emphasis on individual perspective. Its most important narrators belong to the Bundren family, but in such characters as Cora Tull, Doc Peabody, and Samson, Faulkner clearly identifies the community's interest in the journey of that smelly Bundren burial wagon. In *Light in August* the community for the first time becomes a primary element, serving for all practical purposes as a major character.[2]

Narrative structure in the 1932 novel helps delineate the community and its interaction with individual characters. It also reflects a change in Faulkner's attitude towards his reader. In *The Sound and the Fury* and *As I Lay Dying*, the narrating characters' fragmented (and fragmenting) perspectives do not present the stories in a logical or chronological order, forcing the reader to reconstruct the actual sequence of events using internal evidence. Reconstruction directly confronts the reader with the fragmentation which the novels record. The more straightforward plot of *Sanctuary*, on the other hand, is narrated from a generally external perspective. The narrative may reveal what a character sees or hears but virtually never what he thinks. As a result, such a figure as Popeye seems to act without method or reason. *Sanctuary*'s horrific vision of evil, irresponsibility, and spiritual impotence is made all the more frightening by a narrative structure which provides no explanations, no justifications for what many of the characters do. *Macbeth*, at least, explains the circumstances which fuel its protagonist's ambitions, so the audience understands the cause of his evil. *Sanctuary* describes without explaining, affording the reader no basis for understanding, seemingly forsaking the world of rationality, moral codes, and cause-and-effect relationships.

Light in August combines the externality of *Sanctuary* with the internality of *As I Lay Dying*. Four major factors shape its structure. First, the burden of reconstruction shifts from the reader to the characters. Indeed, the community's discussion of events proves to be a favorite pastime. Second, while continuing to emphasize individual perspectives (through such narrators and focal characters as Joe Christmas, Joanna Burden, Gail Hightower, and Byron Bunch), the narrative also portrays a community perspective through town gossip, characters who "symbolize" community opinion, and an external narrator who describes and comments on community reaction. Third, the presence of five major story lines—Christmas, Bunch, Hightower, Lena Grove, and Burden (along with numerous minor ones: Doc Hines and Percy

Grimm, for instance)—necessitates a structure which unifies all the disparate narrative strands. Finally, more than the novels which preceded it, *Light in August* seeks to *explain* the people and events it describes. By employing the perspectives of its characters, it achieves these explanations without sacrificing artistic vigor or intensity and makes them a veritable part of what the novel explores.

The most pervasive structural element in *Light in August* is the uninvolved narrator—the storyteller, overseer to all the action, a central authority connecting various strands of plot and character. In no sense a character or even a person, the narrator and his influence— his "personality"—shape the novel. (Even the masculine pronoun *he* provides only a convenient referent, in no way implying sexual gender). Though he tells the story, he is not Faulkner. Nor does he speak for Faulkner, who uses him as a medium for relaying the story. His presence at best may be theoretical, but his effects are very real.

The external narrator enriches the interrelationships among theme, characterization, and structure. His usually objective perspective contrasts remarkably with the subjective, biased views of the characters. He thus serves as a significant source of characterization. A ubiquitous commentator and analyst, he can intrude into the minds of such individuals as Hightower and Christmas, uncovering their thoughts, articulating their unconscious moods and emotions, pointing to events and people in their pasts which shaped their present-day lives. He also provides a context for the numerous character narratives. Characters who speak at length do so in a narrative framed in Conradian fashion by the external narrator, enforcing the fact of their fallibility. In this role the narrator resembles the unnamed speaker who introduces Marlow in Joseph Conrad's "Youth," "Heart of Darkness," and *Lord Jim.* Conrad's narrator, however, is an actual character who clearly identifies himself with first-person pronouns. Faulkner's narrator never refers to himself, but he works actively in every scene, shaping the story and its telling in a way Conrad's narrator does not. As an organizer, interpreter, moralist, observer, and storyteller, the narrator is the most important structural element in *Light in August.*

The joint use of narrating characters and external narrator, as Olga Vickery has observed, merges experimental and traditional forms in the sort of novelistic structure characteristic of the rest of Faulkner's career.[3] In *Light in August* especially, the fusion of tradition and innovation permits the contrasting of a general community viewpoint with the often quite different perspective of an individual in conflict with the community. In chapter 13, section 4, for example, Byron tries to explain to Hightower why he has moved Lena out to the cabin behind Joanna Burden's house. In chapter 14, section 1, the sheriff and his deputy—both community representatives—discuss the same question. (Each chapter is divided into several sections, set off at beginning and end by line spaces; sections usually center on a single event or focal perspective). The ironic undercurrent of the narrator's presence in both sections suggests ulterior motives to Byron's explanations, ones which he either has not recognized or refuses to admit. Perspectives shift not only among various characters but also between internal and external viewpoints. A character is seen through his own consciousness, from the viewpoints of other characters, from the perspective of the narrator, who himself may work in various ways. Characterization through contrasting perspectives bequeaths the final judgment of a character to the reader. Vickery comments: "Because of the interpenetration and interdependence of the private and public worlds, each character is multidimensional. He is at once subject and object, observer and observed, creator and created."[4] In this novel, which pits one man's agonizing struggle to fathom his identity against an entire community's efforts to understand him, such a narrative mode proves quite appropriate.

Though the narrator is not a character, his personality is easily recognizable and directly responsible for tonal variations from section to section and chapter to chapter. From the first page he establishes himself as an authoritative narrative source—a vehicle through which Faulkner transmits the story and a judge (not always an impartial one) of human character and behavior. He exhibits several obviously human characteristics. Occasionally he pauses to rebuke or correct a character's mistakes, as with the failure of Lena's brother to notice her pregnancy: "Then he remarked her changing shape, which he should have noticed some time before" (pp. 3–4).* He may project objectivity toward his subject, or strong prejudice; he may range in mood from disinterest or amusement to passionate involvement and sympathy.

The narrator also lacks omniscience. Though at points he appears to know everything, at others he seems able only to speculate, especially when examining character motivations. Describing Christmas's attitude towards Mr. McEachern, he explains: "Perhaps he was thinking then how he and the man could always count upon one another,

---

*William Faulkner, *Light in August* (1932; New York: Random House, 1967).

depend upon one another; that it was the woman alone who was un-predictable. Perhaps he saw no incongruity at all in the fact that he was about to be punished" (p. 149). This *conditional* narration occurs when the narrator is unsure of his information, when he either can-not or will not divulge the facts. In one sense, his semiomniscience places him in a position equivalent to that of the citizens of Jefferson, who often can do little more than guess about many characters and events.[5] The lack of authoritative information leaves the reader in a similar position; he too must speculate, which may encourage his identification with the townspeople. The narrative's failure to resolve many of the questions it raises reflects a theme apparent in much of Faulkner's work—the idea that human behavior often remains per-manently inexplicable. When various characters try to explain Christ-mas, they immerse themselves in a search for self-knowledge which often reveals more about their own natures than about his. Condi-tional narrative also indicates the narrator's distinct separateness from Faulkner, who as author and creator possesses total knowledge of what happens in the novel.

While tonal and idiomatic variations may theoretically result from the narrator's multifaceted personality, they ultimately represent the author's purposeful decision. Each episode's prevailing tone directly reflects its structural and thematic purpose. A focal character's emo-tions, thoughts, and personality influence the tone of the scenes in which he appears. The same is true of narrating characters. Tonal variations also occur according to the kind of distance which the nar-rator establishes between himself and his subject. Does he describe only a character's actions? Does he enter the character's mind, reveal-ing his thoughts? Or does he become a spokesman, articulating what the character himself cannot say and does not know? The narrator of *Light in August* may assume one of three general relationships with his subject, although there are many gradations between them. He thus produces one of three types of narrative.

In *external* narrative, the narrator completely separates himself from his subject, an uncommon degree of distance in the novel. Intrusions occur rarely. Characters and events are described objectively, without comment, in a manner which traditional narrative concepts would term "dramatic." The language may seem as direct and terse as the scenario for an Ibsen play:

> Hightower has not moved. He sits erect behind the desk, his
> forearms parallel upon the armrests of the chair. He wears neither

collar nor coat. His face is at once gaunt and flabby; it is as though there were two faces, one imposed upon the other, looking out from beneath the pale, bald skull surrounded by a fringe of gray hair, from behind the twin motionless glares of his spectacles.
[P. 82]

Such narrative simply records dialogue, with the narrator briefly noting physical gestures and identifying speakers. External narrative usually employs present-tense verbs. It emphasizes physical reaction and expression, especially facial and hand movements. In chapter 1, Mrs. Armstid's clashing of stove lids, her neutral voice, and "the savage finality with which she built the fire" (pp. 14–15) reveal her unspoken opinion of Lena. Aware that the older woman probably suspects and disapproves of her condition, Lena averts her eyes, stares at her hands, smooths her dress, and speaks in a voice whose "doggedness has a soft quality, an inwardlighted quality of tranquil and calm unreason and detachment" (p. 15). Other examples of external narrative occur in the conversation between Byron Bunch, his landlady, and Sheriff Kennedy, in chapter 18, section 1 (pp. 396–400); in chapter 14, section 1 (pp. 302–4); and in chapter 1, sections 1, 3, and 5 (pp. 6–9, 14–15, 19–20). The tonal and idiomatic character of such scenes may vary considerably. Although the external narrator may occasionally indulge in mildly lyrical, poetic descriptions, as in the pastoral opening scene, he usually adopts a more detached (occasionally even clinical) tone. His separation from the action is complete; rarely does he express any opinion at all of the characters he describes.

In *internal* narrative the narrator begins to submerge himself in his subject matter. Although he may remain objective and detached, his perspective changes. Not limited to physical description, he enters his characters' minds and reports their thoughts. Except in sections focused entirely on one character, internal narrative often combines with external narrative as the novel's characteristic narrative structure. Double quotation marks identify spoken statements while single quotation marks enclose specific thoughts. When the narrator more generally describes a character's attitudes and experiences, no special punctuation occurs. Importantly, the information which the narrator organizes and refines through internal narrative always comes from the minds of focal characters.

Two internally narrated episodes describe Byron Bunch's glimpse of Joe Brown's escape from Lena's cabin (chapter 18, section 1, pp.

393–403) and Percy Grimm's pursuit of Joe Christmas (chapter 19, section 2, pp. 425–40). These scenes closely resemble one another, especially in perspective. Confrontation with a fugitive marks a climactic moment in each focal character's life. Bunch at last resolves to assert himself, to abandon his passivity and challenge the man on whose behalf (he believes) he has given up Lena. Grimm, on the other hand, feels duty bound by the capture of Christmas to invoke his militant patriotism in defense of Jefferson, justice, and the white race—the event for which he has lived his entire life. Nearly identical moments in each scene occur when Bunch and Grimm catch sight of their quarries. Bunch, about to leave Jefferson for good, turns on his mule and sees the cabin, small and "toylike" in the sun. The word "watches" twice emphasizes his perspective:

> Then, as Byron watches, a man appears as though by magic at the rear of it, already running, in the act of running out from the rear of the cabin while the unsuspecting deputy sits quiet and motionless on the front step. For a while longer Byron too sits motionless, half turned in the saddle, and watches the tiny figure flee on across the barren slope behind the cabin, toward the woods. [P. 402]

A similar distanced description, a cinematic panorama glimpsed through the wrong end of a telescope, occurs when Grimm first sights his prey; the verbs "saw," "watched," "seemed," and "hear" emphasize his observing perspective:

> The he saw Christmas. He saw the man, small with distance, appear up out of the ditch, his hands close together. As Grimm watched he saw the fugitive's hands glint once like the flash of a heliograph as the sun struck the handcuffs, and it seemed to him that even from here he could hear the panting and desperate breath of the man who even now was not free. Then the tiny figure ran again and vanished beyond the nearest negro cabin. [P. 436]

Both scenes center on what the focal characters see. What they *do* see prompts them immediately to action. Despite the generally comic tone of the Bunch episode, it possesses serious implications, for he is voluntarily leaving the only woman he has ever loved. An allusion to the famous *Hamlet* soliloquy ("And Byron Bunch he wouldn't even have to be or not be Byron Bunch" [p. 401]) suggests that if he is not suicidally depressed he is at least wondering about the point of his existence. Grimm, the main antagonist in a tragic episode, proves to be one of the novel's most comically absurd and horrifying figures. His caricaturish personality, with its shallow boy-scout fervor, beguiles such townspeople as Sheriff Kennedy and the American Legion commander into taking him too lightly. That such a person commits the novel's ultimate atrocity—the castration and murder of Christmas— reflects Faulkner's conviction that the distinction between comedy and tragedy is hazy, if indeed it exists at all.

From an external perspective the narrator does little more than report, but internal narrative allows him the freedom to comment and evaluate, if still rather hesitantly. In relaying a character's thoughts, for instance, he can place them in the context of the circumstances and events which created them. He does so in his account of Percy Grimm's life (pp. 425–27) and in chapter 6, section 2, which describes the dietician's fear of betrayal by the young Christmas:

> On the fourth day she became quite calmly and completely mad. She no longer planned at all. Her subsequent actions followed a kind of divination, as if the days and the unsleeping nights during which she had nursed behind that calm mask her fear and fury had turned her psychic along with her natural female infallibility for the spontaneous comprehension of evil. [P. 117]

The passage employs a metaphorical clause ("as if the days and unsleeping nights . . .") to characterize the dietician's behavior—a common enough Faulknerian device. Unlike conditional narrative, which leaves the ultimate judgment of a character up to the reader, such metaphoric language clarifies the reasons for an individual's behavior. Hence, internal narrative can explain as well as describe. It is objective in that the narrator serves only as a reporter, rarely revealing his own opinions; it is subjective in its close reliance on the perceptions of characters. Its access to the conscious mind provides a link between thought and action, allowing a character's own perspective to explain his behavior. Importantly, the internal views of character which it provides often contradict the purely clinical descriptions of external narrative.

Internal translated narrative at its extreme wholly abolishes distance between narrator and subject. The narrator shifts from objective detachment to complete subjective submergence in the focal character's consciousness. For all practical purposes, narrator and focal character fuse. Internal translated narrative penetrates deeply into a character's mind, beneath the levels of consciousness to the realms of emotion, instinct, forgotten memory, and unconscious thought. The narrator articulates these thoughts, placing them in the context of the character's conscious mind and behavior. Unlike internal narrative, where the narrator merely reports what the focal character thinks, translated internal narrative enables the narrator to speak *for* the character. His voice becomes the character's voice, even in its use of the first-person pronoun *I*. Accordingly, translated narrative is usually printed in italics, which distinguish it from internal and external narrative.

Faulkner's use of translated narrative has attracted considerable critical comment. It has been called the direct voice of a character's mind as well as a mixture of traditional narrative with stream-of-consciousness techniques.[6] The mind, of course, especially the unconscious mind, has no voice of its own. Stream-of-consciousness narrative in Joyce's *Ulysses* conveys primarily conscious impressions, how subconsciousness becomes manifest in conscious thought. Without an actively translating narrator, stream of consciousness cannot depict the contents of the unconscious mind. The third section of *The Sound and the Fury*, a Faulknerian stream-of-consciousness monologue, occasionally hints at what lies beneath the surface of Jason's conscious mind, but it never lays his subconsciousness open. Subconscious thoughts occasionally well up during Quentin's narrative, but only because of his insanity (in a sense, the confused commingling of conscious and subconscious thoughts). Faulkner makes the subconscious mind's influence on conscious thought and behavior a minor theme in *The Sound and the Fury*, a theme which stream of consciousness can effectively explore. The same is true in the *Ulysses* Nighttown episode, where Bloom's drunken stupor allows his subconscious mind to manifest itself through hallucinatory fantasies and symbols. The primary distinction between pure stream-of-consciousness narrative (found, for example, in the first three chapters of *Ulysses*) and Faulkner's translated narrative lies in the narrator. A stream-of-consciousness narrator simply reports what the mind is thinking (though such reporting obviously involves some organization); the translating narrator, on the other hand, explains and articulates the mind's contents. The difference proves crucial to *Light in August*, which examines causative links between the unconscious motives, conscious thoughts, and physical acts of Joe Christmas. When the translating narrator intrudes into a character's mind, he moves from reporting spoken words to conscious thoughts to unconscious memories and impressions.[7] When he reports speech and conscious thoughts, the focal character's idiom and personality pervade the narrative, but in the deepest translated intrusions the character's voice fades and is replaced by the typical voice of a Faulknerian narrator. When Christmas first enters Joanna Burden's kitchen at the end of the tenth chapter, he gropes to identify the food which he finds there, to remember what the strange kitchen reminds him of:

> *I'll know it in a minute. I have eaten it before, somewhere. In a minute I will* memory clicking knowing *I see . . . my head bent I hear the monotonous dogmatic voice . . . I see the indomitable bullet head the clean blunt beard they too bent and I thinking How can he be so nothungry and I smelling my mouth and tongue weeping the hot salt of waiting my eyes tasting the hot steam from the dish* "It's peas," he said, aloud. "For sweet Jesus. Field peas cooked with molasses." [P. 217]

Christmas reaches this conclusion after his memory both consciously and subconsciously analyzes numerous vague sensory impressions and images. The passage literally portrays Christmas's act of remembering, but its voice belongs to the narrator, not to Christmas. The narrator speaks *for* Christmas. The kitchen scene occurs at the end of the five-chapter account of his early life in the orphanage and with the McEacherns, a time when he came to see the eating of food (or its refusal) as a self-assertive, rebellious act. The narrator's translation symbolically summarizes the contents of the retrospective chapters by showing their accretive impact upon this one moment of Christmas's life. The scene also provides transition between the past and present times of the novel. Joe Christmas has entered another household where he will resist what he regards as another woman's desire to possess him. Before ever meeting Joanna Burden he rebels against her by eating the food she has yet to offer.

The narrator's subjective interpretations in such translated intrusions invest the narrative with a remarkable analytical objectivity. The additional perspective it provides allows the brief scene in Joanna Burden's kitchen to dramatize the consequences of Joe's life with the McEacherns. In the seventh, eighth, and ninth chapters, which describe the McEacherns from Joe's perspective, the reader easily recognizes the tyrannical atmosphere of the McEachern home and understands why a boy might rebel against it. The translated intrusion, however, reveals the effects of the McEachern household on Joe's psyche. Such adjectives as "indomitable," "monotonous," and "dogmatic" emphasize authoritarianism, while sensory adjectives, contrasting Joe's hunger with his parents' ritualistic piety, suggest his physical deprivation and his essential isolation from the McEacherns

and their religion. Fifteen years after leaving them, his immediate reaction to food discovered in a strange house is to eat it, not out of
hunger but because of the repressive authority against which his entire life has conditioned him to revolt. The brief episode in Joanna
Burden's kitchen implies that the "destiny" which Christmas seeks al-
ternately to embrace and escape results directly from the environment of his childhood and adolescence.

Translated narrative employs the full range of the narrator's voice
and analytical power. It relies strongly on his omnipresence in time
and space, on his ability to "read" a character's mind. Objective and
reliable, he knows what none of the characters can know; he likewise
admits his limitations by using conditional narrative. When such a
character as Gavin Stevens in chapter 19 attempts to serve the narrator's function by explaining another person's mind and behavior, he
cannot succeed. Because Stevens cannot enter Christmas's mind,
know of his past, or directly observe what he does, he can only guess
haphazardly about him. Stevens's personality—his emotional and intellectual character—limits his objectivity. As a result, his explanation
provides only inaccurate stereotypes rather than genuine answers.
Very simply, he lacks the external narrator's abilities. When the narrator does provide information, he does so infallibly, and no character
can speak with infallibility. Because the reader has access to the narrator's knowledge, he knows more about what happens in the novel
than any character, but he never quite learns, or understands, the entire story.

Though translated narrative occurs mainly in brief italicized passages, a few longer sections (all of chapter 5, for example, the novel's
most thorough characterization of Christmas) also fall within the clas-
sification. Such long narratives are not printed in italics. Moreover,
italics serve several minor functions not always related to translated
narrative; they may denote intensity of thought, confusion (especially
at the beginning of chapter 10, after Joe has been beaten up), an anonymous community voice composed of many individuals (section 1,
chapter 13—the communal voice itself results from the narrator's intrusion into a communal "mind"), or printed language (Hightower's
sign; Joanna Burden's will).

In whatever form, translated narrative portrays a moment of heightened awareness, of fear, doubt, epiphany, resolution, or tension, not
merely in a character's life but in the novel's progress as well. In comments on *Sanctuary*, André Bleikasten has effectively characterized
one of the functions of translated narrative. Of Temple Drake's ex-

clamation, "Something is going to happen to me," Bleikasten says, "In the vertigo of imminence the future ceases to be the time of possibility. Temple's present is nothing but entranced anticipation, her present is her future, a past to come, memory before the event." Her past and future merge in a dramatic glimpse of how past and present will lead inexorably towards a specific future destiny.[8] When Christmas likewise exclaims, "*Something is going to happen to me. I am going to do something*" (p. 97), he is surrendering to a fate which his three years with Joanna Burden, which the design and pattern of his entire life's experience, have predetermined.

The portrait in chapter 5 of a depressed, despairing, inexorably doomed Joe Christmas vividly illustrates the consequences of events recorded in chapters 6–12. Using Christmas as a focal character, these chapters employ objective internal narrative, with brief translations, to chronicle the progress of his life from the orphanage through his affair with Joanna. The two introductory sentences to chapter 6 establish that the long biographical retrospection which follows will concern Christmas's memory and experience: "Memory believes before knowing remembers. Believes longer than recollects, longer than knowing even wonders" (p. 111). Loosely paraphrased, these sentences read: "Past events, preserved in memory, shape the individual's identity whether he consciously recalls them or not. Identity is stronger than memory, which can be forgotten, stronger than the mind's attempt to understand events which have formed it." Providing a sort of ritualistic invocation to the retrospective chapters, these opening lines prepare for the narrative investigation of Christmas' life, as if to say, "Here is what made him the man he became." They also indicate that the events in the ensuing narrative reside in Christmas' memory.[9] But the source of these chapters is not Christmas's mind, but rather the narrator's voice. The long retrospection intrudes deeply into the focal character's mind, whose contents the narrator organizes and portrays through internal narrative. The narrator also provides much information which Christmas himself did not possess (about the dietician and the McEacherns, for example). Scenes from his childhood are detailed, specific, and factually drawn. Although he might remember some of these events, it is extremely doubtful he can recall them so exactly. And although he is the focal character, the retrospection does not restrict itself only to what he knows. Whenever necessary, the narrator freely supplies missing information and invokes the perspectives of other characters.

Centered on his life and memory, the retrospective chapters present the crucial episodes in the formation of Christmas's identity: his encounter with the dietician, adoption by the McEacherns, the ordeal of the catechism, the Bobbie Allen affair, his assault on McEachern and subsequent running away. Occasionally the narrator will explain an episode's significance before narrating it. Chapter 7, the story of Christmas's rebellion against McEachern, begins: "And memory knows this; twenty years later memory is still to believe *On this day I became a man*" (p. 137). His previously discussed struggle to remember the taste of cold peas suggests that Christmas does not clearly remember the McEacherns, perhaps has nearly forgotten them. In Joanna Burden's kitchen he recalls McEachern merely as "*the indomitable bullet head.*" Chapter 10 reveals how most events from the past have become blurred and confused in his memory: "the thousand streets ran as one street, with imperceptible corners and changes of scene"; "one place was the same as another to him" (pp. 210, 213). The few important events which he might recall less vaguely are described at length by the narrator, who continues as the presiding observer, organizer, and translator. The same narrative principle works in the life histories of other characters, especially in the accounts of Joanna Burden's family (pp. 228–41) and Hightower's disgrace (pp. 55–66 from community perspective; pp. 441–67 from his perspective). The result is a more objective presentation of past-time people and events responsible for the lives which important characters lead in the novel's present time. Hightower and Burden, of course, have much better memories than Christmas; in fact, their problems result from their remembering *too* well.

Multiple perspectives work as another fundamental component of the novel's structure. The narrator provides one important perspective. Character narrators, focal characters, and the community consciousness provide three others. The combination of an objective, semi-omniscient narrator with numerous subjective character perspectives prevents any one authoritative source of knowledge from being established. Though occasionally expressing his opinions, the narrator never becomes the final arbiter of events and characters. He is basically a reporter; even when interpreting a character's subconscious thoughts, he does so only to convey them to the reader. Ulterior motives do not warp his perspective.

Faulkner emphasizes the potential fallibility of character-narrators by carefully framing their narratives, thus allowing for the undercutting influence of irony. The external narrator introduces all the primary speakers—Byron Bunch, Joanna Burden, Doc Hines, Mrs. Hines, Gavin Stevens, the furniture dealer, and a few others—and describes the circumstances surrounding their talks. Significantly, narrating characters always direct their narratives to other characters. Bunch talks to Hightower, Joanna to Christmas, Stevens to a professor friend, the Hines couple to Bunch and Hightower, the furniture dealer to his wife. Such hearer-teller relationships prevent the illusion of a direct address to the reader, on which the character narratives (not addressed to other characters) of *The Sound and the Fury* and *As I Lay Dying* rely. When a character in *Light in August* tells a story, he does so for a reason which itself belongs to the story. Strangely, Christmas, the main character, never narrates, although chapter 12 reveals that at some point he has told Joanna about his life. His absence as a narrator heightens his isolation and mystery.

Byron Bunch, the most significant character narrator, spends more actual time talking than anyone else. His main narratives occur in chapter 4, sections 1 and 2; chapter 13, sections 2 and 4; and chapter 16, sections 1 and 3. He can, obviously, tell a good story when he wants to, and he chooses Gail Hightower for his audience. He evidently regards the ex-minister as a kind of moral counselor. Perhaps these two men are drawn together because neither has actively participated in community affairs, because each has been an essentially passive observer rather than an active doer. Both express a cynical attitude towards human behavior, though the ex-minister's cynicism seems more deeply entrenched. Byron may also be drawn to Hightower for the same reason he at first becomes interested in Lena, Christmas, and Brown—like everyone else in Jefferson, he is curious about strange people and events.

Byron's narratives reveal as much about his own character as about the people he describes. He talks out of the urge to gossip, like other townspeople, but also in order to justify—to himself and to Hightower—his plans and actions. As he becomes more aware of how he has transgressed against social propriety, his separation from Hightower grows. As his life moves imperceptibly towards involvement, he begins recognizing the minister's unnatural isolation. Their relationship gradually reverses. At first Hightower serves almost as a confessor, a moral catalyst; later he becomes a tool in Byron's scheme to aid Lena and the Hines couple. Finally, Byron becomes the counselor; Hightower the (unwilling) protégé. Byron feels free not only to point out Hightower's faults but also to prepare him, by telling him about Christmas, Grove, and Brown, for the challenges which he eventually must face: the delivery of Lena's child, and his lie that Christmas "was with me the night of the murder" (p. 439). Byron's talking also signifies a tentative grappling with the new potentialities opening up in his life. His changing relationship with Hightower— who at first is his advisor, later a simple listener, then part of a scheme, finally a castoff friend—measures his progress towards full involvement in life.

Ulterior motives also figure in Joanna Burden's narrative. Her attraction to Christmas compels her to recount her history, perhaps in the hope of securing his affection. Gavin Stevens's normal garrulousness, and a northern professor's curiosity, motivate his flawed analysis of Christmas. A somewhat different circumstance molds the narratives of the Hines couple: their grandson's appearance after more than thirty years sets each of them off—Hines in his obsession with getting Christmas lynched, Mrs. Hines in her wish to see her dead daughter's child. The Hines pay no particular attention to their listeners, Byron and Hightower, whom they address mainly because they happen to be available, though the old woman may believe that the ex-minister can save her grandson. The furniture dealer in the final chapter talks because of his desire to make his wife jealous by telling her a humorous story, a mildly lewd anecdote, after making love to her. Shaped by listeners as well as tellers, character narratives project solid, three-dimensional images of the individuals who produce them. They vary the novel's predominant narrative structure by interjecting direct, firsthand narration. Irony helps to insure objective characterization; constantly shifting perspectives balance one character's view of events with the views of other characters, the Jefferson community, and the external narrator.

However, the long monologues of Stevens (pp. 421–25), Burden (pp. 228–40), and the Hines couple (pp. 352–61, 361–65) may also mark a flaw in the novel's structure. Out of context they remarkably exemplify Faulkner's storytelling talent, but they do not fit smoothly into the narrative. The same can be said of the long speech which Hightower, in chapter 20, remembers having delivered to his wife during their train ride to Jefferson (pp. 457–59). On one level the narratives present important firsthand information. Only Mr. and Mrs. Hines could reveal the events surrounding Joe Christmas's birth. Only Joanna could tell her own story, not merely because she knows it better than anyone else but also because it dramatizes so well her personality and her guilt-ridden attitude towards Negroes and the town of Jefferson. Her narrative proves cumbersomely long, however, and her passion for Christmas seems almost an awkward authorial excuse for getting her to talk. But Gavin Stevens's disquisition is undoubtedly the most aberrant element in the novel. Apparently he symbolizes the community, and his analysis of Christmas may well represent the opinions of many townspeople. But he appears so suddenly and speaks at such length, with such emphatic authority, that his voice has too often been identified as Faulkner's, clumsily inserted into the novel to explain Christmas's behavior on the day of his death.[10] Though narrative evidence suggests that Stevens does not speak for Faulkner, his totally unheralded intrusion creates a disturbing imbalance. He provides one of several illustrations of Christmas's impact on the community, but at some cost to the novel's artistry.

A somewhat different type of character narrative is *reported narration*, told by one character to another about what a third said or did. These "secondhand" narratives are framed by the comments of a narrating character or focal character, who in turn is framed by the external narrator, thus adding another level to the transmission of information about Christmas. In a few instances rumor and speculation may pass back and forth among five or six narrators. The most extreme example occurs in chapter 4, section 2, when Byron describes the discovery of Joanna's body and her burning house. First he tells of the countryman who found the fire. The verbs "told" and "said" emphasize that information is being passed along, that he wishes to acknowledge its source: "he told how he suspected there was something wrong" (p. 84) and "The man said how he stood there and he could hear the fire" (p. 85). The countryman reports his discovery of Joanna's body and her burning house to various community members (especially Sheriff Kennedy and his deputies) who later speak to Byron, who finally talks to Hightower; the few instances of direct quotation represent Byron's version of what he has been told the countryman said. News of Joanna's murder travels along four narrative levels: the external narrator, Byron, the townspeople, and the countryman. A similar transmission process underlies Byron's account of how Joe Brown revealed Christmas's responsibility for her death. One of Byron's statements implies five levels: "Because they said it was like he [Brown] had been saving what he told them next for just such a time as this" (pp. 90–91). Brown gives his information to the sheriff and his deputies (the antecedents of "they" and "them"), who later talk to Byron (or more likely to other townspeople who talk to Byron), who finally reconstructs the episode for Hightower, all of which the external narrator records. When Brown goes so far as to report what Christmas told him (pp. 86–88), a sixth level of transmission results.

Reported narrative also works prominently to obscure the facts of Thomas Sutpen's life in *Absalom, Absalom!*, but in *Light in August* it serves more to illustrate community involvement (although hazy uncertainty does enshroud Christmas's life and racial heritage). In chapter 15, section 2, an anonymous Mottstown citizen relates the activities of Doc and Mrs. Hines on the day of Christmas's capture. He gathers the details of his story from several different townspeople— the Mottstown sheriff, deputy, jailer, railroad ticketman, and others. Acting much like an external narrator, he reports their reactions and even describes their thoughts. Of the cafe man he says: "Once he started to call, but he didn't. 'I reckon I misunderstood her,' he says he thought. 'Maybe it's the nine o'clock southbound they want'" (p. 340). In chapter 3, section 1, another anonymous townsman, speaking from the Jefferson community's perspective, tells a stranger about Hightower. In each case the narrating character functions as a reporter, reconstructing events from various community sources, guessing in the absence of firm evidence. The Mottstown citizen speculates about Mrs. Hines: "Maybe she was enjoying herself, all dressed up and downtown all Saturday evening. Maybe it was to her what being in Memphis all day would be to other folks" (p. 339). Such narrative represents the word-of-mouth communication typical of small rural towns. The narrating character, gathering together all the various strands of the town's knowledge, becomes an encompassing symbol of community reaction. Character-symbols usually share three common features: a desire to learn what happened, to understand it, and to explain it to someone else. Byron, Stevens, and Sheriff Kennedy are all character-symbols, like the narrator too in his general concern with describing and speculating over what happens. (A character-symbol also narrates "A Rose for Emily"). Reported narrative vividly delineates community response to a person or event: in chapter 3, section 2, for example, Jefferson reacts to Hightower after his wife's death and his expulsion from his church through specific acts (the Ku Klux Klan attack) and gossip (the rumors that Hightower drove his wife to suicide or murdered her [p. 65], had sexual relations with a Negro man and woman [p. 66], fathered a child by another Negro woman and then killed it [p. 68]). By confronting Jefferson with several people who in some way violate its norms—Joanna, Hightower, Grove, Christmas—and characterizing its reactions through reported and external narration, the novel explores the nature of the community, the limitations of its tolerance, from a number of different vantage points.

In a larger sense these community spokesmen are also archetypal *individuals*, sometimes distantly removed from the novel's action, nevertheless deeply involved in one way or another. The furniture dealer unknowingly enmeshes himself in a complex web of people and events of which he is hardly aware. Yet even as symbols these characters continue to speak fallibly. In fact, their limitations are what make them representative. When the Negro parishioner of chapter 14, section 2, reports Christmas's rampage through his church, the narrator carefully qualifies what he says: "That was what he told, because that was what he knew" (p. 307)—an apt appraisal of each character's cognitive limitations, of the novel's insistence upon them.

Faulkner may also vary perspective by reintroducing as a total stranger a character who has appeared previously, often in a prominent role. Such reidentification shocks the reader into an awareness of an individual's true personality by its almost clinically objective descriptions. It strips away whatever attitudes the reader has already formed and especially discourages him from sympathizing with a character too strongly. In chapter 16, for instance, the Hines couple, described at some length previously in the narrative, enter Hightower's house: "Byron leads them into the study—a dumpy woman in a purple dress and a plume and carrying an umbrella, with a perfectly immobile face, and a man incredibly dirty and apparently incredibly old, with a tobaccostained goat's beard and mad eyes. They enter not with diffidence, but with something puppetlike about them, as if they were operated by clumsy springwork." (pp. 348–49). This cold, indifferent description portrays the Hines couple from a ruthlessly external perspective, reinforcing earlier implications that neither the old man nor his wife is quite sane. Hines engages in reidentification by characterizing himself with third-person pronouns, as if he is discussing a person separate from himself. But his schizophrenic perspective is intensely subjective. Its irony and its narrator's insanity combine in a characterization more bizarre than any other in the novel. When Hines stops his ranting, the reader, along with Byron and Hightower, can react only with "quiet and desperate amazement" (p. 361). Faulkner frequently employs reidentification as a means of characterization—to describe Benjy in the fourth section of *The Sound and the Fury*, or to portray Temple Drake and her father in the Luxembourg Gardens scene at the end of *Sanctuary*.

Because the perceptions of focal characters provide much information about events in this novel, the narrator must be present to correct, or at least to identify, mistaken information. Focal characters react to events instinctively and impulsively; because they are not narrators, they do not attempt to order or objectify their experience, a fact which may or may not affect their reliability. The narrator may counterbalance the focal character's subjectivity in several ways, most commonly by distancing himself or by reidentification. His presence proves especially important to the portraiture of individuals whom the focal character views only from the outside. Such externally viewed characters are seen precisely as the focal character, with all his flaws and limitations, sees them.

In his judgment of other characters, Christmas proves the least reliable focal individual. McEachern is described exactly as Christmas saw him, with only rare intrusions into his perspective. His importance thus lies mainly in his effect on his stepson—who always perceives him as cold, indifferent, and ruthless. Yet occasional adjectives, which the narrator supplies almost surreptitiously, suggest that there might be more to the man than the boy recognizes. Twice, as McEachern tries to force Christmas to learn the catechism, he is called "not unkind," and he is said to feel real shame at having whipped the boy into unconsciousness.[11] Still, Joe's view of him prevails until chapter 9, section 1, which is related entirely from McEachern's perspective. His formerly two-dimensional character develops a heretofore unseen human dimension not afforded by the boy's limited view. Shifts in perspective between Christmas and McEachern create out of chapters 8 and 9 a kind of self-contained unit. The first section of each chapter describes Joe's stealthy departure by rope from the McEachern house on the night of the dance. The chapter 8 version uses the boy's perspective, looking into his stepparents' bedroom window ("he slid down the rope, passing swift as a shadow across the window where the old people slept" [p. 159]). The chapter 9 version employs McEachern's perspective, from within the bedroom looking out the window ("as Joe, descending on his rope, slid like a fast shadow across the open and moonfilled window . . . McEachern did not at once recognise him" [p. 189]). The episode is the climax of Joe's rebellion against his stepfather, of McEachern's efforts to dominate his stepson. Their contrasting perspectives illuminate their grim, stubborn attitudes towards each other, establishing the steady pattern of rebellion and violence which Christmas follows throughout his life.

Joe's narrow perspective also accounts for the warped, stereotyped characterizations of the three important women in his life. The narrative never enters Bobbie Allen's mind at all; it enters Mrs. McEachern's only once, in chapter 9 (pp. 194–96). Joanna becomes a focal character only when she describes her family history (pp. 228–35). Otherwise, these women appear merely as animated façades; to Christmas they are abstractions, "the smooth and superior shape in which volition dwelled doomed to be at stated and inescapable intervals victims of periodical filth" (p. 173).[12] He believes Mrs. McEachern and Joanna desire to conquer him through kindness. In the episode he remembers as the *"day I became a man"* (p. 137), his greatest pride lies not in having refused to learn the catechism but in his rejection of the food Mrs. McEachern brings him. He regards her as a "motionless shadow, shapeless, a little hunched" (p. 145), a "patient, beaten creature without sex demarcation at all save the neat screw of graying hair and the skirt" (p. 155), "that soft kindness which he believed himself doomed to be forever victim of and which he hated worse than he did the hard and ruthless justice of men" (p. 158). Yet the brief intrusions into her thoughts as she watches him riding away conclusively establish what the reader should have suspected already: that she is a human being, not an abstraction, that her fumbling kindnesses are expressions of love and generosity. Her failure with Joe exemplifies the generally repressive atmosphere of the McEachern home as well as Christmas's abnormal attitude towards women, love, and human relations—an attitude which leads him to view Joanna's story of her family history as an attempt to surrender to him "in words." A few shallow intrusions establish the humanity of Mrs. McEachern and Joanna Burden, betraying Christmas's hollow views of them. This rather subtle method of characterization has misled some readers into assuming that Christmas's attitude toward women reflects Faulkner's misogyny. Actually, Faulkner depicts positive as well as negative traits in his female characters, and he successfully avoids most of the traditional sexual stereotypes. His male characters, however, do not. Women in Faulkner's fiction are often victimized by men, and nowhere does Faulkner depict a man being victimized by a woman in the way Christmas believes himself victimized. Narrative structure provides ample evidence that the misogyny in *Light in August* belongs to Joe Christmas, not to his creator.[13]

Characterization may be drawn two-dimensionally for other reasons as well. As the sheriff's men hunt for Christmas, the narrative repeatedly refers to Brown as "he," the "unshaven man," "one of the party" who is "unshaven and muddy" (pp. 309–11). Though Brown's identity soon becomes obvious, the impersonal characterization satirizes his obsessive desire for the reward money. In much of chapters 5 and 14, Christmas is identified only as "he," and in the final moments of his escape attempt in chapter 19 he becomes merely "the man." This reductive characterization, essentially a form of reidentification, strips away physical and psychological features, leaving only thought, emotion, and action. Brown becomes a parody, a comic-strip character as absurd to the reader as to the sheriff's posse. On the other hand, chapter 5 depicts Christmas in a rounded, fleshed-out characterization which vividly contrasts with how he is seen by Byron Bunch and the planing-mill men in the second chapter. The resulting product affords a rich, full portraiture of Joe Christmas—not merely a cold, reclusive, misogynistic, mentally unstable, and murderous man, but also a sympathetic and deeply emotional man, sensitive to nature and himself, intensely self-contained, "more lonely than a lone telephone pole in the middle of a desert" (p. 106). Similarly applied in chapters 13 and 20, reductive characterization portrays Hightower as weak and deluded, wholly isolated from reality.

In his commentary on *As I Lay Dying*, Cleanth Brooks has remarked that multiple perspective "does not commit us to the experience and sensibility of one character whom we see only from the inside and whose world we apprehend only from his point of view. Instead, Faulkner has attempted the much more difficult role of putting us into some kind of sympathetic rapport with an individual character and yet constantly forcing this character into the total perspective of the world."[14] In *Light in August*, multiple perspectives both illustrate and symbolize the intersection of individual and community. Perspective shifts back and forth continuously, preventing the reader from focusing too long on one character without being reminded in some way of his participation in the community. Though an individual may seem unaware of the community, the community is always aware of him.

The portrayal in chapter 1 of the community's reaction to Lena Grove introduces this theme. In the first section she is the focal character, with community response represented by an italicized anonymous voice: "*Lucas Burch? You say you tried in Pocahontas? This road? It goes to Springvale. You wait here. There will be a wagon passing soon that will take you as far as it goes*" (p. 6). In the second section Armstid and Winterbottom, representatives of the community, notice Lena walking down the road and remark that she is "young, pregnant, and a stranger. 'I wonder where she got that belly,' Winterbottom said" (pp. 6–7). The next three sections portray the Armstids' reactions to Lena, paying special attention to Mrs. Armstid, who disapproves of the girl but who also gives her money. The sixth section depicts a group of men on the porch of Varner's store; together they represent the community. As an individual so does Varner. Faulkner carefully contrasts what these men believe Lena is thinking ("of a scoundrel who deserted her in trouble" [p. 22]) with her real thoughts ("how she can . . . buy cheese and crackers and even sardines if she likes" [p. 23]). Variations between the focal character's internal perspective and the observing community's external perspective continue throughout the novel. Chapters 5–12, however, almost exclusively concern the perspective of Joe Christmas. Surrounding chapters counterbalance this emphasis by providing numerous external views of him.

Generally, internal narration through focal characters explores the nature of individual experience. More objective reportorial narrative, which also relies on internal perspectives, explores the community. Character narrators express their personal interpretations of events, but because their knowledge often comes from different community sources, they too may represent a community viewpoint: many of Byron's reports to Hightower are based on community information; so is the Mottstown citizen's account of the Hines couple in chapter 15. There is at least one representative character in the novel for each social, economic, and racial class in Yoknapatawpha County: the sheriff and his deputies stand for law and government; Armstid and the countryman for the farmer; the churchman for the Negro community; Hines, Hightower, and his former parishioners for organized religion; the doctor, Mrs. Beard, and the railroad ticketman for the middle class; the planing-mill workers for the laboring class; Joanna Burden for unwelcome but tolerated intruders. Significantly, the community's diverse composition identifies it as a cohesive group of citizens who may respond similarly to such an event as Joanna Burden's murder, but who also may react in widely varying ways. For instance, the community never suspects the possibility of Christmas's Negro blood until Brown first suggests it in chapter 4 (p. 91), after Christmas has lived in Jefferson for three years. Most people immediately accept the notion, but Sheriff Kennedy hesitates, preferring to call Christmas "that fellow" instead of "nigger." Even those who believe in his blackness find it difficult to explain because he does not behave as the community believes a Negro should. They are forced to call him a "white nigger" (p. 326), to claim that "He dont look any more like a nigger than I do" (p. 330) and "It was like he never even knew he was a murderer, let alone a nigger too" (p. 331). Opinion is hardly unanimous.

Nor does Percy Grimm provoke cohesive community response. The men who support him belong to "an age, a generation, an experience" (p. 433); they are "the younger ones, the ones who had not gone to France" (p. 428), who, like Grimm, were born too late to fight in World War I, "not alone too late but not late enough to have escaped first hand knowledge of the lost time when he should have been a man instead of a child" (p. 425). Grimm, populist and small-town demagogue, coerces the community into tolerating his vigilantism. His decision to establish the patrol first meets with resistance and later earns him only begrudging "respect and perhaps a little awe" (p. 432). The community never fully accepts him. On the day of Christmas's indictment, many townspeople do not even recognize Grimm, mistaking him for a "special officer sent by the governor" (p. 433). When he murders Christmas, he acts entirely on his own, independent even of the men who follow him, who are repulsed at his mutilation of a dying man. At best he represents a small, vindictive community element; at worst, he exceeds the criminal misanthropy of the man he kills.[15]

Jefferson proves surprisingly tolerant of variations in character and behavior. Hightower and Joanna live relatively unmolested lives there, once they have paid the price for violating the community's standards; even Lena, pregnant and unwed, receives comfort and help. Christmas, however, enjoys no such treatment. He fails to observe even the most lenient community standards. Moreover, once the town learns of his "blackness," its racism rigidly mandates his rejection. He has no racial identity. He is neither black nor white—social roles created and demanded by the community. The resulting confusion, in his own mind as well as the townspeople's, destroys him. Hence, the community is generous only to a point; when race becomes an issue, it becomes viciously inflexible.

At critical points in the narrative the community itself "speaks" in a group voice most apparent in chapter 13, in the crowd's response to Joanna's murder. When the sheriff finds a black man to question about the recent tenants of the Burden cabin, the crowd coalesces in a single, unified response:

> It was as if all their individual five senses had become one organ of looking, like an apotheosis, the words that flew among them

wind- or air-engendered *Is that him? Is that the one that did it? Sher-iff's got him. . . .* the dying fire roared, filling the air though not louder than the voices and much more unsourceless *By God, if that's him, what are we doing, standing around here? Murdering a white woman the black son of a* [P. 275]

The great irony of this passage lies in how the community's attitude towards Joanna has changed. Only her murder by a black man could so arouse the crowd's protective fury and sympathy against this woman whom they had previously scorned. Here the community re-acts as an organic entity, ready to lynch an innocent man out of an abstract desire for retribution, a quite different response from the one which leads to Grimm's murder of Christmas. (At points in *Intruder in the Dust*, Chick Mallison "hears" or imagines a similar communal voice, another unified response to the supposed crime of a black man against a white). The communal voice speaks again in chapter 18 when Byron imagines its reaction to his behavior with Lena.

In a different way the community speaks also in the eulogy for the dead Joe Christmas at the end of chapter 19. Because the community serves as a focal character, the translated intrusion can look to its past as well as its future. As Christmas dies, the transition from external narrative to elegiac benediction occurs abruptly. The concluding nar-rative dramatically characterizes the dead man's impact on the town's consciousness—not merely as a flesh-and-blood man but also as a legend: "The man seemed to rise soaring into their memories forever and ever. They are not to lose it. . . . It will be there, musing, quiet, steadfast, not fading and not particularly threatful, but of itself alone serene, of itself alone triumphant" (p. 440). The antecedent of "it" is Christmas's "pent black blood," whose release the entire novel has prepared for. News of this man has passed from mouth to mouth in the community, in traditional legend-making manner, with individu-als such as Byron Bunch serving as bard or town historian. In a sense too the eulogy parallels the town's transformation of Christmas into legend by likewise translating him into art. It richly symbolizes the theme of the individual's intersection with the community. It also is a tribute paid by the town and the novel (perhaps even by Faulkner himself), to the figure of Joe Christmas. Though three weeks after Christmas's death the furniture dealer can speak of him only as a "nigger" that "they lynched" (p. 470), chapter 19's conclusion sug-gests that his agony has indelibly marked the community conscious-ness. Hightower receives a similar tribute at the end of chapter 20, but it is laden with irony and far from laudatory, confirming his essential weakness.[16]

The novel's design also reflects the eminence of another important theme, the meaning of individual experience. Focal characters and character narrators express subjective, internalized interpretations of reality; irony and external perspectives provide a counterbalance by which the reader may judge their views. Certainly, Christmas's own perspective does not explain his character adequately; conclusions which the reader bases only on his perspective, without the perspectives of other characters and the community, must be inherently unreliable. Christmas's life assumes meaning and importance because of the way other characters react to it, because of the narrator's ability to order and represent their perspectives objectively. Finally, however, all perspectives combined fail to explain him satisfactorily. The enigma he represents, like the enigma of every human being, lies beyond explanation. As the archetypal individual—in conflict with his heritage, nature, time, society, himself—he remains at the end the selfsame mystery he was in the beginning.

In a larger context, narrative structure also symbolizes the ultimate interrelatedness of all events and individuals. Several scenes specifically illustrate this theme. As a young boy, Christmas considers his rejection of Mrs. McEachern's food an act of manhood and rebellion. Twenty years later, in Joanna Burden's kitchen, he refuses food again for the same reasons. But a more significant variation of this theme concerns how one person's life can intersect with the lives of many others. Chapter 1 describes how people in Yoknapatawpha County learn of Lena Grove, how she gradually enters into the community consciousness. By the chapter's end, her story has been told four different times. Multiple perspective permits the retelling of such stories, a kind of redundant narration. So does the chronological fragmentation of plot, which allows the first view of the Burden fire in chapter 1, its discovery and Joanna's murder in chapter 4, a description of Christmas's depression the night before the murder in chapter 5, an explanation of how Joanna "forced" Joe to kill her in chapter 12, and in chapter 13 the community's discovery of the crime. Hightower's life story is related on at least three occasions; the dietician's twice. Christmas's death is reported three times—Byron learns of it at the end of chapter 18; in chapter 19 the community discusses it and Gavin Stevens explains it—all before it is ever actually described. Transition between these related but disparate narrative chunks usually occurs abruptly, the result of what Michael Millgate calls "deliberate crudeness."[17] They dissuade the reader from expecting any traditional sequence of events, jolting him towards an awareness that events and people who seem wholly unrelated are in reality intimately bound up in a common destiny.

Multiple perspective, redundant narration, and fragmented chronology evoke the illusion of simultaneity, the impression that several events may be occurring at the same moment, and that what people *believe* may be more important than what really happens. Redundant narration illustrates how various characters learn of events at different times, either by participating in them, witnessing them, or hearing of them through word of mouth. While Hightower worries over the moral implications of Byron's having moved Lena into the Burden cabin, the sheriff and his deputy are just discovering that "there's somebody out there in that cabin. . . . Not hiding: living in it" (p. 302). When the community learns that Christmas has been living at the Burden place for three years, he has already moved out. When the town learns he is a Negro, he himself has believed it for his entire life. This interrelatedness extends beyond the realm of Jefferson, at least as far as the world of the furniture dealer, who has heard vaguely of Christmas and who tells his wife about Lena and Byron. His tale invests their story with a certain permanence; his wife will likely tell it to others who themselves will pass it along. Eventually, it will merge into the community consciousness along with the legend of Joe Christmas.

The center of interrelatedness, the novel's primary catalyst, its main character and protagonist, is Christmas. His experience gives the novel unity and power, becomes an issue to every character. Without his presence, Lena might never have found Brown; her relationship with Byron might have developed much differently; Byron would not have quit his job at the planing mill; Joanna would still be alive; Hightower would have remained in passive seclusion; Doc Hines, Percy Grimm, McEachern, Bobbie Allen, and the dietician, among others, would not figure in at all. The tension created by Christmas's intrusion into the community provokes the townspeople into awareness; his search for identity prompts Byron and Hightower to a similar effort, as it does all of Jefferson. Excluding his murder of Joanna, he works his greatest effect on Byron, the seriocomic protagonist whose inner conflicts ironically mirror the tragic struggles of Christmas. Byron participates actively in every narrative strand; his infatuation with Lena leads to his involvement with the Hines couple, with Brown, with Christmas. He unintentionally helps to convince Mrs. Hines that

Hightower can save her grandson, and so Christmas dies in the ex-minister's dining room. In the terms of a chemical formula, Christmas is the catalyst, Byron the reagent, the climax of *Light in August* the ultimate reaction.[18]

The theme of interrelatedness is closely connected to the theme of community, that social organism in which all things interdepend. It also encompasses the novel's exploration of the development of human identity. Three major retrospections chronicle events and individuals which formed the characters of Hightower, Joanna, and Christmas. Byron requires no such retrospection. His identity continues to develop throughout the novel, and even past the end of the last chapter. Narrative structure enables the reader to glimpse these character-forging influences from the affected individual's perspective, as well as from the perspectives of other characters and the external narrator. Ultimately, the narrative perspectives of *Light in August* combine in an evocation of the nature of all human experience, with Joe Christmas as the archetypal individual, locked into a rigid, fatal pattern, and Byron Bunch—still growing, still becoming—as the archetypal man.

Chapter Three
Pylon

Faulkner's 1935 novel *Pylon* illuminates the lives of a few individuals against an ominous, distant landscape. In this sense it resembles such futuristic or polemical novels as George Orwell's *1984*, Aldous Huxley's *Brave New World*, Arthur Koestler's *Darkness at Noon*, Alexander Solzhenitsyn's *A Day in the Life of Ivan Denisovitch*, and Evgenii Zamiatin's *We*—which focus on characters struggling to survive in an oppressive environment. But *Pylon* is neither primarily futuristic nor political (though economic exploitation is one of its themes). Rather, in a newspaper reporter and a clan of itinerant stunt fliers it embodies Faulkner's evaluation of the modern world, at least as it seemed to him in the mid 1930s, as an isolating, dehumanizing, coldly forbidding place.

At the University of Virginia, Faulkner suggested that *Pylon* concerns the "fantastic and bizarre phenomenon" of the pilots: "they were ephemera and phenomena on the face of a contemporary scene. . . . That they were outside the range of God, not only of respectability, of love, but of God too. That they had escaped the compulsion of accepting a past and a future, that they . . . had no past."[1] Yet the ephemeral character of the pilots is determined not so much by who they are and what they do as by where and when they live—in an artificial, mechanized modern world devoid of meaning, inimical to human endeavor, looming with disaster and annihilation. According to Richard Pearce, who finds the same mood of senselessness and impending apocalypse common in other literature of the 1930s, *Pylon* "conceives and responds to structures that are not organic, have no controlling center, but are all the exploding surface of a totally circumferential form. No organic connections, no controlling center, only energy and the continually changing relations of an exploding circumference."[2] In the city of New Valois, the setting for most of the novel, traditional social structures and values have collapsed. New Valois teems with anonymous crowds celebrating a holiday whose religious origins they have forgotten. Beset by unending poverty, the fliers perform stunts and compete in air races which earn them barely enough money to survive. In fact, their lack of money, their need for it, enslaves them to a vocation which threatens their lives and denies them any semblance of a normal, secure existence.

Because the novel's setting is nearly as important as its characters, the narrative employs a highly charged pattern of figurative language which evokes a specific texture and mood, molding the reader's response to this chaotic, decaying world. Imagery is especially significant. Confronting the reader with an incredibly ironic environment, it sharply contrasts the warm human personalities of individual characters with the impersonally abstract city and airport. Oddly enough, though these characters are alienated from their world, they also feel a natural part of it. The most important among them is the unnamed Reporter, who stands at the novel's center. Aware of the world in which he lives, he knows also of the impossibility of escape, and he reacts with continual bewilderment to the events which he witnesses and in which he becomes involved. Though he is not the controlling intelligence, most of the novel is narrated through his perspective, and his perceptions strongly influence the narrative tone and content. Imagery reflects his emotional state of mind, starkly depicting the psychological consequences of his existence in New Valois. By describing familiar scenes and objects so that they appear totally foreign and unfamiliar, the imagery, together with the prevailing narrative focus, compels the reader to view the landscape to a large degree from the Reporter's own perspective, to share in his bewilderment, to experience firsthand his frustration and sense of estrangement. Despite this "forced" identification, however, the reader remains sufficiently detached to view and judge the Reporter objectively.

Michael Millgate has pointed out the influence of T. S. Eliot's poetry, especially "The Love Song of J. Alfred Prufrock" and *The Waste Land*, on figurative language in this novel.[3] The stark settings of the city and airport both resemble the "Unreal City" of *The Waste Land*. The poem's first section, "The Burial of the Dead," bears special significance, especially in these lines:

> Unreal City
> Under the brown fog of a winter dawn
> A crowd flowed over London Bridge, so many
> I had not thought death had undone so many.
>
> [Ll. 60–63]

Similar anonymous multitudes of "living dead" inhabit *Pylon*. The imagery establishes the motif of a city of the dead, underscoring the isolation of the main characters from their environment. Because of its prominent and unusual character, imagery in *Pylon* is as important a structural element as point of view and is a powerful force in the narrative. It also becomes a form of symbolism, reinforcing Faulkner's portrait of a modern world mired in decay and atrophy. In every sense it plays a significant role in the novel.

Elliptical images fuse at least two, frequently contradictory, words into a single expression, a compound noun or adjective in some way connoting the oxymoronic character of New Valois. The opening scene, for instance, describes an unshaven man's chin as "blueshaven" (p. 8) and a confetti-littered street as a "confettispatter" (p. 11).* Other elliptical images are "lightpoised," "greasestained," "slantshimmered" (p. 7), "bayou-and-swampsuspired" (p. 11), "cheeseclothlettered" (p. 12), "typesplattered," "stillopen" (p. 13), and "blacksplotched" (p. 14). Denoting the slightest of visual impressions—a littered street or a newspaper headline—these images evoke vivid visual impressions by implying much more than they say outright. Reducing a scene to the bare sensory components of sight, sound, texture, and shape, they express the individual observer's unique perceptions. They also intensify mood—evoking an hallucinatory atmosphere which shimmers and changes, stripping familiar scenes and objects of their familiarity, puzzling the reader with the source and meaning of their foreignness. The intensity of a scene's tone and impact varies directly in proportion to elliptical imagery's frequency of occurrence.

Because of its central role in describing setting and creating tone, Faulkner employed elliptical imagery sparingly, using it strategically to emphasize mood or a focal character's perceptions. It often describes key scenes and settings: the airport, the city editor's office, the crowded New Valois streets. In episodes narrated from the main character's perspective, it may also reflect his confusion, depression, drunkenness, or sense of futility. In the sixth chapter, for instance, after Shumann's death, the Reporter drives toward Feinman Airport and looks back upon the city:

> presently the street straightened and became the *ribbonstraight* road running across the *terraqueous* plain. . . . he could still see the city, the glare of it, no further away. . . . He was not escaping it; symbolic and encompassing, it outlay all *gasolinespanned* distances and all *clock-* or *sun-stipulated* destinations. . . . the hot rain

---

*William Faulkner, *Pylon* (1935; New York: Random House, 1965).

gutterfull plaiting the eaten heads of shrimp; the ten thousand
inescapable mornings wherein ten thousand swinging airplants
stippleprop the soft scrofulous soaring of sweating brick and ten
thousand pairs of splayed brown hired *Leonorafeet tigerbarred* by
jaloused armistice with the invincible sun.
[Pp. 283–84, my emphasis]

Elliptical images establish the scene's mood, reflecting the Reporter's
emotions and his contempt both for the city and for the general condition of modern humanity as well. The overall effect is of hope-
lessness, despair. It is complemented by the repetition of "ten thousand," the alliteration of consonants *r*, *s*, *t*, and *th*, and by the obvious
rhythm, which breaks down completely when Faulkner omits punctuation: "the eternal smell of the coffee the sugar the hemp sweating
slow iron plates" (p. 284). (In *Pylon*, as in a number of his other novels, Faulkner frequently uses punctuation to distort and manipulate
rhythm.) The disrupted rhythm temporarily interrupts the flow and
sense of the text. Style momentarily wrests control from the reader,
confusing and overwhelming him just as events culminating in Shumann's death have overwhelmed the Reporter. For an instant, the
reader can glimpse the Reporter's state of mind and share in his de-
spondent bitterness. This scene exemplifies a primary strategy of the
narrative in *Pylon*, which periodically plunges the reader into a character's disordered consciousness and perceptions, then abandons him
to his own means of explanation. Complemented by the interrupted
rhythm, elliptical imagery effects a sensory disruption in the mind of
the reader, who may recognize what is being described, but not without some confusion. The end result forces him to view old familiar
objects in a new, disorienting way—as they appear to the Reporter in
New Valois.

Imagery of stasis, more important than elliptical imagery, signifies
the deadening inertia and artificiality of New Valois. Like elliptical images, static images are typically visual, but they usually depict distance, open spaces, and motion rather than color, shape, or physical
appearance. Confusing and disorienting, static imagery confronts the
reader with the apparent unreality of New Valois, establishing it as a
place where technology has superseded nature, where anonymous
men and women sacrifice their identities to machines and the acquisi-
tion of money. Appropriately, the most significant static images serve
as the defining symbols of this world: the Mardi Gras and air-show
crowds, the airport beacon light, and the loudspeaker voice (an audi-
tory rather than visual image).

Static imagery specifically characterizes the New Valois community, whose presence often seems overpowering. Oddly, several critics have suggested that *Pylon* lacks the unifying sense of community found in such works as *Light in August* and *Absalom, Absalom!*[4] Yet the narrative provides ample evidence to the contrary. New Valoisians enjoy the Mardi Gras festivities together, attend the air show, watch over the search for Shumann's body. There are frequent glimpses of various community members: the elevator operator, the newsboys, the Italian absinthe peddlers, the Greek proprietor of the airport diner. Of course, New Valois does lack the "sense of living tradition" which Cleanth Brooks finds a necessary characteristic of community.[5] New Valois simply differs from the communities found in such novels as *Go Down, Moses* and *The Hamlet*. Its obliviousness to the past is merely one of its defining characteristics, and one of the novel's minor themes. The Mardi Gras celebrations vividly exemplify the deadness of the past. What began as the Shrove Tuesday observance of Lent's approach has degenerated into a meaningless drunken revelry. Moreover, New Valoisians themselves apparently lack the communal self-consciousness apparent in *Light in August*, *The Hamlet*, and the prose sections of *Requiem for a Nun*. Their city isolates them socially and offers no central source of unity or support. With all that it is and is not, their community exerts a major influence on each character in this novel.

Static imagery consistently denotes the characteristic impersonality of the New Valoisian community. The Reporter imagines their reactions to Shumann's death as "the ten thousand different smug and gratulant behindsighted forms of *I might be a bum and a bastard but I am not out there in that lake*" (p. 252). Elsewhere the community becomes merely a "physical curbmass of heads and shoulders" (pp. 54–55), "a floodtide" (p. 57), a "static human mass" (p. 58). The air-show and Mardi Gras crowds seem to behave instinctively, without consciousness, like bees. In the airport terminal, "the rotunda was full of people and with a cavernous murmuring sound which seemed to linger not about the mouths which uttered it but to float somewhere about the high serene shadowy dome overhead" (p. 240). After Shumann's first crash the Reporter hears the crowd's "single long exhalation of human breath," and the mob at the ticketgate turns "suddenly clamorous" to view the disaster (p. 163). During the search for Shumann's body in chapter 6, spectators mill around the lake like ants or carrion birds, and a small fleet of boats appears "as though by magic from nowhere like crows" (p. 236). A mile of automobile headlights illuminates the lake surface as drivers wait for a glimpse of the body.

More than any other image, however, the Hotel Terrebonne most powerfully symbolizes the community's pervasive impersonality. The Reporter describes the hotel as the "tiered identical cubicles of one thousand rented sleepings" (p. 58), the "billboard stage and vehicle . . . immemorial flying buttresses of ten million American Saturday nights" peopled by "shrewd heads filled with tomorrow's cosmic alterations in the form of pricelists and the telephone numbers of discontented wives and highschool girls" (pp. 60–61). It embodies the massive anonymity of the city's inhabitants: "behind a million separate secret closed doors we will slack ourselves profoundly defenseless on our backs, opened for the profound unsleeping, the inescapable and compelling flesh" (p. 63). In such an environment, representative of the city as a whole, sincere personal relationships prove difficult, if not impossible. The Reporter's own isolation thus comes as no surprise. He is like every other New Valoisian. The Hotel Terrebonne symbolizes neither history nor tradition, only a numerical quantity of people. Its character is forged not by the awareness of the past but by integers. Its name, the French words for "good earth," is an irony which Faulkner surely intended.

The most significant static image in *Pylon* is the airport beacon light, first mentioned in the opening chapter. Controlling the mood of the search for Shumann's body in chapter 6, it repeatedly punctures the Reporter's perspective. His sense of guilt in this episode for Shumann's death leaves him emotionally numb, and he functions merely as an unthinking observer. Accordingly, the narrative focuses primarily on his physical sensations—what he sees and hears. His consistently benumbed reactions intensify the already bizarre nighttime landscape. The beacon light and other static images clearly reflect his depression. They also establish the significance of what he observes, for at no other point in *Pylon* does the atmosphere become more nightmarishly surreal. The dredgeboat searching for the body becomes "something antediluvian crawled for the first time into light" (p. 237); the small boats surrounding it are "like so many minnows in the presence of a kind of harmless and vegetarian whale" (p. 252). The lake bottom where the plane has settled is "composed of refuse from the city itself—shards of condemned paving and masses of fallen walls and even discarded automobile bodies—any and all the refuse of man's twentieth century" (pp. 236–37). The Reporter muses over what the "crabs and gars" will do to Shumann's body (p. 241). He is especially sensitive to his own breathing (pp. 242–43, 245, 249–50, 256–57) and to the hissing of the wind through the palm trees along the beach (pp. 242, 245).[6] But he seems most aware of images of light in contrast to the nighttime darkness—the dredgeboat searchlight, the headlamps of the cars, the curving shoreline's diffuse luminescence "twinkling faintly away into darkness" (p. 248). The central image of the beacon light appears nine times (pp. 240, 242, 246, 247, 252, 254, 255, 256, 257); it is a "swordsweep," a "flick," a "swordstroke sweeping steadily up from beyond the other hangar until almost overhead and then accelerating with that illusion of terrific strength and speed which should have left a sound, a swish, behind it but did not" (p. 247).

Like the mindless simulacrum of a god, the beacon mechanically presides over the airfield and beyond, enveloping the entire setting in a strange, distorting light. Though it appears to occupy a god's place, its sterile light, devoid of divine warmth, illuminates without hope or salvation. Its unsentient eye, "turning" and "yellow" (pp. 240, 254) sweeps with a "peremptory, ruthless and unhurried" (p. 257) motion described in chapter 7 as a "steady and measured rake" (p. 285). It also seems to signify time's passage, a grim cosmic clock. When the Reporter awakens from a nap on the lakeshore, he sees that "the steady clocklike sweep flick! sweep. sweep flick! sweep of the beacon had accomplished something apparently, it had checked something off" (p. 256). The beam revolves smoothly, inexorably, like a second hand, a comparison enforced by such metaphors as "nebulous swordstroke" (p. 247) and the "long sicklebar" that moves "with clocklike and deliberate precision" (p. 252). Suggesting the onset of temporal atrophy, its movement changes nothing, continuing on even as morning light drowns it out. Indifferent to both natural and human events, it fosters the illusion that some event will bring meaning and resolution to the world, at the same time portending that no such event can ever occur. As the ultimate symbol of pessimism, the beacon symbolizes the world's meaninglessness, all human effort's futility.

Similar to the beacon is the loudspeaker voice, which blares constantly during the air show. Man-made and electrically powered like the beacon, it too serves an unnatural purpose, again not unlike an impotent god: "the voice of the amplifier, apocryphal, sourceless, inhuman, ubiquitous and beyond weariness or fatigue" (p. 39). Its function reinforces the air show's absurdity: describing to the spectators events which they are witnessing at the same moment with their own eyes, as if human senses no longer work, as if the air show lacks the required drama and suspense which the voice must supply by investing each airplane with a human personality and life history. The loudspeaker characterizes the aviators, speculates about Shumann's marital problems, cracks jokes, poetically narrates a parachute jump, urges a faltering plane safely back to earth. The audience has no sense organs of its own, no ability to see and react, no emotions. It lives through the loudspeaker's words, the mechanized expression of thought and emotion.

Ironically, the beacon's meaningless illuminations are paralleled by the loudspeaker's inability to describe the air show with any accuracy. Its characterization of the aviators especially seems to depart from reality:

> Above the shuffle and murmur of feet in the lobby and above the clash and clatter of crockery in the restaurant the amplified voice still spoke, profound and effortless, as though it were the voice of the steel-and-chromium mausoleum itself, talking of creatures imbued with motion though not with life and incomprehensible to the puny crawling painwebbed globe, incapable of suffering, wombed and born complete and instantaneous, cunning intricate and deadly, from out some blind iron batcave of the earth's prime foundation. [Pp. 28–29]

Elsewhere, the narrative repeatedly emphasizes the flesh-and-blood reality of the fliers, their very real suffering and poverty. The loudspeaker only increases the misunderstanding of the crowds who watch the fliers perform; it also completely fails to recognize the real motive for their participation in the air show—not glory but money, which they need badly. Yet the Reporter, like the spectators, believes in the images which the loudspeaker creates. Ironically, the loudspeaker announcer himself, "the microphone's personified voice" (p. 149), is a former aviator whom all the pilots know by name. His physical appearance at the fourth-chapter meeting bears no resemblance to the distorted, abstracted voice of the loudspeaker. The nature of his job exaggerates the distortion: the air-show management employs him as a "labor lawyer" (p. 149) to mediate disputes with the pilots. Despite his "softened and whitened" calluses (p. 150) and his labor badge, his speech at the meeting shows that his allegiance lies with the fliers. Like so many other characters in the novel, he too has been victimized and corrupted by economic pressures.

As a medium of communication, the loudspeaker fails. So also do other images of printed and written communication: headlines, programs, newspaper stories, signatures, street signs. Even the beacon light flashes out a meaningless Morse code *F*—the initial of the man who financed the airport. All communication images in *Pylon* are characterized by their inability to communicate.[7] Headlines are representative examples. Intended to call attention to a day's events, in some way to relay a coherent if tenuous meaning, they produce the opposite result. Jumbled and incoherent, they fragment the world, reducing it to a level of absurdity:

BURNHAM BURNS
VALOISIAN CLAIMS LOVENEST FRAMEUP
Myers Easy Winner in Opener at Feinman Airport
Laughing Boy in Fifth at Washington Park
[P. 64]

---

or of fundamental meaninglessness:

FARMERS REFUSE   BANKERS DENY   STRIKERS
DEMAND   PRESIDENT'S YACHT   ACREAGE
REDUCTION   QUINTUPLETS GAIN   EX-SENATOR
RENAUD CELEBRATES TENTH ANNIVERSARY AS
RESTAURATEUR. [P. 75]

The form in which the narrative presents these headlines (their printed appearance on the page) forces the reader to *see* them along with the Reporter, to experience his frustration at their incoherence and their failure to reveal meaning. Like most other forms of communication, headlines become a visual image in the novel's text, which the reader must *look* at as well as read. In particular they serve as the primary symbol of the Reporter's inability to use language. They are the

> cryptic staccato crosssection of an instant crystallised and now
> dead two hours, though only the moment, the instant: the sub-
> stance itself not only not dead, not complete, but in its very
> insoluble enigma of human folly and blundering possessing a
> futile and tragic immortality [P. 85].

The drunken Reporter's efforts to decipher them reveal their nature more clearly:

> he held the page up into the gray down as though for one last
> effort, concentrating sight, the vision without mind or thought,
> on the symmetrical line of boxheads . . . the fragile web of ink

and paper, assertive, proclamative; profound and irrevocable if only in the sense of being profoundly and irrevocably unimportant . . . the dead instant's fruit of forty tons of machinery and an entire nation's antic delusion [P. 111].

The visual appearance of other forms of language reinforces its incoherence. A sales receipt becomes a "cryptic scribbled duplicate of the sale" (p. 11) while a newspaper presents a "thick heavy type-splattered front page filled with ejaculations and pictures" (p. 13). André Bleikasten has observed that all such printed words in the novel dissolve meaning into meaninglessness.[8]

The Reporter's reaction to the printed word mirrors his inability to produce it. He is especially obsessed with newspapers, buying three copies in the third chapter alone. But his attempts to write for them, like his efforts to understand them, do not succeed. He misunderstands or simply cannot fulfill a newspaper's purpose: to provide a coherent narrative of events, the "living breath of news" (p. 42) as his editor, Hagood, puts it. Hagood regards the Reporter's writing as nonsense, "like trying to read something in a foreign language. . . . Can it be by some horrible mischance that without knowing it you listen and see in one language and then do what you call writing in another?" (p. 43) The Reporter yearns for explanations beyond the ken of journalism, beyond even the capacity of language to express or the human mind to comprehend. Yet he is not the only character puzzled by words. Jiggs cannot decipher the letters on the street sign where the Reporter lives, while officials of the air show convene a meeting to speculate over the import of a check endorsement. Spoken language is as powerless as written. Jiggs misinterprets the Reporter's description of "tiered identical cubicles" as "teared Q pickles" (p. 58). A telephone is a "dead wirehum . . . cold space . . . the profound sound of infinity, of void itself filled with the cold unceasing murmur of aeonweary and unflagging stars" (p. 75). In every form language proves ineffective, purposeless. The Reporter's final scrawled note to Hagood, along with his two equally unsatisfactory stories of Shumann's "funeral," gives concluding expression to the novel's futilitarian pessimism.

Communication's failure severs the bonds of social kinship. New Valois lacks the unifying communal force of oral communication, a basic means of social interaction, the foundation of community in such a novel as *Light in August*. The city newspaper, a source of information about local events, in some sense a substitute for oral communication, can be read in total isolation, requiring no contact among its readers. The newsboys reinforce its isolating symbolism: like mythological harpies, they swirl, scream, and hover around the Reporter, shouting out the news "apparently as oblivious to the moment's significance as birds are aware yet oblivious to the human doings which their wings brush and their droppings fall upon" (p. 55). The newspaper symbolizes one of the important themes in *Pylon*—that communication's failure isolates the individual intellectually, emotionally, and socially, making lasting relationships an impossibility. In such an environment narcissism can be the only love—the self-gratification of Jiggs's desire for the boots, the Reporter's lust for Laverne.

The Reporter is the prime example of New Valoisian isolation. Aware of his aloneness, he seethes with confusion. He fails to establish a lasting relationship with his mother, Hagood, Laverne, the other fliers, even with such anonymous townspeople as the absinthe sellers. His efforts to communicate, to establish bonds with other people, constitute his major activity in the novel. Perhaps the ultimate irony lies in how he himself is misperceived. Hagood regards him as a "creature who apparently never had any parents . . . who apparently sprang full-grown and irrevocably mature out of some violent and instantaneous transition like the stories of dead steamboatmen and mules" (pp. 41–42). The fliers see him as "something which had apparently crept from a doctor's cupboard and, in the snatched garments of an etherised patient in a charity ward, escaped into the living world" (p. 20). Alluding to his "skeleton frame," they refer to him as Lazarus. Jiggs wonders whether "they locked the graveyard up before he got in last night" (p. 23). The Reporter, of course, returns their misunderstanding. *Pylon* brims with a misunderstanding which stems from the failure of communication and the collapse of conventional social bonds. The narration of much of the novel through the Reporter's misperceiving perspective establishes him as the primary symbol of incoherence and isolation.

The impotence of language reflects only one of the traditional forms and conventions which have collapsed in *Pylon*'s world. Human beliefs and values seem to have little place. Machines, technology, and faceless crowds predominate. Without the binding power of language, the inhabitants are alone and isolated. Rather than merely describing this world, figurative language compels the reader to experience and feel it, exactly as the Reporter does, to understand the Reporter from within as well as without, finally to *be* the Reporter in such a crucial episode as the search for Shumann's body in chapter 6.

Of the various narrative and structural elements, figurative language exerts the most powerful force on the reader's emotional and intellectual apprehension of this novel. It supplements the frequent contrasts in perspectives, especially between the Reporter and the external narrator. The imagery in *Pylon* is its distinguishing characteristic, one of the features which makes this novel seem so different from Faulkner's better-known works.

Yet similar imagistic patterns occur frequently in other Faulkner novels: in the contrasting linear and circular images of *As I Lay Dying*, for instance, or in the motifs of water, money, and clashing palms in *The Wild Palms*. Perhaps the closest parallel lies in *Absalom, Absalom!*, whose composition Faulkner interrupted to write *Pylon*. As a number of French critics have pointed out, both *Pylon* and *Absalom* investigate the incoherence of language.[9] Communication imagery in *Pylon* is paralleled in *Absalom* by Charles Bon's letter to Judith Sutpen and by Mr. Compson's letter to Quentin about Rosa Coldfield's death. (One is reminded also of Cecilia Farmer's scrawled signature on a windowpane in *Requiem for a Nun*). In both novels, the main focal characters, Quentin and the Reporter, become obsessed with discovering and explaining a truth which they finally conclude is inexpressible. Further similarities lie in the figurative language which describes settings. In emotional impact *Pylon*'s central image is the airport beacon light, symbolic of the novel's fundamental concern with meaninglessness and decay. Less central, but still important, are the images which characterize the two main places of narration in *Absalom*: the bug-stained lightbulb, Mr. Compson's pipesmoke, and the fragrant Mississippi wisteria, which contrast with the "strange iron New England snow" and the frigid air outside Quentin and Shreve's Harvard dormitory room.[10]

In *Pylon*, however, figurative language serves a more central role than in *Absalom, Absalom!* and the other novels. Perhaps Faulkner found himself confronted with a meaning more inexpressible (if that is possible) than the themes of *Absalom*, where Quentin's curiosity, frustration, and despair provide an appropriate means of exploring and expressing theme. In *Pylon*, figurative language, rather than any particular character or event, is the most important expression of the novel's themes, perhaps because, finally, the Reporter alone proves wholly inadequate as a symbol. He is as incoherent a character as he is a newspaper writer.

Pylon's narrative structure marks a transition between the communal perspectives of *Light in August* and the individual narrators of *Ab-*

salom, Absalom! Although the Reporter usually serves as the focal character, he is not the controlling intelligence—the opening scene is narrated from Jiggs's perspective, for example, and the external narrator relates several important episodes which do not involve the Reporter. Hence, internal narrative predominates, but considerable external narrative occurs as well. Retrospective narratives describe the early lives of Roger and Laverne. Character narratives, such as the Reporter's long telephone diatribe to Hagood in chapter 2 and his unsuccessful stories about Shumann's death in chapter 7, also occur. Mood and tone vary significantly—the Reporter's long, hysteric monologues stand apart from the more subdued external and internal narratives. Characterization is achieved mainly through contrasts between different character perspectives and between internal and external narrative. Though not as structurally diverse as *Light in August* nor as complex as *Absalom, Absalom!*, *Pylon* employs similar methods, and with relative success. It certainly is not, as some have contended, artificial or contrived. Its themes of isolation and failed communication strongly influence its fundamental form.

The juxtaposition of misperceptions alongside realities exemplifies the misunderstanding and isolation which pervade New Valois. Variations in perspective afford numerous views of character, most of them inaccurate, warped and tainted by the viewer's personality. Only external narrative can characterize reliably. Laverne, the object of desire and curiosity among so many characters, is described more fully than anyone else in the novel. She is seen from a number of perspectives—Jiggs, Shumann, the Reporter, the external narrator. Jiggs views her first, in a pair of dungarees, "topped by a blob of savage mealcolored hair" (p. 19), "Iowacorncolored" hair (p. 22). To the deputy sheriff who wants to rape her, she is "the ultimate shape of his jaded desires . . . clothed in the very traditional symbology—the ruined dress with which she was trying wildly to cover her loins, and the parachute harness—of female bondage" (pp. 196–97). The Reporter idealizes her and feels not a little lust; after Shumann's fatal crash he can grieve only because she "told me to go away. I mean, to go clean away, like to another town" (p. 238). Despite his romantic feelings, he does not view her much differently than does the deputy sheriff or the reporters in the diner in chapter 6. Entranced by her sexual mystery, he senses in her a world to which he can never belong. His desire to gain her favor motivates much of his behavior in the novel.

Roger Shumann, Laverne's husband, does regard her differently. Though she is never viewed from his perspective, his affectionate, respectful behavior clearly reflects his feelings. He and Laverne are husband and wife, the parents of a child, partners in the air show. They obviously love one another but make no open avowals, first because the narrative rarely portrays them in private settings, second because such avowals are not in their natures. The most convincing evidence for their love lies in Roger's determination to support his "family" with money won in the air races, a determination which eventually leads to his death. Of course, Laverne and Roger hardly share a conventional marriage; Jiggs and Jack also belong to their family, and there is some evidence that Laverne sleeps with Jack, who may have fathered her unborn child. On the other hand, the evidence is rather flimsy. Laverne does tell Dr. Shumann that Jack fathered her unborn child, but probably only because she knows what the old man wants to hear. Only Jiggs suggests that she sleeps with both Roger and Jack. The narrative obscures this aspect of the Shumann relationship, but it does not obscure Laverne's open display of affection for Roger, an emotion which she is not seen expressing toward Jack.

External narrative, free of biased character perspectives, portrays Laverne objectively. The definitive view comes in chapter 1, "Dedication of an Airport," where she changes out of her grease-stained dungarees into conventional women's street clothing. The scene emphasizes her three-dimensional humanity and traditional womanhood; in no way has her work on the airplane "unsexed" her. She displays numerous "feminine" traits: modesty, neatness, cleanliness, for example. This "real" Laverne contrasts significantly with the illusions of other characters. Later scenes afford further glimpses into her true nature. She confesses to Roger that "all I want is just a house, a room; a cabin will do, a coalshed" (p. 165)—a conventional desire for hearth and home. In the final chapter, she nobly gives up her son to Roger's parents so that both he and her unborn child can be properly provided for. Such instances portray her admirably. Joseph McElrath regards her as the novel's center, a woman doing her best to survive in an environment where survival seems of doubtful value.[11] Those who misunderstand her, including Shumann's parents, are repulsed, or attracted unnaturally, by her sexuality, and they exploit her, sexually and otherwise, for their own purposes. Finally, however, Laverne even misunderstands herself, telling Dr. Shumann that she was "born bad and could not help it" (p. 307). Despite her unorthodox lifestyle, however, she behaves consistently with prudence and courage, assuming full responsibility for her life, whether she is working alongside the mechanics on Shumann's plane or giving up her child for his

own well-being. She is more nearly "normal" than any other character but Shumann. And she is also the prime victim of the world which
Pylon portrays.

Other individuals are similarly characterized. Shumann's behavior—reported by the narrator, Jiggs, and others—reveals his humanity, undermining the Reporter's and the loudspeaker's idealization of
him as a nonhuman creature of the air. Shumann risks his life in Ord's
defective plane to earn money for Laverne's unborn child; just before
the plane crashes he uses the last bit of control to steer it out over the
lake, away from the spectators, sacrificing any chance to save himself.
His every act reveals his sober, responsible personality.

The Reporter, who finds the aviators so perplexing, perhaps proves
the most confusing character of all. Faulkner's characters are always
fallible, always imperfect, but the Reporter seems remarkably so—
physically, mentally, and emotionally. His behavior repeatedly illustrates his immaturity, irresponsibility, naïveté, drunkenness, sexual
fantasies, bad judgment, selfishness, and foolishness. Often he seems
little more than a caricature. Yet he is a human being, a sentient if
misguided creature whose perceptions form the main source of narrative. Though he knows he cannot escape his world, he still fantasizes
about taking over Roger's role as pilot and husband to Laverne. To
him the fliers represent escape, if only vicarious, of which Laverne is
an important part. But events in the novel soon teach him that they
inhabit the same imprisoning world as he. Rather than escaping from
it, he helps cause Roger's death and the collapse of the Shumann
group.

If the Reporter is a tragic hero, as some critics suggest, his fall occurred long before the novel's beginning. His flaw is the fallen world
he lives in, a world which prevents communication and the development of an understanding that might lead him to a fulfilling, creative
existence. He recognizes the horror of his environment and suffers as
its victim. Chronically affected with incoherence, perpetually doomed
to wonder, he can only experience and observe. Unlike others in the
novel, he may possess a philosophical self-awareness, but it leaves
him no better able to cope with his life than anyone else. Bitterly, pes-
simistically, he acquiesces to his condition, "not only not to hope, not
even to wait: just to endure" (p. 284).

Perspective in *Pylon* varies between internal narrative focused on
the Reporter (the main focal character), internal narrative focused on
other characters, such as Jiggs or Hagood, and external narrative.
Retrospective narratives by Jiggs, the Reporter, and the external nar-

rator chronicle the early lives of Laverne and Roger. Jiggs ultimately provides the information in these narratives: he either talks himself, serves as a focal character, or passes information to the Reporter, who later relays it to Hagood. Internal narrative from the Reporter's perspective may occasionally do nothing more than record his observations and experiences without relaying his thoughts and emotions. In such cases internal narrative becomes practically equivalent to external narrative; the reader observes exactly what the Reporter observes. Chapter 1 describes his initial meeting with the fliers from this perspective, which also occurs in the search for Shumann's body in chapter 6. When the Reporter begins to theorize about what he observes, however, internal narrative assumes its more familiar function (unless he is talking aloud to Hagood or to another character). Significantly, chapter 1 balances the Reporter's view of the first meeting by also describing it from the fliers' perspective. Their Prufrockian allusions to the Reporter as an "etherised patient" (p. 20), a "skeleton frame" (p. 21), and a "Lazarus" (p. 33) reflect their initial reactions to him, and provide one of the few descriptions of his gangling physical appearance.

One way *Pylon* symbolizes theme is through contrasting two or more distinctly isolated character perspectives. In *Light in August* character perspectives overlap and intersect, creating a pervasive community consciousness which helps define the individual. No overlapping occurs in New Valois, thus no communal consciousness. The typical New Valoisian perceives himself only from his own viewpoint. The elevator man, for example, knows only what he reads in the newspaper and glimpses when his elevator door opens for a few brief seconds. Contrasting character perspectives—isolated centers of consciousness—provide the basic structure for at least two chapters, the third and the seventh.[12]

Chapter 3, "An Evening in New Valois," founds its three-part structure on the interaction between the isolated perspectives of Hagood and the Reporter. The chapter's beginning and end are narrated internally from Hagood's perspective, as he reacts to the Reporter in face-to-face and telephone conversations. The Reporter, trying to explain what he has learned about the fliers, narrates the middle section, and he also talks some in the introduction and conclusion. At several points the narrative hints at a close kinship between these two men. As a veteran newspaper editor and confirmed habitué of the city, Hagood seems indifferent to the ironies of his world. The Reporter, of course, is obsessed with them. He looks up to Hagood as a father figure, while Hagood paternally indulges his frequent requests for money, tolerates his incompetence and unreliability, and urges him to impose order on his life. His curiosity about the Reporter's past, his occasional bitter frustration with him, hint that he may glimpse something of his former self in the younger man.[13] Despite their potential closeness, however, "An Evening in New Valois" emphasizes their estrangement. Though they might wish to establish a closer friendship, their inability to communicate prevents them from doing so. Moreover, the philosophical truths for which the Reporter yearns are simply unattainable, a fact which Hagood must realize. When the Reporter tries to explain the "truth" about the fliers, for example, he forsakes logic and reality completely:

> They aint human, you see. No ties; no place where you were born and have to go back to it now and then. . . . Because they dont need money; it aint money they are after anymore than it's glory because the glory can only last until the next race and so maybe it aint even until tomorrow. And they dont need money except only now and then when they come in contact with the human race like in a hotel to sleep or eat now and then or maybe to buy a pair of pants or a skirt to keep the police off of them. [Pp. 46–47]

Narrative emphasis on the humanity of the fliers, on their fundamental needs and desires, on their victimization and eventual destruction by financial need contradicts this mistaken view. Hagood's reactions suggest he recognizes its inaccuracy. The Reporter's compulsive recitation of facts and theories to his unsympathetic editor is curious enough. His regard for Hagood as a father figure perhaps explains it, along with his belief that a city editor should be interested in air-show aviators. The fliers and the lives they live pose a riddle which the Reporter's diatribes obsessively, repeatedly try to answer. But a more basic reason also accounts for the Reporter's talks to Hagood. Like Byron Bunch, his attraction to a woman has led him into involvement with people and problems he is wholly unfamiliar with. He goes to Hagood (much as Byron did to Hightower) to justify his involvement on moral and journalistic grounds, thus cloaking a more primary motive: lust for Laverne.

Given his characteristic impatience, Hagood's ability to listen to the Reporter's prolonged monologues without exploding seems highly unlikely. Because it is improbable that the Reporter would speak aloud and at such length without stopping for at least a drink of water, his speeches are essentially unrealistic, more closely related to the character narratives of *The Sound and the Fury* than the spoken narratives of *Light in August*. Perhaps Faulkner meant them to symbolize the Reporter's personality. Several narratives in *Absalom, Absalom!* serve a similar purpose (Rosa Coldfield's, for instance). Rather than imitating spoken language, they reflect a state of mind, the accumulated impact of knowledge and experience on a human psyche. Though the Reporter's narratives may achieve such a reflection, their structural context clearly identifies them as spoken. Hagood listens to them and occasionally interrupts. The newsroom and telephone booth where the Reporter talks are concretely described, signifying the setting of a conversation, however one-sided it might be. Hence, the Reporter's narratives represent a flaw in the novel's structural realism. Still, they vividly reflect his incredible mental confusion.

Transition in the third chapter between the perspectives of the Reporter and Hagood occurs abruptly, indicating their utter separation. The first transition occurs after Hagood tells the Reporter to "go home and write it" (p. 49). As the elevator door is closing, the editor watches the Reporter clownishly trying to light a match; the instant the door shuts, the perspective switches to the Reporter, reading headlines in the elevator about Lieutenant Burnham's death. Transition occurs more abruptly at the chapter's end, as the Reporter is talking to Hagood on the telephone. An operator interrupts with a request for coins; the Reporter hears the "dead wirehum" of the connection and shouts into the phone. Perspective then immediately shifts back to Hagood, sitting at his desk:

> "Hello! Hello!" he [the Reporter] bawled. "You cut me off; gimme my . . ." But now the buzzing on the editor's desk has sounded again; now the interval out of outraged and apoplectic waiting: the wirehum clicked fullvoiced before the avalanched, the undammed:
> "Fired! Fired! Fired! Fired!" the editor screamed. He leaned halfway across the desk beneath the greenshaded light. [P. 74]

The ensuing description of the desk reorients the reader to Hagood's perspective. The visual image of the Reporter in a phone booth, with Hagood as a disembodied voice, is replaced by its antithesis—the Reporter's voice heard by Hagood through the telephone on his desk. Similar shifts elsewhere in the novel emphasize isolation and the absence of communication. But the theme of failed communication particularly dominates chapter 3, where nothing more than an electronic connection, a "dead wirehum," links the Reporter and Hagood.

The chapter's middle section, framed by the two shifts in perspective, focuses on the Reporter. Typically, the external narrator records the focal character's conscious thoughts and emotions along with what he does and says. In the absence of translated intrusions, subconscious impulses can only be guessed at. The narrative's objective use of a focal perspective becomes apparent in the metaphoric descriptions of the Reporter:

> When he approached her she looked full at him for a moment, with pale blank complete unrecognition, so that . . . he seemed to walk solitary and chill and without progress down a steel corridor like a fly in a gunbarrel, . . . thinking (while the irrevocable figures clicked and clicked beneath the dim insistent bulb and the child slept on his bony lap and the other four smoked the cigarettes which he had bought for them . . .)—thinking how he had not expected to see her again. [P. 62]

The Reporter thinks and speaks in images, symbols, and figurative language derived from the kind of sensationalist literature and journalism which he has grown up reading, and which he ends up writing himself in the final chapter. His self-conscious rhetoric strikes some, especially Jiggs, as silly and confusing. The reader, along with Hagood (whose cynicism proves the proper attitude), reacts to it negatively. Neither spontaneous nor natural, the Reporter's manner of speech springs from his delusions about himself and his world. It also encourages others to misunderstand him, prevents the reader from sympathizing too strongly with him, and occasionally exposes him to justly scornful ridicule.

"The Scavengers," the seventh and final chapter, employs a similar though less symmetrical structure. Centering on the Reporter, it concludes his involvement with the fliers and brings the novel to an end. Oddly, he remains fairly passive through the chapter's first half, listening quietly to the newsmen in the diner gossip about Laverne. His passive listening here parallels his passive watching in chapter 6. The predominant imagery is also a diminished version of that in the previous chapter. Throughout the diner scene the Reporter periodically flicks his cigarette ashes onto the floor. The flick of ashes ("he held himself rigid, watching the calculated hand flick the ash carefully from the cigarette" [p. 294]) replaces the "flick" of the chapter 6 beacon light (alluded to a last time on p. 285). The trivial greasyspoon restaurant dramatically undercuts the beacon's magnitude, symbolizing the intensely ironic gap between the gossip of chapter 7 and the reality of Shumann's death in chapter 6. If the Reporter wanted, he could correct every inaccuracy in the conversation of the other reporters. The reader, who knows what the Reporter knows, cannot help but do so. Why does the Reporter not speak? Because he realizes the futility of trying to explain the Shumanns to these men. He has spent the last three days trying to understand them himself, and with no success. His grief over Shumann's death and his loss of Laverne, his sense of responsibility for the fatal plane crash, also prompts his silence. Although much of the chapter is external narrative, emphasis on the Reporter's taciturnity, his flicking cigarette ash, and the gossiping newsmen creates the *effect* of internal narrative without ever intruding into the focal character's mind.

In the chapter's second half, the Reporter moves from passivity to action. A newsman's suggestion that Laverne has gone to leave her boy with Roger's parents sets the narrative's final events in motion. When the Reporter returns to New Valois, Jiggs confirms this speculation as fact. External narrative continues to reflect the Reporter's state of mind. His strained appearance and behavior indicate his approach towards nervous collapse: "His face wore again that faint wrung quiet grimace as with the other hand he continued to try to put Jiggs' hand aside even after Jiggs was no longer offering to touch him. He began to apologise to Jiggs for having disturbed him, talking through that thin wash over his wasted gaunt face which would have been called smiling for lack of anything better." (p. 296). Jiggs responds sympathetically: "'It's all right, doc,' Jiggs said, watching him, blinking still with a sort of brutal concern. 'Jesus, aint you been to bed yet? Here; you better come in here; me and Art can make room—'" (p. 296). After watching the dropping of the funeral wreath, he begins "shaking slowly and steadily" (p. 298). A newspaper headline gradually materializes before his eyes: "AVIATOR'S BODY RESIGNED TO LAKE GRAVE" (p. 299). Literally, the headline denotes the finality of Shumann's death. Metaphorically, it expresses the ultimate significance of the Reporter's involvement with the fliers, his desire for Laverne, his life in New Valois. Like the gossiping newsmen in the diner, it provides another meaningless reaction to the aviators.

The Reporter's apprehension of the meaninglessness in the headline heightens his tension and drives him to begin drinking again. Intrusions emphasize his exhaustion and focus on little more than his physical sensations: "He had himself in hand fine now; he did not feel at all: just the liquor flowing slowly down him, fiery, dead, and cold" (p. 300). He speaks his thoughts aloud as soon as they occur to him—another symptom of his condition. As he grows drunk, he begins to identify with the dead Shumann on the lake bottom: "the dredgeboat hanging over him for twenty hours and then having to lie there too and look up at the wreath dissolving, faintly rocking and stared at by gulls, away and trying to explain that he did not know" (p. 301). Next he imagines that he could have been Laverne's lover, even her child's surrogate father: "I just thought . . . we would go up and she maybe holding my arm and him looking at us over the cockpit and she would say, 'This is the one back in New Valois that time. That used to buy you the icecream'" (p. 301). The reality of the newspaper headline destroys this fantasy, confronting him with the knowledge that he will never sleep with Laverne, that because of Shumann he never could have. Realizing that his life will continue on unchanged, weighed down by the burden of the events he has been a part of, he finally exclaims, "Something is going to happen to me. I have got myself stretched out too far and too thin and something is going to bust" (p. 300). Joe Christmas makes a similar exclamation in *Light in August* and then commits the murder which ultimately leads to his death. But in *Pylon*, the Reporter commits no equivalent act. He informs Hagood by note that he is going off to get drunk, and the novel ends, his built-up tension and despair unresolved.

"The Scavengers" illustrates human futility in several different forms—gossiping reporters, the misplaced funeral wreath, meaningless headlines, Shumann's death, the Reporter's fantasies and reckless drinking. It is interrupted, however, by an interpolated narrative, much calmer and more subdued in tone, of Laverne's visit to Shumann's parents in Myron, Ohio. The source of this episode has occasioned some debate. Does the external narrator produce it, or is it drawn, as several French critics suggest, from the Reporter's clairvoyant imagination? Whatever the answer, the interpolation proves a unique break in the predominant structural pattern and a characteristic example of the novel's narrative form. The transition from the perspective of the drunken Reporter at his typewriter to the Ohio-bound railroad car occurs abruptly, unmarked by spacing or punctuation. One moment the Reporter is typing; the next a wholly different scene begins:

> He [the Reporter] could not feel his fingers on the keys either: he just watched the letters materialise out of thin air, black sharp and fast, along the creeping yellow.
>
> During the night the little boy slept on the seat facing the woman [Laverne] and the parachute jumper, the toy aeroplane clutched to his chest; when daylight came the train was running in snow. [P. 302]

When the interpolation ends, perspective returns even more abruptly to the newsroom, where a newsboy is piecing together the Reporter's torn story (p. 313). Sudden, unannounced transitions characterize Faulknerian narrative, occurring as early as the Benjy section in *The Sound and the Fury* and as late as *The Mansion*. There is nothing unusual about them in *Pylon*. The Reporter attempts to summarize his experiences in two typed stories and a scrawled note—his epilogue, his last frustrated utterances. The interpolated narrative, coming where it does, provides the fliers a much different epilogue, one emphasizing their humanity and their hardships. Complemented by, contrasting with the Reporter's stories, it suggests a last time the futility of their lives. The emphatic contrast between what the Reporter writes and what actually happens likewise emphasizes his inability to explain his experiences or understand human character, again stressing his essential isolation and the inadequacy of language. It also confirms, for the last time, the disastrous consequences of his involvement with the Shumanns. Nowhere else in the novel do illusion and truth clash more emphatically.

Several French critics, however, suggest that the Reporter imagines the events in the interpolated narrative as he sits before his typewriter. They regard the last chapter as his apotheosis, his transformation and redemption. He finally creates the "literature" which Hagood told him to go home and write. Like Lazarus, according to François Pitavy and Michel Gresset, the Reporter arises after four days in his New Valois "tomb" and achieves through suffering a compassionate understanding of human nature. His newly altered imagination, freed from the restraints of time, space, and personality, at last fully appreciates Laverne's character. Noting that the change in perspective is not signaled, Pitavy suggests that the interpolation is less tortured in mood than elsewhere in the novel because it has been produced solely by the Reporter's vision.[14] French critics thus view the last chapter's portrayal of the Reporter as strongly optimistic.

Despite the strength of its argument, neither the novel's structure nor evidence in the text supports the French view. The interpolation is narrated with an authoritative force and sensitivity which the Reporter lacks, which the narrative in no way has prepared him to acquire. It reports facts he cannot possess; he bases his vague notion of where Laverne has gone on gossip and what little information he and Jiggs have gathered. Throughout his career, Faulkner always carefully identified his narrative sources, especially when these sources were characters. *Absalom, Absalom!*, his most structurally complex work, consistently identifies narrative sources. Furthermore, Faulkner's characters rarely acquire information through such an unnatural means as clairvoyance—Darl's instability only partially (and unsatisfactorily) explains his psychic abilities in *As I Lay Dying*. That the Reporter has matured sufficiently to fully value the fliers' humanity and Laverne's nobility also seems doubtful. Just before the interpolation begins, he has gotten drunk and fantasized himself into the dead Shumann. His cynicism, egotism, and self-destructiveness remain apparent in his news stories and his scrawled note to Hagood. His reports of Shumann's funeral in particular bear no relation to the tone or content of the Myron, Ohio, episode. Has he changed? Not much, at least not enough to be able to imagine Laverne's trip to Ohio or to create literature.

Similar scenes elsewhere in the novel also suggest that the external narrator produces the interpolation. The Reporter obviously speaks aloud the two second-chapter character narratives: both bear the features of spoken language, are addressed to a listener, and are identified with quotation marks. The source of the loudspeaker voice becomes a symbol of language's distorting influence. In the sixth chapter, Jiggs talks about the early lives of Roger and Laverne (pp. 274–78), basing his discussion on what they have told him (Jiggs says that Laverne "told me something about" her first meeting with Shumann [p. 276]). Structurally, however, Laverne's parachute jump in chapter 5, retrospectively narrated (pp. 194–201), most closely resembles the interpolation. The bedroom scene between Roger and Laverne, in which her knowledge that he will race a dangerous plane leads to sexual intercourse, moves logically into the account of an event where danger once before had sexually aroused her. Transition between the two scenes is typographically unmarked; the retrospection's first sentence clearly establishes, however, the beginning of a different episode focused on Roger's perspective. The Reporter knows nothing of this incident. Though Jiggs alludes to minor details, he evidently knows little about it either. When the parachute narrative ends, a present-tense internal narrative from the Reporter's perspective follows. The unmarked transition from Shumann's perspective to the Reporter's again occurs abruptly: suddenly the Reporter is walking down a street, unaware of the events just described. His ignorance of this important episode from Roger and Laverne's relationship contributes directly to his misunderstanding of them.

Clearly, the external narrator relates the story of Laverne's trip to Myron, Ohio. The contrast between the interpolation and the Reporter's own stories emphasizes his essential failure as a human being, and Laverne's success. His sudden ability to value compassion over lust, sacrifice over selfishness, would radically contradict his earlier behavior and the novel's fundamental philosophical pessimism. The interpolation also confirms that the Reporter is not the novel's controlling intelligence. His perspective may predominate, but not with authority. He *is* the main character, however, and the nature of his personality, of the world he inhabits, is the main subject. The concatenation of numerous perspectives—internal and external, character and narrator—on people, scenes, and events, combined with their impact on the reader, and his subsequent reactions to them, make up the novel's authentic presiding intelligence.

Pylon may be Faulkner's most unusual, atypical book. But it explores themes which remained of interest to him throughout his career— isolation, economic exploitation, the powerlessness of language, the individual in conflict with his environment. Atypicality alone might explain the neglect accorded the book by contemporary readers and critics. But it admittedly is not one of Faulkner's great achievements. Despite its emotional power and its brilliant evocation of setting, it simply does not measure up to *Absalom, Absalom!*, *Light in August*, or *Go Down, Moses*. Its unrelentingly intense moods grow tiresome. The Reporter seems too unbelievable, his long tirades too often little more than rhetorical bombast. Nevertheless, the strains of modernism which run through its pages offer significant clues to Faulkner's general attitudes towards the twentieth century. Its bitterness is perhaps explained by his difficult struggle with the writing of *Absalom, Absalom!*, his dissatisfying screenwriting job in Hollywood, and the financial pressures of the Depression. As his most despairing evaluation of modern society, it belongs with other, much better American novels of the modern wasteland—*The Sun Also Rises*, *The Great Gatsby*, *The Day of the Locust*, and Tom Cromer's *Waiting for Nothing*. Still, *Pylon* is more respectable than many have recognized, and it deserves rescue from its relative obscurity. It may well be a novel that Faulkner *had* to write, one which allowed him to vent unhealthy frustration and despair, cleansing his mind and imbuing him with the blend of passion and detachment necessary for the creation of great art. *Pylon* also gave Faulkner an opportunity to perfect the narrative strategies which became the structural core of *Absalom, Absalom!*—the most important novel of his career, one of the crowning achievements of modern literature.

Chapter Four
Absalom, Absalom!

Absalom, Absalom! (1936) marks Faulkner's most intricate, convoluted, and artistic exploration into the potentials of narrative form. No novel in American literature can match its achievement. It stands alone in its realization of the novelist's desire to find a shape and a set of aesthetic principles uniquely suited to his genre. Among Faulkner's contemporaries, only Joyce, on the eastern side of the Atlantic, attempted an equivalent feat in his much different novel *Ulysses* (1922). In both these books form is an important element of narrative content. For some readers, however, it has also proven a source of difficulty. Interpreters of Joyce have done a much better job of explaining the form of *Ulysses* than have Faulkner critics with *Absalom, Absalom!*—perhaps because structure in Joyce's fiction has always seemed inherently a part of the narrative, while Faulkner's fiction may so emphasize the story that form can be overlooked or completely ignored. Of course, form in Faulkner's fiction so thoroughly affects the story's telling that it ultimately becomes part of the story.

Strangely enough, numerous critics have set themselves to explaining the narrative structure of *Absalom, Absalom!* Such interpretations usually fall either into the "Detective" or "Impressionist" schools of criticism. Detectives emphasize form. They focus primarily on the characters who narrate the novel, suggesting that because they have little direct knowledge of the story, they create a "fiction" which bears little relation to the historical truth. This created "fiction" is the novel's real subject. The reader must evaluate the evidence which the narrators present and reconstruct the real story, if reconstruction is possible. Detectives often devalue the Sutpen story and pay too much attention to the characters who try to tell it. Impressionists, on the other hand, hold that the novel accurately presents the basic facts of the story, that minor discrepancies in detail and opinion understandably result from the contrasting character narrators, or even from Faulkner's carelessness in composing the novel. Impressionists grant less importance to the narrators than to Sutpen and his family; occasionally, they ignore the narrators altogether.[1] Although there are a number of good Detective and Impressionist critics, the two critical attitudes may stretch to absurd lengths. Radical Detectives may attest to the absence of *any* reliable information, while Radical Impressionists may insist that what Wash Jones thinks or Shreve McCannon says directly represents the opinions of William Faulkner.

Faulkner made several oddly equivocating comments on the novel's structure and its story's accuracy. At the University of Virginia he implied that the stories which the narrators tell are essentially correct— suggesting, for instance, that Shreve's theories about Bon's vengeful mother are true, that Sutpen is the main character, that Bon did know his father's identity. After reportedly rereading the book, however, he expressed a different attitude:

> I think that no one individual can look at truth. . . . You look at it and you see one phase of it. Someone else looks at it and sees a slightly awry phase of it. But taken all together, the truth is in what they saw though nobody saw the truth intact. So these are true as far as Miss Rosa and as Quentin saw it. Quentin's father saw what he believed was truth, that was all he saw. But the old man was himself a little too big for people no greater in stature than Quentin and Miss Rosa and Mr. Compson to see all at once. It would have taken perhaps a wiser or more tolerant or more sensitive or more thoughtful person to see him as he was. It was . . . thirteen ways of looking at a blackbird.

Quentin's view was "just one of the thirteen ways to look at Sutpen, and his may have been the—one of the most erroneous. Probably his friend McCannon had a much truer picture of Sutpen from what Quentin told him than Quentin himself did." Of narrating characters, Faulkner said that "Every time any character gets into a book, no matter how minor, he's actually telling his biography. . . . Quentin was trying to get God to tell him why, in *Absalom, Absalom!* as he was in *The Sound and the Fury*."[2] Because he often spoke inconsistently about his fiction, and his memory sometimes failed him, Faulkner's comments must be taken with a grain of salt. Yet they clearly suggest that he regarded *Absalom* as about both Thomas Sutpen *and* the narrators who try to tell his story.

In fact, *Absalom* must be viewed from both perspectives. To interpret it solely from the frequently limited Detective or Impressionist viewpoints, to worry exclusively over the truth of Bon's racial heritage or the sociopolitical meaning of Sutpen's Design, to force this finely wrought, intricately compelling work into a narrow, rigid, unbending mold—this is to miss the novel's meaning entirely, and to grant it a shallow artistic merit.

Absalom explores the lives of Thomas Sutpen and the people he influenced. It also concerns how certain individuals came to regard and be affected by his life as they tried to reconstruct and explain it. Finally, it chronicles Quentin Compson's gradual recognition that the past, the forces which compel human behavior, even the basic significance of human existence are essentially unknowable. Three separate but interwoven areas of interest can thus be identified: (1) Thomas Sutpen's life; (2) his life as others perceive it; (3) his life as others wrongly perceive it. The discerning reader will likely react to the narrative in two stages. Because traditional novels tell a story, the reader initially pays attention to the events of Sutpen's life as they unfold in the early chapters. The narrative frame, along with Miss Rosa's and Mr. Compson's talks with Quentin in the first four chapters, at first seem little more than conventional ways of getting the story told. As discrepancies and contradictions begin to multiply, as Quentin's curiosity and emotional involvement mount, the reader expands his attention to include the characters who tell the story—primarily Miss Rosa, Mr. Compson, Quentin, and Shreve. This added concern with narrators as *characters* casts doubt on the credibility of what they say. On the one hand the reader wonders about the meaning of a story whose truth, on the other hand, he is forced to question. Despite these suspicions, he experiences the novel on both levels, realizing, perhaps even sensing unconsciously, that the narrators cannot be divorced from the Sutpen story, that the meaning of *Absalom, Absalom!* resides in their union.[3]

Absalom presents a series of speculative narratives containing information of questionable authenticity (but which, in its effect on the narrators, might as well be authentic if it is not). These narratives suggest something about the nature of Thomas Sutpen's life and those it affected. They reveal virtually nothing about his motives, and they also fail to explain the behavior of several members of his family. Nor do they uncover the significance of his life. Explanations, more than facts, are what the narrators yearn for, especially Shreve and Quentin. Though only one of them knew him personally, each becomes intensely interested in Sutpen. Quentin becomes obsessed, and he is a major character as a result. But his obsession does not enable him to understand the story better than any of the other characters. It probably has the opposite effect. The narrators often disagree and even in-vent facts to fit into the story. None ever reaches a wholly satisfying or logical conclusion. The reader must sift through fact and conjecture and evaluate the different interpretations which the narrators offer. In the end, he achieves no greater success in ascertaining the truth than the characters do. The joint participation of readers and characters in unraveling and understanding the Sutpen mystery lies at the core of the novel's narrative design.

An early reviewer, while calling *Absalom, Absalom!* "one of the most formidable [novels] of our generation," attacked the "multiple point of view" which lacked justification, did not provide the contrasting perspectives "for which it was invented," and was unnecessary to the narrative structure.[4] This amazing assessment sums up Faulkner's principal strategy quite well. Since different views of Sutpen's character became a major concern, structure emphasizing individual perspective provided an obvious advantage. The result was a series of character narratives—framed by an uninvolved external narrator—predicated on a carefully developed relationship between the speaking character and his listener. Rather than speaking directly to the reader, characters talk to each other, usually to Quentin. Denied a traditional relationship with first-person narrative—direct address by the speaking character—the reader instead finds himself an eavesdropper to the talk of two individuals about events which occurred forty years before the time of narration (1909–10). Character narratives are a distinguishing feature of Faulkner's fiction. They are important in *The Sound and the Fury, As I Lay Dying, Light in August, Pylon*, and the entire Snopes trilogy. *The Reivers* (1962) is a single sustained character narrative, the only one of Faulkner's career, while *The Unvanquished* (1938) is a series of closely related narratives given by the same character. In *Pylon*, the narratives of Jiggs and the Reporter concern events about which neither has much direct knowledge; the Reporter's consequent misconceptions are counterbalanced by events in the story, other character perspectives, and the external narrator. *Absalom* presents similar misconceptions as fact, but neither the external narrator nor any of the characters intrude to identify them; the reader, and the reader alone, must recognize and try to correct them. For example, only Shreve's desire for what he regards as dramatic justice supports his theory that Henry, not Bon, was wounded at Shiloh. The narrative offers not a shred of evidence in his favor. Yet both he and Quentin adopt this revised version of the story without hesitation. The narrative likewise offers little evidence to confirm Rosa's portrayal of Sutpen as an evil demon, or Mr. Compson's adornment of Sutpen, Henry, Judith, and Bon with the raiments of his own personality and philosophy. The careful reader should instinctively mistrust such irrational viewpoints. He should also be warned against the speaker's misinterpretations by a listening character's reactions. After Quentin returns from his visit to Sutpen's Hundred, he corrects his father on a number of points, while Shreve's affected cynicism often counters Quentin's deep emotional involvement in the story. Of course, Shreve is no more reliable than the other narrators. In fact, he is probably the least reliable. His characterization of Sutpen seems the combination of three other mistaken perspectives—Rosa's, Mr. Compson's, and Quentin's—and it is compounded by his essential unfamiliarity with southern history and custom.

Absalom utilizes three main types of character narrative. Simple character narrative usually occurs in the present time of the novel and involves reminiscence about past-time events. The narrating character speaks in a style and diction consistent with his personality. Simple character narrative occurs in the stories of *The Unvanquished*, most of which Faulkner wrote while he was working on *Absalom*. It also occurs in "That Evening Sun" (1931), where Quentin narrates an episode from his childhood, and in "A Justice" (1931), where he relates a tale told him by Sam Fathers. In simple character narrative the speaker describes something he has seen or heard; his apparent objectivity is usually a defining characteristic (though he may be much less objective in fact than he seems on the surface). Even though Bayard, in *The Unvanquished*, recounts events from his own childhood, he generally suppresses his emotions, allowing the reader to reach conclusions based mainly on the narrative content. In "A Justice" and "That Evening Sun" Quentin's characteristic passivity makes him an ideal observer; in *Absalom*, however, it also reflects his emotional involvement and his despair. All the narrating characters frequently reveal their curiosity and confusion, two important motives in their quest to explain the story. They prompt General Compson to devise his theory of Sutpen's innocence and compel Quentin's father to view Sutpen as a doomed tragic hero. Making no pretense of detachment, the narrators openly involve themselves. They are eager to express their prejudices and opinions. Rather than lifeless, rhetorical sources of information, they become vital parts of the story they tell. Though they honestly desire to uncover the truth, their lack of objectivity is perhaps their single most important characteristic.

Rosa Coldfield's monologue in chapter 5, on the other hand, uses a kind of translated character narrative similar to the narrative in *As I Lay Dying* and the first three sections of *The Sound and the Fury*. In contrast to simple character narratives, translated narratives do not always reflect the narrator's speaking voice, implying instead an external narrator's presence. Such narrative evokes the speaking character's personality, environment, sensibility, weakness and strength. Appropriately, Cleanth Brooks calls Rosa's narrative "poetry" and suggests that her personality justifies her often wind-blown, melodramatic rhetoric.[5] In fact, chapter 5 presents a fusion of what Miss Rosa says with what Quentin thinks and feels as he listens to her. Translated narrative establishes the retrospective, searching tone of the novel as a whole and of the characters' attitudes towards Sutpen and his family in particular.

The third type of character narrative is directed narration, which implies the presence of the hearer-teller relationship and provides the basic foundation of the novel's structure. In *Light in August* and the Snopes trilogy, directed character narrative signifies the speaker's and listener's participation in the community, the transmission of knowledge from one person to another, from one generation to the next. In *Absalom* directed narration concerns the community only indirectly. Though nineteenth-century Jefferson discovered much of what it knew about Sutpen through social interaction, the twentieth-century narrators are only casually interested in the community's response. (In *The Hamlet*, of course, the community's reaction to Flem Snopes is a major theme). Yet the narrators do occasionally discuss various citizens of Jefferson, so they do not neglect the community entirely. Their greatest interest centers on Sutpen family relationships—Henry and his father, Bon and Henry, Henry and Judith, Clytie and Judith. Moreover, in the last four chapters, Quentin's relationship with his sister Caddy and with Shreve helps motivate his interest in relationships of the past. (Caddy's influence on Quentin in *Absalom* should be regarded cautiously, however; she is never mentioned and may not figure in at all).

Appropriately, the hearers and tellers of directed narrative share more than casual relationships. General Compson, his son, and his grandson belong to the same family. Shreve and Quentin are roommates and close friends. On two occasions Sutpen approaches General Compson as a friend, the only person to whom he felt free to speak candidly. Miss Rosa, according to Mr. Compson, selects Quentin to hear her story because he is descended from the "demon"'s friend: she thus believes he bears inherited responsibility for the events she describes. She also evidently harbors some desire for immortality and wants her side of the story remembered. "So maybe you will enter the literary profession," she tells Quentin, "and maybe some day you will remember this and write about it. . . . you can write this and submit it to the magazines. Perhaps you will even remember kindly then the old woman who made you spend a whole afternoon sitting indoors and listening while she talked about people and events you were fortunate enough to escape yourself" (pp. 9–10).* The hearer-teller relationship motivates the bequeathing of a heritage from one generation to the next. More specifically, the Sutpen story becomes a Compson family legacy, passed from grandfather to son to grandson. Hence, hearer-teller relationships provide the rationale for the narrators who talk about Sutpen in the first place.

Although Quentin may appear to be the novel's primary narrator, in only one chapter, the seventh, does he ever talk at length. Usually he merely listens to and thinks about what others tell him. He is the final recipient of all the accumulated knowledge, gossip, speculation, and theorizing about the Sutpens. Throughout the novel the external narrator consistently describes from Quentin's perspective:

> yellow slashes full of dust motes which Quentin thought of as being flecks of the dead old dried paint. [P. 7]

> [Quentin] could almost see her, waiting in one of the dark airless rooms. [P. 88]

> But Quentin was not listening, because there was also something which he too could not pass—[P. 172]

> So it is zero outside, Quentin thought. [P. 217]

> "University of Mississippi," Shreve's voice said in the darkness to Quentin's right. [P. 360]

> *I dont hate it* he thought, panting in the cold air, the iron New England dark; *I dont. I dont!* [P. 378]

The opening lines of each of the last four chapters describe Shreve's words and movements exactly as they appear to Quentin. In chapter 8, during the apparent union of Quentin's and Shreve's perspectives, Shreve continues to talk, and what he says is transmitted through Quentin's listening perspective. Because his thoughts and reactions

---

*William Faulkner, *Absalom, Absalom!* (New York: Random House, 1936).

are repeatedly emphasized and each of the narratives is channeled through his mind, because he ultimately receives all the information about Thomas Sutpen, Quentin is the focal character of the novel—a sustained internal narrative from his perspective. The external narrator frames the various character narratives and notes their effect on Quentin. In each chapter he provides clear evidence of Quentin's listening role.[6] The narrative's pervasive orientation to his perspective gradually influences the reader to identify with him, an identification encouraged by Quentin's characteristic hesitation, his passivity and silence, his ultimate frustration.

As the focal character and the individual whom Miss Rosa has appointed to listen to her talk, Quentin comes into the possession of information as much as a century old, passed down to him in various and often contradictory forms. First, he breathes the "eighty years' heritage of the same air which the man [Sutpen] himself had breathed between this September afternoon in 1909 and that Sunday morning in June in 1833 when he first rode into town" (p. 11). Community knowledge accumulates much like a legend, growing out of the accretion of actual events, gossip, apocrypha, speculation, and outright invention in the communal Jefferson mind. The entire town participates in the heritage's growth. Similarly, in *Light in August* and *The Hamlet* the crimes of Joe Christmas and the rise of the Snopeses become popular topics of conversation. Such individuals as V. K. Ratliff and Byron Bunch embody community opinion, while other characters occasionally appear to reflect the general population's interest. While community knowledge does not figure prominently in *Absalom*, it remains always in the background, and narrating characters allude to it freely. It is the wellspring of much of what they know. The first section of chapter 2 chronicles Jefferson's initial reaction to Sutpen. Of the community representatives who appear, a coonhunter named Akers is twice mentioned as a source of Sutpen lore: he first claims to have stumbled across one of Sutpen's slaves sleeping in the mud (p. 36) and later reports that Sutpen "stole the whole durn steamboat" (p. 44) to acquire furnishings for his mansion. Akers's stories bear the definite mark of the tall tale, and certainly much of what the community "knows" about Sutpen is apocryphal. His taciturn refusal to talk about himself generates stories and gossip which the town passes eagerly back and forth. This communal legend making is inherent in the description of Sutpen's mysterious arrival, "as though . . . out of thin air" (p. 32), and in the subsequent talk: "the stranger's name went back and forth among the places of business and of idleness and

among the residences in steady strophe and antistrophe: *Sutpen.
Sutpen. Sutpen. Sutpen"* (p. 32). Once the nature of Sutpen's uneasy
relationship with the community becomes clear, focus shifts to specific individuals—primarily General Compson—who themselves belong to the community, but who become involved with Sutpen for
more substantial reasons than idle curiosity.

Although General Compson, Miss Rosa, Mr. Compson, and Quentin do represent various community reactions, their importance lies
in their contrasting personalities, in their own perspectives. Their
narratives reflect their individual perceptions and maintain the novel's
central focus on Sutpen. They also know more than the rest of the
townspeople about his activities, which they chronicle with general,
though not fastidious, accuracy. General Compson and Miss Rosa
knew him personally. They are the second and most important means
by which Quentin receives information—from personally involved
individuals who pass the story on for the significance of the lives it
chronicles and the meanings which they can find in it. Contrary to the
amorphous community heritage, this is the specific transmission
of human history, of narrative, from one person to another down
through time. Two of the major themes of *Absalom, Absalom!* grow out
of this acquired knowledge: the influence of the past on the present,
and the unknowable nature of truth.

As focal character, Quentin becomes linked to a chain of transmitted
information reaching back in time to the people who knew Sutpen and
to the very man himself. In the final chapter Quentin actually becomes part of the story when he discovers Henry in the ruined mansion. His awareness of the complex and unlikely way the story has
sifted down to him, of the various narrators' deep involvement, encourages his interest in discovering the facts. It likewise sparks his
frustration, for he finds himself confronted repeatedly with the impossibility of discovering those facts. Each link in the chain carries the
potential for distortion and fabrication. The oldest information concerns Sutpen's childhood during the first two decades of the nine-
teenth century and his life in Haiti during the 1820s. Sutpen provides
the only source of information for these years, though he confesses to
not remembering them clearly. His directed character narrative to
General Compson circa 1835 (chapter 7) is the first link in the narrative chain. General Compson adds the second link when, much later,
he relays Sutpen's story to his son Jason in a narrative (or narratives)
which the novel does not record. Mr. Compson welds a third link
when he relays the story to Quentin (again in an implied, unrecorded

narrative), who finally tells it to his roommate in 1910. Shreve's speculative narrative in chapter 8, a fifth link, bears the obvious marks of the individuals who have passed the story down to him along a chain stretching more than a hundred years into the distant past.

At each link in the chain, the process of transmission grows more complex. At first, only Sutpen's memory and his desire to make a good impression on General Compson mar his narrative's reliability. Yet as each succeeding narrator passes Sutpen's childhood reminiscence along, the probability of distortion grows. Each narrator embellishes the tale with new information—from the community's heritage, members of the Sutpen family, personal experiences, and personal opinion. When Sutpen first talks in 1835, General Compson has already heard much of the rumor and gossip about him. He has also had the opportunity to witness Sutpen's behavior on several occasions and has thus developed opinions. He begins interpreting Sutpen's story even as he hears it. When Sutpen talks to him for the second time in 1864, Compson has the advantage of knowing about his career as a planter, his marriage to Ellen Coldfield, the appearance of Charles Bon, and the rumored break with Henry. By the time the General talks to his son, he knows also of Bon's murder, Henry's disappearance, Sutpen's final years, his death and the death of Judith. The contextual web of all this accumulated knowledge exerts a force whose influence he cannot escape.

Moreover, General Compson's motives for telling his son about Sutpen must also be significant. Though the narrative never suggests what they are, they can probably be accurately guessed at. Many fathers do, of course, talk a great deal to their sons. Perhaps Compson sees in Sutpen's life an object lesson about ambition and ruthlessness, property and class distinctions, by which his son might profit. He also evidently enjoyed reminiscing and speculating about the past. His theory of innocence and of Sutpen's lifelong misunderstanding of human nature are his means of explaining the past. Of course, he might also have been trying to answer his son's questions about a prominent community legend—the probable subject of frequent dinner-table conversations. Jason Compson's motives for talking were likely somewhat different. Unlike the old general, he knows only one of the story's participants—Miss Rosa—and probably not well. Nor does he seem too interested in teaching moral lessons. In place of his father's apparent magnanimity, Mr. Compson's dissipated cynicism and tastes for classical literature influence his view of Sutpen as an example of tragic decline and destruction (in his terms, Destiny and

Retribution). Charles Bon, whom he depicts as a sort of Creole roué, especially attracts him. Quentin, perhaps because of his own private obsessions, fixes on Henry's relationship with Judith and Bon. The Henry-Bon friendship also draws Shreve, whose unfamiliarity with the South initially piques his interest. Shreve and Quentin's apparently close friendship probably also influences their interpretation of the Bon and Henry relationship. Each successive link in the chain of transmission incorporates an additional level of knowledge (however poorly grounded in logic and fact), a different storyteller and listener with a new set of motives and complicating characteristics. Not only the passage of time shapes the story's telling, but also the wavering complexities of very distinct and individual human personalities.

How Quentin learns about Sutpen is of central importance to the novel's meaning. Of course, he inherits the community tradition. He also hears much of the story from his father. What his father tells him compounds, complements, sometimes contradicts Rosa's narrative of a few hours before. Rosa, an actual participant in some of the events which Mr. Compson had only heard about, provides a much different perspective. Instead of affecting detachment and wry amusement, she seems obsessive, illogical, and clearly prejudiced. Quentin comes to regard her as a relic out of antiquity, a living symbol of Sutpen's life and the past. She compels him to experience and feel the story in an intensely emotional way which his father cannot provoke. Quentin learns more of the story from Bon's letter and from his visit to Sutpen's Hundred. He may also have learned something important from Henry Sutpen himself, though this is only speculation. Shreve, the final source of information, repeats much of the story back to Quentin in the process of trying to understand it and adding his own embellishments. He completes the chain of transmission, the final link who gathers all the evidence together in an attempt at a definitive account of what happened. Indeed, Shreve assumes this summarizing role willingly. Quentin hazards no conclusions, perhaps because the various incarnations of the story have confronted him with the painful knowledge that the real truth can never be uncovered.

The nature of the story's transmission provides the foundation of the Detective critics' argument, for, they say, knowledge acquired in such a fashion can never be better than speculative. The novel does not present, for instance, one shred of evidence which would hold up in a court of law. Miss Rosa, neither uninvolved nor objective, is the only firsthand witness, but she talks about events some forty years in her past. The best the other narrators can do is offer hearsay testimony. Virginia Hlavsa maintains that every character could be disqualified as a reliable trial witness for one reason or another. The narrative structure's effect, she suggests, "is that the reader feels he knows the story in essence before he knows it in substance," but the facts themselves rest upon the flimsiest evidence.[7] The letter which Mr. Compson says Bon wrote Judith is the only concrete evidence, but Estella Schoenberg, noting the absence of date, salutation, or signature, even questions its authenticity.[8] The novel presents no evidence against Bon's authorship of the letter, nor does it suggest that General Compson's wife lied about Judith's having given it to her. The letter provides Quentin with his most substantial link to the past. The process of transmission, however, holds the authenticity of other "facts" in abeyance. Though some are very likely true, others are not, and there is simply no way to be sure. The story's basic outline may come clear, as Cleanth Brooks suggests, but its details, its reasons and motivations and meanings, remain shrouded in mystery.[9] The ambiguity heightens Quentin's awareness of a very real and concrete past—as real as the present in which he lives—but by the end of the final chapter he knows he can never recover it.

From the beginning Faulkner apparently intended the facts of Sutpen's life to be shrouded in doubt. "Evangeline," written in 1931, represents the earliest extant stage in the composition of *Absalom*. Its narrator, an unnamed reporter, summons his friend Don to investigate a "ghost" in a "small Mississippi village."[10] Don learns about a man named Sutpen who once lived in a now-ruined mansion outside the village. In simplified form, much of the basic structure of *Absalom* occurs in "Evangeline." Within the frame of character narrative, Don and the reporter discuss the Sutpens, often bantering back and forth in a quick, eager repartee typical of Quentin and Shreve. Don learns much of the story from Negroes who live near the mansion. An old mulatto woman who turns out to be Henry Sutpen's half-sister talks a great deal, but she seems unsure of the truth. The facts remain unclear, and the best Don and the reporter can do is to guess at their outline. The story's climax comes when the reporter climbs to the old mansion's second floor and discovers Henry Sutpen on his deathbed. According to Joseph Blotner, a fragmentary early draft of the novel, under the title of "Dark House," names the two narrating characters Chisholm and Burke, who in a later draft became Quentin and Shreve. Still later, Faulkner experimented with making the two narrators separate halves of Quentin's "divided consciousness" (elements of which remain in the published version). Blotner's biography reproduces a kind of diagrammatic sketch in which Faulkner outlined his early interest in the transmission of information. The sketch shows how General Compson would pass information along to his son and on to Quentin; it also identifies Rosa as a primary information source and Sutpen as the center of attention.[11]

Yet sufficient evidence also exists to suggest that Faulkner never intended to relegate Thomas Sutpen's life and family to an uncertain existence in a hazy legend. In a February 1934 letter to Harrison Smith, he described the book's plot: "It is the more or less violent breakup of a household or family from 1860 to about 1910. . . . The story is an anecdote which occurred during and right after the civil war; the climax is another anecdote which happened about 1910 and which explains the story. Roughly, the theme is a man who outraged the land, and the land then turned and destroyed the man's family. Quentin Compson, of the Sound & Fury, tells it, or ties it together; *he is the protagonist so that it is not complete apocrypha*" (my emphasis). In another letter written to Smith later the same year, Faulkner called *Absalom* "the story . . . of a man who wanted a son through pride, and got too many of them and they destroyed him."[12] Both letters show Faulkner's specific concern with the Sutpen story. In at least one instance prior to the novel's publication, he cast an *Absalom* episode in a narrative form which left no doubt as to the truth of its story. "Wash" (published in the February 1934 issue of *Harper's*) generally corresponds to the novel's version of Sutpen's death (chapter 7, pp. 280–92). Mr. Compson, speculating freely and unreliably about Wash's thoughts, narrates the episode in the novel. An apparently omniscient external narrator, employing Wash as a focal character, tells the story. Both story and novel contain virtually the same information about Wash, especially his thoughts on the events leading to Sutpen's murder. The story in no way suggests that Mr. Compson tells Wash's tale accurately, but it does indicate that in either form the episode possesses a literary value separate from any interest which narrators show in it. That Faulkner did not intend the Sutpen story to possess meanings of its own, independent from but closely related to the narrators who try to tell it, is incredible. Truth's mystery is undoubtedly a major theme, but the Sutpen story has its own themes too. To divorce these two aspects of the novel, to overemphasize one at the other's expense, would likely lead to an utter misunderstanding of both.

Although Faulkner told parts of the Sutpen story elsewhere, only in *Absalom, Absalom!* does he use a series of narrators attempting to discern a link between past and present, to uncover truth but failing at every turn. He employed this particular narrative strategy nowhere else in his work, though in some of his other novels characters do spend considerable time speculating about human nature and behavior. In *The Hamlet*, for example, an external narrator uses the accounts of various characters and of the entire community to chronicle the rise of the Snopes clan. V. K. Ratliff, in his travels as a "sewing machine salesman," comes to be regarded as the county authority on Snopeses. In this sense Ratliff is like Quentin, but he has the advantage of being able to see and talk to the Snopeses face to face. On several occasions he even plots against these adversaries, but they always outwit him, as they do also in *The Town* and *The Mansion*. But Ratliff is fooled only by his misunderstanding of human nature, by his own self-deception. Quentin faces more formidable obstacles of time, truth, and human mortality.

When characters in *The Hamlet* talk about the Snopeses, they usually do so in a realistic context—the narrative gives the impression of people actively talking back and forth. Most of the conversations (to be exact, the directed monologues) in *Absalom* are not realistic. The narrative frame establishes a relationship between two characters—one talking, the other listening; the focus falls on the speaker and what he says. The speaker or external narrator may occasionally refer to the listener, who may briefly interrupt (Quentin's "no'mes" and "yessums" in chapter 1; his comments and questions in chapter 6; Shreve's imploring "Wait . . . for Christ's sake wait" in chapter 7, p. 289). Hence, "conversation" serves as a convention allowing a single character to speak coherently, incisively, and vividly for more than an hour at a time without pause. In the fourth chapter, Mr. Compson speaks virtually uninterrupted for forty pages. At an average speaking rate of two minutes per page (not a slow speed), his narrative would last eighty minutes. In chapter 5 Rosa's monologue (which is actually translated rather than directed narrative) would last about the same period; chapter 7 about two hours and fifteen minutes; chapter 8 an hour and forty minutes (though only an hour is said to have passed between the beginning of chapter 8 and the end of chapter 9). Clearly, Faulkner does not attempt, nor ask the reader to accept, the verisimilitude of spoken language. Narrating characters are no less important for this fact; they simply do not speak normally. They serve as an important means of telling the story, describing characters, and illustrating theme.

The use of spoken narrative as an expository device rather than a realistic imitation of speech is the author's prerogative. The Elizabethan soliloquy is not "realistic," but as a dramatic convention presenting a character's innermost thoughts, it is indisputably valuable. In *Absalom*, under the pretense of conversation, characters express their opinions and individual perspectives in detail. In the frame of a structure which contrasts four distinct viewpoints, character narrative illuminates each speaker's personality in an intimate manner which realistic dialogue could not achieve without fundamentally altering the novel's form and meaning. Hence, the suspension of realism, the illusion that character narrators *do* talk, is simply one of the basic components of the narrative structure. Albert Guerard calls such conversation a literary language, an elevated style unlike normal prose, permitting the author several advantages: "It allows the writer to use, whenever he pleases, his full rhetorical inventiveness and skill. The convention frees the writer from that obligation to imitate impersonal speech. . . . But, more important to the reader, the high language helps 'carry' (or lend necessary distance to) events of tragic, mythical grandeur. Or, to change the figure slightly, the language helps carry the reader out of his everyday rational world of disbelief in major tragic confrontation and plight."[13] The departure from realism (and Faulkner could certainly manage realistic dialogue when he chose to) allows authentic characterization and description, the examination of human motives, and the illustration of theme in both the narrators and the characters they discuss. It also permits the speech of characters whose concerns are usually more mundane to evoke the poetic, tragic, and mythical aspects of their story. In fact, *Absalom* works as much like a long poem as it does a novel. Its lack of realism in this respect contributes directly to its artistry.

Obviously, character narrators are the most important element of the narrative. They talk both in the present time (where there are four of them) and in the past, where they present narratives which eventually filter down to one or more of the present-time narrators. The external narrator, not a character, ranges freely between past and present, summarizing and describing what the characters themselves cannot; his objectivity counterbalances the subjective perspectives of characters. Though not part of the story (he does not try to discover the truth about Sutpen; he merely reports what the narrators discover), he witnesses all of it. His function is rarely apparent on the surface, primarily because the more personable character narrators overshadow him. He also is not omniscient—at least he does not exercise omniscience, often speaking in a conditional, speculative manner suggesting his uncertainty about, or unwillingness to divulge, the truth. But his ability to travel in time and space, his detailed descriptions, and his one sustained external narrative (at the beginning of chapter 2, pp. 31–43) suggest that he occupies a better position to "know" about events than any of the characters. He rarely expresses opinions of his own, and, of course, in no way at all is he equivalent to William Faulkner, whose opinions come forth only in the novel's impact as a whole. The external narrator is an important aspect of narrative structure, a summarizing, unifying observer—and a literary fiction, the author's creation.[14]

The external narrator both frames and visualizes. His very presence, sometimes indicated by only a few words, places each speaker in a narrative context, distancing him from the reader, preventing a speaker such as Shreve or Mr. Compson from assuming too much authority. He describes the speaking character, his listener, the setting, and other relevant aspects of the hearer-teller relationship. His characterization of Quentin and Shreve in chapter 8 suggests the effect of their friendship on what they tell each other. Because he repeatedly emphasizes their status as characters, he insures that their stories do not eclipse them. He also adds another link to the chain of transmitted information, further complicating the themes of truth and the past's relation to the present. His role as a visualizer is especially significant. He can intrude to describe a scene which the speaking character himself is about to describe or remember. In chapter 6, for example, Shreve asks about Quentin's visit to the Sutpen burial ground (pp. 187–88). Though the visit represents one of Quentin's memories, he does not narrate it. Instead, the external narrator relates it for him, never wavering from his perspective, imposing a form and objective coherence on the episode which Quentin probably could not muster. In effect, two narratives occur simultaneously, the external narrator's and the character's, the first based upon the second, but only the first recorded in the novel. In chapter 9, when Quentin relives his visit with Rosa to the ruined Sutpen mansion, the narrator visualizes his memories for him. This visualizing function directly affects the narrative tone, allowing Faulkner considerable license in describing an event while still remaining true to character perspective. The abrupt shift from subjective character narration to objective external narration invests the story with a dramatic, heightened energy. A character's memories, emotions, and imaginings suddenly come alive, are made real. Alternation between external and character narration also creates a powerful structural dynamic which keeps the reader aware of the novel's double-edged concern with the narrators and with the Sutpen story.

Though the external narrator's attitude never changes, each of the narrating characters reacts differently to the story. They are representative Faulknerian individuals—with sharply contrasting personalities and ways of looking at the world, confronted with the vicissitudes of time, history, and human nature, in their own particular ways trying to make sense of these ineffable mysteries. The strengths and weaknesses of their personalities affect their interpretations of what they discover. Mr. Compson's fin de siècle sensibility clearly shapes his portrayal of Charles Bon. His tendency to force events into the tragic patterns of sin, retribution, and destiny provides a useful, interesting, if finally irrelevant explanation. Quentin's weaknesses grow rather obvious once one recognizes how easily Shreve's romantic imagination can manipulate him. Yet Quentin's failure to understand Sutpen, his native South, or the meaning of human existence is no mere quirk of personality. He is unfortunate enough to confront questions whose answers lie well beyond any human being's grasp. His neuroses allow Faulkner a convenient way of externally dramatizing the internal tensions which events of the past can create in an inhabitant of the present. Quentin's final rejoinder "*I dont hate it!*" symbolizes not only his twisted, strained consciousness but also *any* individual's ultimate reaction to the problems which he faces. Yet his neuroses do distinguish him from the other narrators. Parallels which he senses between the Sutpen story and his own life exacerbate his reactions and further hinder his objectivity.[15]

Each chapter in *Absalom, Absalom!* employs a common set of narrative elements: a narrator, listener, place of narration, and subject. In each chapter these elements are combined differently. Two chapters—6 and 7—contain within their primary structure a secondary narrative framework bearing its own characteristics, the result of a present-time narrator who passes on a past-time narrator's story. The identification of each chapter's essential characteristics allows a number of interesting patterns to emerge:

CHAPTER 1—September 1909, middle to late afternoon.
NARRATOR: Miss Rosa—primary source.
LISTENER: Quentin.
SUBJECT: Introduction of Sutpen; Rosa's attempt to justify her and Ellen's relationship with him.
PLACE OF NARRATION: Miss Rosa's house.

CHAPTER 2—September 1909, twilight.
NARRATOR: Mr. Compson, relying on General Compson and the community heritage.

LISTENER: Quentin.
SUBJECT: Sutpen's arrival in Jefferson (external narrative); his court-ship and marriage to Ellen Coldfield.
PLACE OF NARRATION: Porch of the Compson house.

CHAPTER 3—September 1909, early evening.
NARRATOR: Mr. Compson, relying on the testimony of his parents and his own speculation.
LISTENER: Quentin.
SUBJECT: Rosa, especially her attitude towards Bon and Judith; Mr. Coldfield's death, Ellen's "butterfly summer," Henry and Bon's dis-appearance.
PLACE OF NARRATION: Porch of Compson house.

CHAPTER 4—September 1909, early evening.
NARRATOR: Mr. Compson.
LISTENER: Quentin.
SUBJECT: Judith, Bon, and Henry, with emphasis on Bon's character and relationship with Henry.
PLACE OF NARRATION: Porch of Compson house.

CHAPTER 5—September 1909, middle to late afternoon (same day as the previous chapters).
NARRATOR: Miss Rosa, as remembered by Quentin.
LISTENER: Quentin.
SUBJECT: Rosa's relationships with the Sutpens, especially Judith and Thomas.
PLACE OF NARRATION: Miss Rosa's house.

CHAPTER 6—January 1910, late evening.
NARRATOR: Shreve, relying on information told him by Quentin; Mr. Compson, as a past-time narrator, relying on secondhand tes-timony.
LISTENER: Quentin.
SUBJECT: Judith, the Sutpen fortunes after the Civil War, Bon's progeny.
PLACE OF NARRATION: Present time—Harvard dormitory room. Past time—Sutpen graveyard.

CHAPTER 7—January 1910, late evening.
NARRATOR: Quentin, relying on information from past-time narra-tors, Sutpen and General Compson, whose talks have been relayed to Quentin by his father.

LISTENER: Present time—Shreve. Past time—Quentin, Mr. Compson, General Compson.
SUBJECT: Sutpen's childhood and his experiences in Haiti; his design, his murder by Wash Jones.
PLACE OF NARRATION: Present time—Harvard dormitory room. Past time—Sutpen's Hundred; General Compson's office; probably the Compson house porch.

CHAPTER 8—January 1910, late evening, between midnight and 1:00 A.M.
NARRATOR: Shreve, relying on what Quentin has told him.
LISTENER: Quentin.
SUBJECT: Bon and Henry; the dilemmas which Shreve believes they faced.
PLACE OF NARRATION: Harvard dormitory room.

CHAPTER 9—January 1910, around 1:00 A.M.
NARRATOR: There is little character narrative, though the thoughts and memories of Quentin, the focal character, make up most of the chapter's contents.
SUBJECT: Quentin's discovery at Sutpen's Hundred; the effect on him of all he has learned.
PLACE OF NARRATION: Harvard dormitory room.

As the focal character in each chapter except the one he narrates, Quentin possesses by the end of the novel all the transmitted information about the Sutpens. The two main places of narration are Jefferson, Mississippi, in September 1909, and Cambridge, Massachusetts, in January 1910. According to Joseph Blotner, Faulkner at one point set the entire novel in the Harvard dormitory room, making most of the first five chapters a retrospective narrative from Quentin's perspective.[16] The published novel's division into geographical halves—one southern and the other northern—joins with Shreve's unfamiliarity with the South to emphasize the tension which Quentin feels between his experiences in Mississippi and his attempts to explain them in Massachusetts.

Specific images and motifs emphatically distinguish the northern and southern places of narration. Although imagery contrasts the two settings, it also binds them together and serves as a unifying force in the novel. Chapters are organized so as to create disunity and confusion, which mirror Quentin's state of mind as well as the failure of the events of Sutpen's life to fit together coherently. While the episodes of the Sutpen story are not described in the order of their occurrence, their narration does occur chronologically. The first four chapters follow logically one after the other. The last four chapters also occur in chronological order, evidenced by their occasional references to the passage of time. Chapter 5, the novel's pivotal narrative, proves a crucial exception. Chapter 1 describes the circumstances of Miss Rosa's talk, but most of her narrative does not occur until the fifth chapter. Certain chronological ironies lend drama and suspense. As his father tells him about Sutpen in chapters 2, 3, and 4, Quentin is waiting to accompany Rosa to the mansion where he will discover Sutpen's son Henry. Because the story is uncovered only in apparently unrelated bits and pieces, the reader must determine the actual sequence of events, thus participating in the same process as the narrating characters.

Each chapter presents a distinct body of knowledge and experience often related only indirectly to other chapters. What the narrators know determines when and how they reveal information. Because there are several narrators, not all of whom have been in contact with each other, information flows in a discontinuous and often contradictory or repetitious manner. Each chapter begins as a seemingly new narrative, with no apparent relationship to any other, and concludes on a note of unresolved tension and mystery. Such discontinuity, according to Michael Millgate, violates the reader's concept of the traditional novel:

> Again and again, Faulkner stops us short of elucidation, constantly reinforcing in this way a suspense which . . . is created not so much by the withholding of narrative facts . . . as by the continual frustration of our desire to complete the pattern of motivation, of cause and effect. The movement of the book becomes wave-like—surging forward, falling back, and then surging forward again—and it is notable that most of the chapters, including the last, end on such moments of checked resolution.[17]

The disunity in the Sutpen story creates unity in the process of its telling. The reader's awareness of a disorderly narrative but of an orderly narrative process invests the novel with its greatest continuity. When the reader himself enters the reconstruction process, as he must, the novel assumes an even greater cohesiveness.

The novel offers numerous examples of how the narrative enforces unity and disunity simultaneously. Nearly every chapter begins by invoking imagery characteristic of the place of narration. For Mississippi the important motif is wisteria, mentioned in chapters 1, 2, 3, and 5 (chapter 4 consists mainly of Mr. Compson's narration). Wisteria is a flowering vine (p. 7), an odor (p. 31), a color (p. 89), and "*the substance of remembering*" (p. 143). Quentin associates it with listening to his father and Miss Rosa talk about Sutpen (p. 31), while Rosa links it to the summer of her short-lived womanhood (pp. 143–44). For Quentin, and the novel as a whole, wisteria evokes the Mississippi landscape, the act of reminiscing about events from the distant past. Other images—Mr. Compson's cigar smoke, fireflies, the dust and heat, and the bug-stained light bulb above the Compson porch—likewise characterize the narrative landscape. The last four chapters associate with New England a different set of images—primarily the cold, the radiator, the snow. These two imagistic patterns interweave and contrast throughout the narrative; at important points they fuse the two environments in Quentin's mind. His father's letter about Miss Rosa's death injects the Southern wisteria into a foreign setting: "that dead summer twilight—the wistaria, the cigar-smell, the fireflies—attenuated up from Mississippi and into this strange room, across this strange iron New England snow" (p. 173). At times the images themselves fuse: Shreve's pipe smoke pervades the Massachusetts dormitory room just as Mr. Compson's cigar smoke wafted through the summer Mississippi air. Significantly, the novel's concluding lines juxtapose Quentin's protest that he does not hate the South with the "cold air, the iron New England dark" (p. 378).

Chapter endings, in addition to their evocation of suspense, create unity and disunity by sometimes echoing, almost word for word, a previous chapter's ending, or by hinting at information to be later revealed. Faulkner understood that chapters divide a novel into units which directly affect the reader's response. For many readers the end of a chapter is a natural point to lay the book aside until later. Even if a reader wades straight through such a novel as *Absalom* (an unlikely feat), he will still perceive it in terms of the units which divide it: the distinct individuality of the chapters in *Absalom* encourages such a perception. As a result, the chapter endings encourage the impression of a novel which gets nowhere and resolves or reveals nothing— an impression that subtly prompts the reader to share in Quentin's frustration.

The end of chapter 3, narrated by Mr. Compson from Rosa's perspective, cites without explanation Wash Jones's question "Air you Rosie Coldfield?" (p. 87). Chapter 4, also narrated by Mr. Compson, moves towards the same question from a different direction using

Bon's character and Henry's infatuation with him, Mr. Compson's theory of why Sutpen ordered Henry to prevent the marriage, and Bon's letter to explain the previous chapter's conclusion before repeating it again, this time with the new information that Henry has killed Bon "dead as a beef" (p. 133). Miss Rosa describes her reactions to the murder in chapter 5, which ends with her cryptic statement, "There's something in that house" (p. 172). Suddenly the reason for her night-time trip to the ruined mansion begins to emerge. Vaguely hinted at in the first five chapters, her visit has not seemed important until now. Of course, the "something in that house" strongly implies a connection with the Sutpens. Tension, suspense, and anticipation result and are not resolved until the last chapter. Significantly, Bon's murder, alluded to dramatically at the end of two chapters and a climactic event in two others, is never itself described. The reader can react to it only through the perspectives of the characters involved.

A more subtle rhythm of repetition runs through the final four chapters. The end of chapter 6 again alludes to the "something" out at Sutpen's old mansion, prompting Shreve's breathless "For God's sake wait" (p. 216). Each chapter's beginning alludes to the dormitory room's coldness. The beginnings of chapters 6 and 7 also describe Shreve's hand; chapters 7 and 8 allude to the cold window and Shreve's deep-breathing exercises, which he has evidently completed by the beginning of chapter 9 because the window is open. The time of evening is noted at the beginning of chapters 8 and 9. Shreve's exclamatory "Wait" at the end of chapter 6 expands into a comment on the room's coldness and is repeated at the end of chapters 7 (p. 292) and 8 (p. 359): "Come on. Let's get out of this damn icebox [refrigerator] and go to bed." His suggestion is neither selfish nor impatient—at the beginning of chapter 9 he considerately offers to bring overcoats to Quentin, who is shivering (p. 360–61—echoing Bon's offer of a cloak to Henry in chapter 8, [p. 356]). The ninth chapter's concluding allusion to the New England coldness, contrasted with Quentin's panting denial that he does not hate the South, ironically echoes the closing lines of the two preceding chapters. Such carefully calculated repetitiveness intensifies tone and suspense, effectively demonstrating how deeply the narrators have become involved in the story.

The analyses which follow focus on the important implications of narrative structure in each chapter of *Absalom, Absalom!*: characterization, irony, the narrator's credibility, figurative language, the transmission of knowledge. These chapters reveal the gradual merger of narrative structure with the theme of knowing—how narrators come to learn about the Sutpens, what they do with their knowledge, how they pass it on, how their personalities and their relationships affect what they say. Each chapter's singular structural composition reflects numerous levels of experience and interpretation, every one of which must be accorded its proper place in the firmament of the novel's meanings.

Chapter 1. The first chapter sets the entire novel in motion, especially the Mississippi chapters, and introduces Quentin's at first reticent interest in the Sutpen family. Emblematic motifs characterize the southern landscape: the "weary dead September" heat, the wisteria, and the dust, associated at important points with the past and the process of trying to discover it. Framed by the external narrator, Rosa Coldfield does most of the talking (except for a brief intrusion by Mr. Compson), addressing Quentin, the primary listener and focal character. Like most of the novel, chapter 1 employs internal narrative. The external narrator remains uninvolved, revealing only the attitudes of the characters whose narratives he frames. Accordingly, he filters Rosa's first description of Sutpen through Quentin's perspective:

> Out of quiet thunderclap he would abrupt (man-horse-demon) upon a scene peaceful and decorous as a schoolprize water color, faint sulphur-reek still in hair clothes and beard, with grouped behind him his band of wild niggers like beasts half tamed to walk upright like men, in attitudes wild and reposed, and manacled among them the French architect with his air grim, haggard, and tatter-ran. [P. 8]

Quentin's imagined vision of this demonic figure assumes the form of what has been called a tableau, an image of arrested time and motion epitomizing the essence of a character's perspective.[18] Pricked by an emotionally stimulating scene or idea, Quentin's empathetic imagination often vividly visualizes what others describe to him. This tendency grows along with his interest in discerning the events of Sutpen's life.

Occasional instances of translated narrative also occur. The most important is the "dialogue" between the "two separate Quentins" (p. 9), one a southerner, the other a prospective freshman at Harvard University in the North. This metaphorical exchange signifies the tension and confusion which Quentin begins to feel as he listens to Miss Rosa. The incredulous repartee anticipates Quentin and Shreve's dialogue at the beginning of chapter 6 (p. 176), Sutpen's debate with himself after being turned away from the Virginia mansion in chapter

7 (pp. 234–35), and the cryptic exchange between Quentin and Henry Sutpen in chapter 9 (p. 373). It also marks the first of several occasions when a character confronts a confusing and insoluble dilemma: "*It seems that this demon—his name was Sutpen—(Colonel Sutpen)—Colonel Sutpen. Who came out of nowhere and without warning upon the land with a band of strange niggers and built a plantation—(Tore violently a plantation, Miss Rosa Coldfield says)—tore violently.*" (p. 9). The passage embodies Quentin's conflicting attitudes of acceptance and rejection towards his native region. It also reflects his inability to remain indifferent to Miss Rosa's story, for which Mr. Compson has suggested he may bear some responsibility: Rosa "may believe that if it hadn't been for your grandfather's friendship, Sutpen could never have got a foothold here. . . . So maybe she considers you partly responsible through heredity for what happened to her and her family through him" (p. 13). The impact of this suggestion grows as Quentin learns more about the Sutpens. By the end of chapter 5, he lies firmly within its grip.

The first chapter also establishes the apocryphal nature of the Sutpen story, passed down through the years by word of mouth and community speculation: "the first part of it, Quentin already knew. It was a part of his twenty years' heritage of breathing the same air and hearing his father talk about the man Sutpen; a part of the town's—Jefferson's—eighty years' heritage of the same air which the man himself had breathed" (p. 11). Rosa brings the heritage to life. She bases her narrative on her own experience, as well as on what her sister Ellen and her maiden aunt had told her. The attitudes of these two women, along with the "insult" she suffered from Sutpen, severely warp her ability to interpret the story objectively and often lead her to simplistic conclusions: her assertions, for instance, that Sutpen caused Ellen's death, Henry's disappearance, and Charles Bon's murder. The truth proves considerably more complex than she makes it.

Rosa's narrative possesses a carefully developed logic and form, much like a legal brief. The forty-three years since Sutpen's "insult" gave her ample time to plan how she might explain and justify her connections with the "demon." The first half of her argument hinges on her thesis that he "wasn't a gentleman. He wasn't even a gentleman" (p. 14). The semantic thrust is negative: all but the first paragraph are prefaced by an interjectory "No," echoed at the end of the first section by Quentin's "No'me" (p. 20). Then follows a transition paragraph, prefaced by "But," expressing Rosa's amazement that Sutpen chose to associate with her father "of all of them that he knew"

(p. 20). Quentin responds this time with "Yessum" (p. 21), introducing the second half of her argument, affirmative in thrust, contending that "Yes," he was a demon, that Fate, or Ellen, had delegated her to protect Judith and suffer the demon's onslaughts. She presents her own case in the best possible light, and Sutpen's in the worst, making herself the victim and him the victimizer. She never manages to ascribe human motives to his behavior. The reader's recognition of her extreme prejudice should prompt a desire for information from other sources. It certainly does so for Quentin.

Despite her prejudice, Rosa speaks with more personal force than any other narrator. Sutpen touched her directly, changed her life. She is prima facie evidence for her testimony. Though Quentin senses this fact, he also finds her an obscure and eccentric fossil. He thinks of her as a "fading and ancient photograph" (p. 14), a "dream which the sleeper knows must have occurred, stillborn and complete, in a second" (p. 22). In a translated narrative, he muses over why she is talking to him: *"It's because she wants it told,* he thought, *so that people . . . will read it and know at last why God let us lose the War: that only through the blood of our men and the tears of our women could He stay this demon and efface his name and lineage from the earth"* (p. 11). Later he decides her voice might once have been a cry of "young and indomitable unregret, of indictment of blind circumstance and savage event; but not now: now only the lonely thwarted old female flesh embattled for forty-three years in the old insult" (p. 14). He finds her as strange as her story.

Chapter 1 introduces three of the four important narrators and uncovers the skeleton of the Sutpen story. It also vaguely foreshadows Quentin's climactic meeting in the last chapter with Henry Sutpen (only hours away in the time of the novel) by revealing that Rosa "had dismissed him [Quentin] at last with his promise to return for her in the buggy" (p. 12). With its imagery of dust and its characterization of Rosa in her "dim hot airless room with the blinds all closed and fastened for forty-three summers" (p. 7), and its concern with people long dead and nearly forgotten, the first chapter introduces the novel's basic themes and essentially reminiscent tone.

Chapter 2. The second chapter chronicles Sutpen's early days in Jefferson—his arrival, his building of the mansion, his marriage to Ellen Coldfield. The first section (pp. 31–43) portrays the community heritage alluded to in the first chapter, while the second section (pp. 43–58) relies on the perspectives of Mr. Compson and his parents to relate specific episodes. Mr. Compson knows only what he has heard from his parents and other townspeople. Although General Compson, Sutpen's friend and a man of relative probity, was a first-hand witness, Quentin receives his testimony secondhand from Mr. Compson. The general's objectivity, especially compared with Rosa's mania, strengthens the reliability of the few facts which Quentin learns. The theories surrounding those facts, however, are another matter.

The first section describes the community heritage through Quentin's perspective. Several references to General Compson (pp. 33, 34, 36, 37, 41) suggest that Mr. Compson has previously discussed Sutpen's early days in Jefferson with his son. The townspeople themselves may have learned much of what they knew about Sutpen from Quentin's grandfather, the only one among them who knew the man well. At any rate, the narrative alludes to General Compson as a reporter of community opinion. In several instances the external narrator intrudes to characterize Jefferson's attitudes towards Sutpen, which often resemble Rosa's: "they saw him, on a big hard-ridden roan horse, man and beast looking as though they had been created out of thin air and set down in the bright summer sabbath sunshine" (p. 32). His name quickly becomes a topic of conversation, spoken back and forth "in steady strophe and antistrophe: *Sutpen. Sutpen. Sutpen. Sutpen*" (p. 32). His mysterious background, unknown source of money, and taciturnity, along with the fact that he is an outsider, an intruder, encourage their reaction. Oddly, the community's reaction divides along class boundaries. Landowners ride out to visit Sutpen while he is building his mansion; lower-class citizens hurl taunts and garbage after his wedding. This distinct social dichotomy appears elsewhere in the novel, and is ironically reflected in Sutpen's chapter 7 tale of being turned away from the Tidewater Virginia mansion. The narrator also frequently notes the limits of the townspeople's knowledge. Once they learn his name, "that was all that the town was to know about him for almost a month" (p. 32). Their opinion of his courtship of Ellen proves equally limited:

> In their surprise they forgot that Mr Coldfield had a marriageable daughter. They did not consider the daughter at all. They did not think of love in connection with Sutpen. They thought of ruthlessness rather than justice and of fear rather than respect, but not of pity or love: besides being too lost in amazed speculation as to just how Sutpen intended or could contrive to use Mr Coldfield to

further whatever secret ends he still had. They were never to know: even Miss Rosa Coldfield did not. [P. 43]

Like Miss Rosa, the town mythologizes Sutpen. The chapter's second half, Mr. Compson's narrative, for the first time humanizes him, counterbalancing these distorted views.

At the beginning of the second section, the clause "Mr Compson told Quentin" (p. 43) reestablishes the hearer-teller relationship of directed narrative, with Quentin listening and his father talking. Double quotation marks precede each paragraph to reinforce the occurrence of spoken narrative.[19] Though Mr. Compson treats Sutpen more kindly than do Rosa and the townspeople, his personality directly affects his talk. His misogyny, for example, often surfaces in his discussions of Ellen and her maiden aunt. While Rosa demonizes Sutpen, Mr. Compson fills women with absurd and illogical motives, occasionally making Sutpen the victim rather than the victimizer. Characteristically, he suggests that Ellen and the aunt forced Sutpen to agree to a big wedding (pp. 51–52). He also seems to admire Sutpen's idealism and determination, traits which he lacks. His fatalism especially colors his account of the wedding, to him a symbol of Sutpen's entire life: "He did not forget that night, even though Ellen, I think, did, since she washed it out of her remembering with tears. Yes, she was weeping again now; it did, indeed, rain on that marriage" (p. 58). Despite these defects, however, he succeeds in making Sutpen believable, finding in him the potential for such human qualities as love, shame, embarrassment, and common sense, as well as ambition and greed. As a result, his view is probably more accurate than Rosa's. But while he may have the facts, more or less, he lacks explanations.

The second section's specific concern with Sutpen's courtship and wedding required a more informed perspective than that of community gossip. Mr. Compson thus focuses upon his father and Mr. Coldfield, who were directly involved. The general himself was privy to information now revealed for the first time. His friendship with Sutpen insures a more sympathetic portrayal, a more unbiased effort to view events from Sutpen's vantage point, or what he and his son consider his vantage point. Yet the general's association with Sutpen does not deter him from a good deal of informed speculation. Mr. Compson agrees with many of his father's opinions, especially the idea that marriage was a crucial part of Sutpen's design, and he is eager to pass them on to Quentin. Theories abound, woven from incredibly tenuous threads; a slight change in Sutpen's appearance prompts this hypothesis: "he was not fleshier either; your grandfather said that was not it: it was just that the flesh on his bones had become quieter, as though passive after some actual breasting of atmosphere like in running" (p. 48). Another theory concerns Sutpen's reasons for marrying Mr. Coldfield's daughter: "Sutpen . . . wanted, not the anonymous wife and the anonymous children, but the two names, the stainless wife and the unimpeachable father-in-law, on the license, the patent" (p. 51). Such theories usually concern motivations for behavior, not the behavior itself. Mr. Compson, like most of the other narrators, is more interested in *why* rather than *what*.

By the chapter's end, Quentin can add his grandfather's testimony, modified and transmitted by his father, to what he has learned from Miss Rosa. Numerous discrepancies between these contradictory portraits of Sutpen heighten the tension which he is beginning to feel, strengthening his desire to hear more.

Chapter 3. Mr. Compson narrates the third chapter, with the external narrator intruding three times, in italics, to identify speakers. The opening lines frame Mr. Compson's talk and reinforce the hearer-teller relationship. Compson consciously acts as an educator, explaining what his son does not know or understand:

> If he threw Miss Rosa over, I wouldn't think she would want to tell anyone about it *Quentin said.*
>
> Ah *Mr Compson said again* After Mr Coldfield died in '64, Miss Rosa moved out to Sutpen's Hundred to live with Judith. [P. 59]

Mr. Compson has learned most of his information from his parents; in addressing his son he is probably reenacting a similar conversation of years before with his own father. Much in the story appeals to him—Sutpen's ambition, the personalities of the Sutpen women, the romantic figure of Bon, the tragic patterns into which he can fit their lives. He theorizes freely and creatively, especially about women; consequently, his peculiar sensibility, deductive reasoning, and philosophy of human behavior pervade the entire chapter.

Because his main subject is Rosa and her relationship with her father and sister Ellen, Mr. Compson's misogyny becomes particularly prominent. Ellen, for instance, he describes as a butterfly in metamorphosis: "At this time Ellen went through a complete metamorphosis, emerging into her next lustrum with the finality of actual re-birth" (p. 64); "Ellen at the absolute halcyon of her butterfly's summer" (p. 74); "Apparently Ellen had now served her purpose, completed the bright pointless noon and afternoon of the butterfly's summer and vanished" (p. 78); "Ellen the butterfly, from beneath whom without warning the very sunbuoyed air had been withdrawn" (p. 80). She talks, he says "the most complete nonsense, speaking her bright set meaningless phrases out of the part which she had written for herself" (p. 69). In contrast, Judith has reached the height of adolescence: "young girls . . . not in themselves floating and seeking but merely waiting, parasitic and potent and serene, drawing to themselves without effort the post-genitive upon and about which to shape, flow into back, breast; bosom, flank, thigh" (p. 67). The style and vocabulary of this description is typical of Mr. Compson. When he relies closely on what his father has told him, however, his vocal characteristics grow less evident. Women to him are little more than mindless erotic vessels which rarely act according to recognizable logic. His misogyny seriously warps his analysis of Rosa. Beginning in chapter 6, Shreve, who reminds Quentin of his father, echoes similar attitudes.

Compson's decadent, self-consciously time-worn sensibility also shapes his portrayal of Bon. Significantly, he envisions Bon's appearance much as the townspeople viewed Sutpen's arrival: Bon was a "personage who in the remote Mississippi of that time must have appeared almost phoenix-like, fullsprung from no childhood, born of no woman and impervious to time and, vanished, leaving no bones nor dust anywhere" (p. 74). Though Mr. Compson is unaware at this point of Bon's parentage, these comments ironically foreshadow the later revelation that Sutpen is Bon's father. He also plants in Quentin's mind the image of a peculiarly close relationship between Judith and Henry, a relationship he describes with a paradoxically homosexual metaphor: "something of that fierce impersonal rivalry between two cadets in a crack regiment who eat from the same dish and sleep under the same blanket and chance the same destruction and who would risk death for one another" (p. 79–80). Such descriptions may well stimulate Quentin's serious interest in Judith and Henry, who likely remind him of his relationship with his own sister. Compson mythologizes Bon, Henry, and Judith just as Rosa mythologized Sutpen. In the last four chapters, when Shreve assumes Mr. Compson's place in the hearer-teller relationship with Quentin, he also identifies with Bon and preserves the mythologizing process.

Mr. Compson's tastes for classical literature appear in his discussions of Rosa, Clytemnestra, and Sutpen. While Rosa denied Sutpen's humanity by insisting on his demonic nature, Compson denies the humanity of the actors in his drama (though constantly professing to believe in it) by forcing their lives into rigid patterns ruled by an indifferent Fate rather than by individual choice and responsibility. He insures that Rosa will fulfill the role he assigns her:

> When [Sutpen] returned home in '66, Miss Rosa had not seen him a hundred times in her whole life. And what she saw then was just that ogre-face of her childhood seen once and then repeated at intervals and on occasions which she could neither count nor recall, like the mask in Greek tragedy, interchangeable not only from scene to scene, but from actor to actor and behind which the events and occasions took place without chronology or sequence. [P. 62]

He speaks of her "Cassandralike listening beyond closed doors" (p. 60). He also makes a Cassandra out of Clytie in a particularly flatulent instance of speciousness: "I have always liked to believe that [Sutpen] intended to name Clytie, Cassandra, prompted by some pure dramatic economy not only to beget but to designate the presiding augur of his own disaster" (p. 62). Sutpen, of course, becomes the tragic hero:

> he acted his role too—a role of arrogant ease and leisure. . . . he was unaware that his flowering was a forced blooming too and that while he was still playing the scene to the audience, behind him Fate, destiny, retribution, irony—the stage manager, call him what you will—was already striking the set and dragging on the synthetic and spurious shadows and shapes of the next one. [Pp. 72–73]

Mr. Compson's narratives are also affected by his dissipation. There is no reason to believe that his alcoholism and financial difficulties in *The Sound and the Fury* do not persist in *Absalom, Absalom!* His personal problems help explain his obsession with failure and ruined lives. Like Sutpen, he is the head of a family, and he takes no small consolation, if not satisfaction, in the similarities between Sutpen's failure and his own. Yet there is much in Sutpen which he can envy too. Again, Quentin cannot be unaware of these similarities.

Chapter 3 exemplifies how each of the novel's divisions possesses its own characteristic form. Though Mr. Compson continues to talk to Quentin, always the listener and focal character, a second narrative structure emerges within the chapter's general structural frame. Because Mr. Compson talks about Rosa from what he believes to have been her perspective, she serves as his focal character. He also intrudes occasionally into the minds of other characters, such as Ellen and Sutpen. Relying on some facts and considerable theorizing, he assumes the role of an omniscient narrator producing internal narrative. To his credit, he does not camouflage his theories. He probably believes they are good ones, that he can judge character astutely. As a result, he reports thought and dialogue, analyzes character motivations, and draws conclusions quite persuasively. Yet his very persuasiveness, in the novel's overall context, identifies him as a fallible source of fundamentally unreliable narrative. Unlike his son, he exhibits no great commitment to uncovering the truth about the people he discusses. He becomes interested in them mainly because of the confirmation which their lives provide his opinions of human nature.

Chapter 4. Chapter 3 ends with Wash Jones's question, "Air you Rosie Coldfield?" (p. 87). Chapter 4 leaves that question unanswered, instead chronicling events in the relationships of Henry, Judith, and Bon which lead to Wash's revelation of Bon's murder at the chapter's end. Framed by the external narrator, Mr. Compson continues talking, relying on information from the community heritage and his parents, especially his mother's account of Judith. The external narrator introduces the chapter with the representative southern imagery and with a comment on Quentin's plans to travel somewhere with Rosa: "He could almost see her, waiting in one of the dark airless rooms in the little grim house's impregnable solitude" (p. 88). This description sets in contrast the two places where Quentin hears about Sutpen— Miss Rosa's house and the Compson porch; by extension, it also calls to mind Quentin's Harvard dormitory room, linking the three main settings of narration together.

Mr. Compson abandons for a time the previous chapter's theorizing by attempting to create some concrete details. He builds his narrative around three events: Bon's engagement to Judith, Sutpen's command to Henry that the marriage cannot occur, and Bon's death. The letter provides factual evidence of these events, but Mr. Compson seems unaware of its significance. Instead, he proposes a number of facts which the narrative later reveals as false. He suggests that Sutpen forbade the marriage because he learned in New Orleans that Bon had married a mulatto. He speaks of "the body which Miss Rosa saw" (p. 104), though she is obsessed in her chapter 5 narrative with never having seen the body and even has difficulty accepting its existence. He also speculates that Judith invited Rosa to live with her after Bon's murder, but Rosa clearly states in chapter 5 that the move was her idea. The New Orleans trip during which he suggests Bon introduced Henry to his mulatto wife has no factual basis. He relates a number of events he could have learned of only from Henry, whom neither he nor his father could have talked to after the break with Sutpen. Despite these elaborate embellishments, Mr. Compson recognizes the shaky foundations on which his theories rest. He admits as much in a passage epitomizing one of the novel's major themes:

> It's just incredible. It just does not explain. Or perhaps that's it: they dont explain and we are not supposed to know. We have a few old mouth-to-mouth tales; we exhume from old trunks and boxes and drawers letters without salutation or signature, in which men and women who once lived and breathed are now merely initials or nicknames. . . . Yes, Judith, Bon, Henry, Sutpen: all of them. They are there, yet something is missing; they are like a chemical formula exhumed along with the letters from that forgotten chest . . . you bring them together again and again nothing happens: just the words, the symbols, the shapes themselves, shadowy inscrutable and serene, against that turgid background of a horrible and bloody mischancing of human affairs.
> [Pp. 100–101]

Mr. Compson's awareness of the story's fragmentary nature does not dissuade him from continuing to tell it. He offers more detail than ever about what characters thought and said, perhaps as the result of his compulsion to understand. He seems willing, occasionally, to acknowledge Henry, Judith, and Bon as independent individuals capable of free choice. Yet when they speak, they usually sound just like Mr. Compson, mouthing his words and opinions. When Judith brings Bon's letter to General Compson's wife, she expresses a suspiciously familiar attitude:

> You get born and you try this and you dont know why only you keep on trying it and you are born at the same time with a lot of other people, all mixed up with them . . . and it cant matter, you know that, or the Ones that set up the loom would have arranged things a little better, and yet it must matter because you keep on trying . . . and then all of a sudden it's all over and all you have left is a block of stone with scratches on it. [P. 127]

At a few points Compson does seem to penetrate through to the emotional essence of the dilemmas which Henry, Bon, and Judith might have faced. He suggests how torn Henry must have felt between his devotion to Bon and his certainty that his father would not lie: *"I will believe; I will. I will. Even if it is so, even if what my father told me is true and which, in spite of myself, I cannot keep from knowing is true, I will still believe"* (p. 90). He also credits Judith with stoic courage after Bon's disappearance with Henry: *"I love, I will accept no substitute; something has happened between him and my father; if my father was right, I will never see him again, if wrong he will come or send for me; if happy I can be I will, if suffer I must I can"* (p. 121).

Mr. Compson's depiction of these intensely emotional dilemmas attracts his son's interest more than any other element of the story. As earlier suggested, Quentin's interest in Henry and Judith may stem from his own obsessions with his sister Caddy. Mr. Compson knows of his son's concerns, remembering his claim of incest with his sister (recorded in *The Sound and the Fury*). Consciously or not, he goads Quentin by describing the Sutpen children in language brimming with metaphors of incest; Henry and Judith were "that single personality with two bodies both of which had been seduced almost simultaneously" (pp. 91–92); "Yes, it was Henry who seduced Judith: not Bon" (p. 97). Quentin's belief in the potential for incest between Judith and Bon, for homosexual incest between Bon and Henry, grows along with his knowledge of the story. To some degree, Faulkner relied in *Absalom* on situations he had developed in *The Sound and the Fury* (and the reader's memory of them) to provide further explanation for Quentin's obsession with the past.

The chapter's most significant factual contribution to the story is Bon's letter. Elisabeth Muhlenfeld regards it as the novel's only authentic evidence about Bon, suggesting that it reveals him as intelligent, mature, and genuinely in love with Judith.[20] Untainted by narrative personalities and word-of-mouth distortions, the letter is undeniably important. Oddly, it tells the narrating characters very little. Compson interprets Bon's statement *"We have waited long enough"* (pp. 101, 131) as fatalistic acceptance of the South's defeat. Shreve and Quentin focus on the same statement in their narratives of Henry and Bon during the last days of the Civil War. With these exceptions, however, the letter is generally ignored. An artifact removed from its cultural context, separated by time and space from the hand which wrote it, it belongs to the mystery it embodies, a symbol of the absolute gap between past and present: Quentin "read the faint spidery script not like something impressed upon the paper by a once-living hand but like a shadow cast upon it which had resolved on the paper the instant before he looked at it and which might fade, vanish, at any instant while he still read: the dead tongue speaking after the four years and then after almost fifty more" (p. 129). The absence of date, salutation, or signature magnifies the enigma. The personality of the letter's author seems just recognizable enough to remain incomprehensible. Bespeaking a reality of human personality and emotion to which Quentin and his father seem oblivious, the letter constitutes fundamentally important evidence. Emphasizing the separation between the narrating characters and the story they seek to explain, it provides a genuine self-portrait which the reader can compare to portraits of Bon offered by narrating characters.

In Bon's resigned conclusion that *"you and I are, strangely enough, included among those who are doomed to live"* (p. 132), the letter ironically foreshadows Bon's murder, and Rosa's account of its aftermath in the following chapter. It is also linked to Mr. Compson's much different letter in chapters 6 and 9, a unifying and encapsulating frame in the last four chapters.

Chapter 5. Rosa Coldfield talks throughout this chapter, but the narrative records her voice only as Quentin, the focal character, hears it. The italicized narrative reflects what Quentin thinks and feels as he hears Rosa's words. A passage at the end of her narrative reinforces his focal perspective: "But Quentin was not listening, because there was also something which he too could not pass—that door, the running feet on the stairs beyond it almost a continuation of the faint shot, the two women, the negress and the white girl in her underthings" (p. 172). Chronologically, Rosa talks on the afternoon before Quentin's evening conversations with his father. The placement of her talk *after* rather than before Mr. Compson's narratives indicates the changes in Quentin's attitude towards what she tells him. Once he has learned more from his father about Sutpen, Bon, Judith, Henry, Ellen, and others, what at first seemed an old woman's rambling prattle assumes a far greater significance. The poetic intensity of chapter 5 shows as much about the nature of Quentin's involvement with the Sutpens as about Rosa's. Her words revolve constantly in his mind. They come to represent the essence of his experience with the Sutpens, of the novel's attitudes towards the past. Thus, the chapter's pivotal location in the narrative.

Rosa's narrative at first seems closely related to the monologues of *The Sound and the Fury* (1929) and *As I Lay Dying* (1930), where speakers reveal their personalities and experiences in a voice whose articulate objectivity suggests an external narrator's presence. Rosa's discussion of her *"summer of wistaria,"* for example, resembles one of the Dewey

Dell chapters in *As I Lay Dying*: "The dead air shapes the dead earth in the dead darkness, further away than seeing shapes the dead earth. It lies dead and warm upon me, touching me naked through my clothes . . . I feel like a wet seed wild in the hot blind earth."[21] Through a series of similarly stylized narratives, *As I Lay Dying* creates the illusion of participating wholly in a character's inner life. Yet Darl, Dewey Dell, Anse, Vardaman, and the others talk to no one in particular; their narratives thus lack the social motive of conversation, of directed narration. Rosa addresses a listening focal character. Her story merges with his thoughts and reactions and is filtered through his consciousness by the external narrator.

Chapter 5 fully and richly evokes Rosa Coldfield's character. It reveals much which she would probably refuse to acknowledge, such as *"the miscast summer of my barren youth which . . . I lived out not as a woman, a girl, but rather as the man which I perhaps should have been"* (p. 144). Other passages similarly utilize a language and insight wholly uncharacteristic of her. Thwarted fulfillment is one of her main themes; she attributes it to several causes: her father, the Civil War, Sutpen's insult, and his death. Since she might be unable or unwilling to discuss these subjects openly, the narrator does so for her. He intrudes into her mind, fuses her words, thoughts, emotions, and memories with Quentin's perspective. Occasionally he distills and articulates dimensions of her experience which she is probably wholly unaware of. As a result, her words often become indistinguishable from his, as in this description of Judith after Bon's death:

> *There were two afternoons in the late fall when Judith was absent, returning at supper time serene and calm. I did not ask and I did not follow her, yet I knew and I knew that Clytie knew that she had gone to clear that grave of dead leaves and the sere brown refuse of the cedars—that mound vanishing slowly back into the earth, beneath which we had buried nothing. No, there had been no shot. That sound was merely the sharp and final clap-to of a door between us and all that was, all that might have been—a retroactive severance of the stream of event: a forever crystallized instant in imponderable time.* [P. 158]

Occasionally she is made to speak in a way to which she would violently object, but which is appropriate nonetheless: *"I who had learned nothing of love, not even parents' love—that fond dear constant violation of privacy, that stultification of the burgeoning and incorrigible I which is the meed and due of all mammalian meat, became not mistress, not beloved, but more than even love; I became all polymath love's androgynous advocate"* (p.

146). Such language is authentically poetic. Because of it, because of the complex narrative perspective, chapter 5 provides the novel's most revealing and compassionate exploration of character. Rosa symbolizes her own story, the Sutpen story, and she affects Quentin tremendously.

As in chapter 1, Rosa's ostensible purpose for talking is to justify her relationship with the Sutpens. She expresses constant disbelief at how he insulted her: "*I could take that many sentences, repeat the bold blank naked and outrageous words just as he spoke them, and bequeath you only that same aghast and outraged unbelief I knew when I comprehended what he meant*" (pp. 166–67). Her first sentence reflects her belief that she has already become an object of community speculation: "*So they will have told you doubtless already how . . .*" (p. 134). At the end of her narrative she expresses humiliation at being a "jilted" woman: "*They will have told you how I came back home. Oh, yes, I know: 'Rosie Coldfield, lose him, weep him; caught a man but couldn't keep him'—Oh yes, I know (and kind too; they would be kind): Rosa Coldfield, warped bitter orphaned country stick called Rosa Coldfield*" (p. 168). Quentin provides her with a chance to vindicate herself in the eyes of the community. He is also an excuse to vent a long withheld burst of despair and rage.

The chapter 5 narrative brims with dream imagery and symbolism. Rosa often remembers the past as a nightmarish hallucination, musing at one point that after Bon's death perhaps she had expected Henry to wake her from a bad dream (pp. 140–41). She can confront reality, but she cannot accept it. Occasionally she distorts it grotesquely, and she is especially fond of believing herself the victim of supernatural forces. Of Sutpen's return from the war she says:

> *He himself was not there, not in the house where we spent our days. . . . The shell of him was there, using the room which we had kept for him and eating the food which we produced and prepared. . . . Something ate with us; we talked to it and it answered questions; it sat with us before the fire at night and . . . talked, not to us, the six ears, the three minds capable of listening, but to the air, the waiting grim decaying presence, spirit, of the house itself.* [P. 160]

Cleanth Brooks suggests that this sort of "demonizing" results from Rosa's ignorance of the reason for Henry's murder of Bon.[22] She also gothicizes, romanticizes, and often dehumanizes the characters of her narrative into abstractions: Bon is the "*abstraction which we had nailed into a box*" (p. 153); Wash, "*that brute progenitor of brutes*" (p. 134); Sutpen, a "*shape which rode away*" (p. 167), the "*light-blinded bat-like im-*

age of his own torment cast by the fierce demoniac lantern up from beneath the earth's crust" (p. 171). Such ploys allow her to concoct explanations commensurate with her outrage, to protect herself from the truth. Her narrative strains constantly for words, images, and metaphors appropriate to a story whose horror she deems beyond description.

Encompassing all that precedes and follows it, chapter 5 is the pivot of the novel's structure. Its first lines, with Rosa's instructions to Wash Jones, who has just arrived with news of Bon's murder, hearken back to the concluding sentences of chapters 3 and 4. The final lines, focused on Henry's announcement to Judith that he has killed Bon and on Rosa's revelation, "There's something in that house. . . . Hidden in it. It has been out there for four years, living hidden in that house" (p. 172), forge similar links. Her revelation hints at the cause of her desire to go out to Sutpen's Hundred and foreshadows Quentin's discovery, in only a few hours, of Henry Sutpen. The terse exchange which he imagines between Henry and Judith after Bon's murder anticipates his own dialogue with Henry in chapter 9. It also anticipates Rosa's second trip to Sutpen's Hundred, which ends with the burning of the mansion and her death, described by Mr. Compson's letter in chapters 6 and 9.

Chapter 5 intensifies the building momentum and suspense and indicates Quentin's acceptance from Rosa (from his father and grandfather too) of the burden of the Sutpen story's mystery and meaning.

Chapter 6. The first chapter narrated from Quentin's Harvard dormitory room occurs some four months after the time of the Mississippi chapters. It contains four sections: introduction and Shreve's narrative (pp. 173–81); italicized internal narrative of Sutpen's death (pp. 181–87); Mr. Compson's narrative (pp. 187–215); Shreve's final comments (pp. 215–16). The subject is the aftermath of the Civil War: Sutpen's death, the life of Charles Etienne Saint-Valery Bon, Judith's "widowhood" and death. How these narratives develop is determined largely by the form in which Mr. Compson originally gave the information in them to Quentin. Mr. Compson develops the theme that St.-Valery Bon and Jim Bond ironically symbolize the decline of Sutpen's dream, since they, along with Clytie, were his last surviving descendants. The theme of decline also influences Shreve's conception of the post–Civil War South. His interest in what Quentin has told him introduces him as the fourth major narrator. In addition to his attempts to continue the story's telling, he also serves as a kind of prompter—asking incredulous questions, venting sarcasms, suggesting theories in order to wrest some response from Quentin. Of all the narrators, he is the furthest removed from the place and time of the Sutpens. He has learned everything he knows from Quentin, who during their months together as roommates has evidently talked a great deal.

Quentin's interruptions, such internal narrative comments as *"I didn't need to listen then but I had to hear it and now I am having to hear it all over again"* (p. 211), and his comparisons of Shreve to his father signify his presence as a listener. Although neither Shreve nor Mr. Compson possesses all the information revealed in the sixth chapter, Quentin does. Because he has heard portions of the story from his father and discovered other parts for himself, then related them to Shreve and listened to Shreve relate them back again, he finds himself constantly forced back to the events of Sutpen's life. In a cyclic pattern enforced by the novel's structure, he repeatedly faces his inability to make sense of it.

Mr. Compson's letter at the chapter's opening injects the Mississippi environment into a Massachusetts dormitory room and leads to an internal narrative of Quentin's thoughts and emotions as he rode towards Sutpen's Hundred with Rosa some four months before. The dust cloud rising behind their carriage "speaks" in an italicized narrative which marks his awareness that figuratively and actually he is moving back through time towards Sutpen's house and what it contains. Shreve's interruption at the end of this retrospective narrative (p. 176) suggests that Quentin may actually describe the trip to his roommate, the external narrator relaying the essence of what he says in the internal narrative. When Shreve begins narrating after his interruption, he first asks a series of unbelieving questions, subordinate noun clauses completing his initial "You mean that this old gal, this Aunt Rosa———" (p. 176). To each question Quentin numbly answers, "Yes." Shreve elevates Rosa's demonizing in an equally unsatisfactory literary characterization by transforming Sutpen into "this Faustus, this demon, this Beelzebub fled hiding from some momentary flashy glare of his Creditor's outraged face" (p. 178). His questions prod Quentin into a revery about Sutpen's death. The transition from external descriptions of Quentin to internal narrative and to translated narrative is easy to follow:

> "Yes," Quentin said. *He sounds just like father* he thought, glancing (his face quiet, reposed, curiously almost sullen) for a moment at Shreve leaning forward into the lamp, his naked torso pink-gleaming and baby-smooth, cherubic, almost hairless, the twin

moons of his spectacles glinting against his moonlike rubicund face, smelling (Quentin) the cigar and the wistaria, seeing the fire-flies blowing and winking in the September dusk. *Just exactly like father if father had known as much about it the night before I went out there as he did the day after I came back* thinking *Mad impotent old man who realized at last that there must be some limit even to the capabilities of a demon . . .* [P. 181]

The participle "thinking" establishes the italicized narrative's source as Quentin's mind. Shreve's cynicism, especially evident in his discussion of Sutpen after the Civil War (p. 181), suggests Mr. Compson's own cynicism, which in turn (along with Shreve's pipe smoke) evokes Quentin's memory of waiting on that Mississippi September evening to ride to Sutpen's Hundred, which then reminds him of what he discovered there, which finally leads him to remember what his father told him about Sutpen's last attempt to father an heir. These wavelike shifts (or progressions) in narrative subject mirror the ramblings of Quentin's mind, an example of how Faulkner often simulated the patterns of his focal character's thoughts in the structural patterns of the fiction they inhabit.

Although his words go unrecorded, Shreve continues talking throughout the italicized translated narrative. At one point Quentin rouses from his revery to answer "Yes" (p. 185) to something Shreve has said. What Shreve says probably reflects the general content of the translated narrative, which characterizes Sutpen as the "demon" and "Faustus," Rosa as the "aunt," and Wash Jones as "*this gangling malaria-ridden white man.*" Such expressions are characteristic of Shreve. The italicized narrative also contains Quentin's thoughts and memories as he listens to Shreve talk about Sutpen's death. Thus it bears not only his mark but also Rosa's and Mr. Compson's, and it provides much more detail than Shreve alone could give.

The retrospective account of the graveyard visit is also narrated from Quentin's perspective—his memories articulated by the external narrator. Within this framework Mr. Compson narrates, with the external narrator occasionally intruding to describe the graves or Quentin's thoughts. At two points lengthy references to Quentin in his dormitory room as he remembers the graveyard visit interrupt. In the first (pp. 207–8) Quentin recalls Mr. Compson's discussion of Bon's letter, then thinks about a conversation (which his father must have told him about) between Judith and Charles Etienne. The second (pp. 210–15) relates Quentin's feelings about Judith's death and leads to an italicized narrative reflecting his reactions to Shreve's talk—Quentin again is clearly marked as the narrative source by two occurrences of the participle "thinking" (p. 211) and by his thought that Shreve _"sounds just like father"_ (p. 211). In both cases, italicized narrative depicts Quentin's present-time memory of past-time events.

Faulkner's use of narrative structure as a metaphor for Quentin's state of mind—in constant flux between past and present, fact and fiction, the voices which tell and which people the Sutpen story—accounts for the structural complexity of chapter 6. Shreve's prompting role enables him to influence the direction of Quentin's comments. At the University of Virginia, Faulkner suggested that "Shreve was the commentator that held the thing to something of reality. If Quentin had been let alone to tell it, it would have become completely unreal. It had to have a solvent to keep it real, . . . believable, creditable, otherwise it would have vanished into smoke and fury."[23] Shreve keeps Quentin in rein. His narratives in chapter 6, generally free of his speculation and embellishments in later chapters, probably accurately reflect what Quentin has told him, a likelihood supported by Quentin's continual assent to (and failure to correct) what he says.

Chapter 7. Faulkner's most thorough portrait of class distinctions, the seventh chapter divides loosely into three sections, each narrated by Quentin to Shreve. In the first, Quentin relates what Thomas Sutpen told General Compson about his childhood and Haitian experiences. Despite the complexity of this episode's transmission—from Sutpen to General Compson to Mr. Compson to Quentin to Shreve—none of the characters who pass it along seem to doubt its authenticity. Much of the story is not recorded as Sutpen told it; rather, Quentin relays his grandfather's account of it, with Sutpen as focal character. Sutpen's own words (as passed down to Quentin) are relayed only once (pp. 239–43). Quentin agrees with his father and grandfather that Sutpen spoke honestly: "He was telling a story. He was not bragging about something he had done; he was just telling a story about something a man named Thomas Sutpen had experienced, which would still have been the same story if the man had had no name at all" (p. 247). This first section encompasses three distinct narrative moments: (1) the time of the events Sutpen describes (1810–35); (2) the time of Sutpen's first talk with General Compson (circa 1835); (3) the time of Quentin's narrative to Shreve (January 1910). The hunt for the escaped French architect occasions Sutpen's talk. When he and General Compson pause during the hunt to rest, he begins talking. Quentin's description of the architect's attempts to escape (pp. 218–20, 238–39, 243–45, 256–58) creates a satiric parable of ownership and human chattel, another ironic counterpoint to Sutpen's Tidewater Virginia and Haitian experiences.

The next section concerns Sutpen's second talk in General Compson's law offices in 1864. Again Quentin uses Sutpen as a focal character and relies upon his grandfather's account of their meeting. He relays Sutpen's words only once (pp. 263–65). When he talked the first time, Sutpen was just beginning the task of fulfilling what the narrating characters call his "design," and he evidently felt no need to defend his behavior. When he talks the second time, however, his design's success has been jeopardized by the war and perhaps also, General Compson speculates, by Charles Bon. He seems much more concerned with explaining and justifying his life:

> Now fog-bound by his own private embattlement of personal morality: that picayune splitting of abstract hairs while (Grandfather said) Rome vanished and Jericho crumbled . . . that Father says men resort to in senility . . . sitting there and talking and now Grandfather not knowing what he was talking about because now Grandfather said he did not believe that Sutpen himself knew because even yet Sutpen had not quite told him all of it. [Pp. 271–72]

Sutpen devotes much of his talk to what went wrong with his design, which "he had long since given up any hope of ever understanding" (p. 263). He also evidently discusses the existence of a child borne him by his first wife, to whom he relinquished his property when he divorced her "in order that I might repair whatever injustice I might be considered to have done by so providing for the two persons whom I might be considered to have deprived of anything I might later possess" (p. 264). His confusion about the design's failure prompts General Compson's innocence theory, an explanation so persuasive that it colors the speculation of all the succeeding narrators.

The transitional passage (pp. 277–80) between the second and third sections exemplifies the difference between directed and external narrative. When Shreve interrupts to begin telling the story, Quentin protests, "Wait, I tell you! . . . I am telling" (p. 277); Shreve stubbornly persists: "No . . . you wait. Let me play a while now" (p. 280). During this brief interruption, the external narrator intercedes with internal and translated narrative. As Quentin waits for Shreve to begin, he thinks, in translated narrative: "*I am going to have to hear it all over again I am already hearing it all over again*" (p. 277); then the external narrator recapitulates Sutpen's return after the war to learn of Bon's death (pp. 277–78), ending with a reference to Wash. Italicized narrative follows (pp. 278–80) with a general, often abstract analysis of Sutpen's efforts to renew the fulfillment of his design. His fear that his determination (characterized phallically as *"the old gun, the old barrel and carriage"* [p. 279]) will fail leads him to propose the "experiment" to Rosa. The italicized narrative, ostensibly given by Mr. Compson but utilizing the rhetoric of other narrators as well, represents Quentin's thoughts about Sutpen's dilemma after the war. It appropriately prefaces Quentin's narrative of Sutpen's final attempt to father a son and his consequent death.

The third section (pp. 280–92) transmogrifies a few bare facts and sketchy thirdhand testimony into a full-fledged narrative of Sutpen's murder. Quentin reports the incident as his father described it to him, though Mr. Compson had heard the story of Sutpen's demise only from his father and perhaps some townspeople. The one generally accepted fact is that Wash killed Sutpen. The rest of the story is based on the testimony, much of it speculative, of witnesses: customers of Sutpen's store report that he fathered a child by Wash's granddaughter Milly. A Negro midwife says that after Sutpen compared the newborn child to a horse, Wash became enraged and killed the old man with a scythe. A Negro boy discovers the body and glimpses Wash's face in a window of the shack. Major de Spain and other townsmen report the murder of Milly and her child and witness Wash's death. Except for the fact of Sutpen's murder, the entire episode is reported information. Because the various witnesses tend to corroborate each other, many or most of the facts may be accurate, but there is no way to be sure.

The real speculation, the creation of what cannot be less than a total fiction, however likely it might be, is Mr. Compson's detailed characterization of Wash Jones. Compson acts confidently as an omniscient narrator who possesses complete knowledge of Jones's personality, feelings, thoughts. Yet his frequent references to his sources of information—his father, the midwife, the townsmen, and others—reflect his utter separation from the events he describes. Perhaps he feels free to speculate because of his sense of superiority over Wash, also because the story complements General Compson's theory of Sutpen's innocence so well. Mr. Compson likes to use parables; the tale of Wash offers a parable of the destruction of the landed upper class at the hands of a landless, subservient lower class. It neatly mirrors Sutpen's 1835 account of being turned away by the Negro servant of a

Virginia plantation house (Wash too was often turned away from Sutpen's house by Clytie, a black servant). Mr. Compson is thus able to bring Sutpen's rise and fall to an artistic, if artificial close.

Chapter 7 is the only section of the novel which Quentin predominantly narrates. Shreve, his interest aroused, interrupts occasionally with the usual exclamations, questions, and sarcasms. At one point he reacts suspiciously to how much Mr. Compson knew ("He seems to have got an awful lot of delayed information awful quick" [p. 266]), but Quentin explains that he had given his father new information the day after his visit to Sutpen's Hundred (pp. 266–67). Such interruptions force Quentin to explain the story more fully. In a sense he and Shreve represent two sides of a single personality: "born half a continent apart" but joined "by that Continental Trough, that River which runs not only through the physical land of which it is the geologic umbilical, not only runs through the spiritual lives of the beings within its scope, but is very Environment itself" (p. 258). The contrast between the Mississippi heat and the New England cold, where two individuals sit talking in a room "dedicated to that best of ratiocination" (p. 280), creates an allegorical framework in which slavery, the Civil War, national history, and individual human lives are weighed in an increasingly complex, never-resolved debate.

Chapter 7 exemplifies Faulkner's ability to conflate different episodes in order to illustrate a single theme from several angles. But no one character speaks for him. His opinions are evident only in the novel's overall structure and content. General Compson suggests that Sutpen's discovery of class distinctions led to his "design." Other narrators accept this theory, sometimes modifying or further developing it. Three parables of conflict between landed and landless, owner and owned, master and slave offer different interpretations of the Sutpen story and different views of the narrators who propose them. They present authentic views of human life, even if, in the novel's framework, they reveal nothing credible. Indeed, Mr. Compson's theory of innocence may be a more valid interpretation of American history and social class structure than of Thomas Sutpen.

Chapter 8. The eighth chapter, narrated by Shreve, relies heavily on imagined reconstruction. The external narrator intrudes often to point out fabrications, paying so much attention to Shreve and Quentin that they become, on one level, the narrative subject. His main concern is Bon and his desire for recognition from Sutpen, as well as the possible 1865 meeting at which Sutpen supposedly reveals Bon's Negro blood to Henry. The details which Shreve imagines, with Quentin's agreement or acquiescence, have no factual basis. Though Henry may indeed have met with his father—in chapter 7, General Compson recalled such a meeting—the novel provides no factual evidence of its purpose. Examining the people involved, influenced by his own fatalism (like Mr. Compson), and employing metaphors he has earlier developed, Shreve arrives at a plausible account of what might have occurred, but he provides no concrete proof.

Shreve's most apparent fabrication is the lawyer who he claims represents Sutpen's first wife and serves as a counselor for Bon. Though Faulkner seemed to verify, twenty years after writing *Absalom*, the lawyer's existence ("There probably was a lawyer. . . . yes, yes, there was a lawyer"),[24] the narrative itself provides no such evidence. The external narrator calls the lawyer one of the "people who perhaps had never existed at all anywhere, who, shadows, were shadows not of flesh and blood which had lived and died but shadows in turn of what were (to one of them at least, to Shreve) shades too" (p. 303). The lawyer personifies several ideas suggested earlier in the narrative. Having previously referred to Sutpen as a demon, a Faustus trying to elude his Creditor, Shreve uses the lawyer to provide a rational explanation for what he cannot otherwise explain. The lawyer, in fact, becomes the Creditor—constantly computing (in italics) the potential value of Sutpen's property and family to the first wife's desire for revenge. Adopting Mr. Compson's misogyny, Shreve thinks it logical for an abandoned woman to desire revenge. The lawyer is very much the product of Shreve's mentality, which possibly has been influenced by lawyers in the novels of Charles Dickens and by Shylock in Shakespeare's *The Merchant of Venice*, works which a Harvard freshman likely would have read. Though the lawyer may reveal much about his creator's personality, he is weak evidence, if evidence at all, for events of the past. Moreover, the success of his schemes depends on the cooperation of a much more submissive and passive Bon than other narrators have portrayed, than Bon's letter to Judith suggests.

Frequent references to mistakes and fabrications in Shreve's narrative emphasize the chapter's reliance on unfounded speculation. When Shreve imagines flowers blooming in the Sutpen garden at Christmas time, the narrator notes the mistake, adding, "But that did not matter because it had been so long ago" (p. 295). Later he contrasts Shreve and Quentin's account of Bon and Henry's New Orleans visit with Mr. Compson's version. He also compares their differing views of Bon (p. 335). Bon's mother is what "Shreve and Quentin had likewise invented and which was likewise probably true enough" (p. 335). Conditional verb tenses, along with frequent references to what "Shreve and Quentin believed" (p. 335) and to the limitations of their knowledge, draw attention to the peculiar circumstances of the narrative's creation:

> In fact, Quentin did not even tell Shreve what his father had said about the visit. Perhaps Quentin himself had not been listening when Mr Compson related it that evening at home; perhaps at that moment on the gallery in the hot September twilight Quentin took that in stride without even hearing it just as Shreve would have, since both he and Shreve believed—and were probably right in this too—that the octoroon and the child would have been to Henry only something else about Bon to be, not envied but aped if that had been possible. [P. 336]

The passage brings several structural elements into view: the external narrator's lack of omniscience (note the frequent use of the word "probably"); his possession of more information than the characters; Quentin's source of information; Shreve's limited knowledge; their disagreement with Mr. Compson; the accuracy of their speculation. Requiring analysis on several different levels, in every way the chapter presents a narrative about narrative. It is also the one instance in the novel where a narrator's lengthy speculations occasionally become rather tedious.

Shreve and Quentin's changing relationship contributes significantly to the chapter's imaginative qualities. Although Shreve appears to dominate and speak for Quentin, both of them are caught up in a mutually envisioned story: "Not two of them in a New England college sitting-room but one in a Mississippi library sixty years ago" (p. 294); "both thinking as one, the voice which happened to be speaking the thought only the thinking become audible, vocal" (p. 303); "Shreve ceased. That is, for all the two of them, Shreve and Quentin, knew he had stopped, since for all the two of them knew he had never begun" (pp. 333–34); "both of them were Henry Sutpen and both of them were Bon" (p. 351). They communicate almost telepathically: vague pronouns become immediately clear ("neither of them said 'Bon'" [pp. 304, 305, 310–11]), and such phrases as "both thinking as one" occur frequently. Yet Quentin's passivity, his surrender to the futility of trying to discover the truth, is probably a more likely explanation than telepathy for the mutuality of their narrative.

Everything Shreve knows and believes about the story he has learned from Quentin. It is only logical that many of Shreve's theories and speculations would seem likely to his roommate, or at least plausible. Besides, Quentin's interest in incest and homosexuality, his memory of what Rosa and his father have told him, have imbued him with a fatalism inherent in his silence and his violent shivering at the beginning of chapter 9. Since almost any explanation could be possible, Quentin probably thinks, why not Shreve's?

The narrative source of Sutpen's 1865 meeting with Henry at first seems ambiguous. The episode reverberates with a more authoritative tone than the rest of the chapter, and not until the second half of the italicized narrative is Quentin and Shreve's joint imagination (though Quentin remains the focal character) clearly marked as the source: "They were both in Carolina and the time was forty-six years ago . . . smelling the very smoke which had blown and faded away forty-six years ago from the *bivouac fires burning in a pine grove*" (p. 351). The episode emphasizes the drama of the meeting it purports to record. Its vividness stems from the external narrator's description of the scene from Quentin's and Shreve's perspectives, through internal translated narrative. But is the imagined meeting factual? It seems more so than the lawyer, and it also has what Cleanth Brooks has called the "ring of truth."[25] General Compson earlier suggested the occurrence of some sort of meeting (p. 276). If Henry knew of Bon's Negro blood, as Quentin says, then the meeting with Sutpen would have been his only opportunity to learn of it. With much scene-setting and dialogue, this dramatic episode is convincing and persuasive, but it also portrays Bon and Henry as the narrators have developed them; it even alludes to Bon's unlikely "wound" at Shiloh.[26] There is simply no way to determine the scene's credibility. But it belongs to the story which the narrators tell. For Quentin it is too real. Its consequence— Henry and Bon's final confrontation at the gates to Sutpen's Hundred—obsesses him. If the 1865 meeting cannot be accepted as fact, at least its metaphoric importance and emotional impact are undeniable.

Chapter 9. The concluding chapter's internal narrative describes Quentin's memory of his visit to the ruined Sutpen mansion with Rosa. Throughout, the Quentin who remembers the visit in his Harvard dormitory room stands in contrast to the Quentin who becomes an active participant in the Sutpen saga when he meets Henry. Occasional interruptions by Shreve or the external narrator suggest that as

Quentin relives the trip, both by remembering it and by talking about it, his memories are being refined and presented through internal narrative. His memory of the climactic meeting symbolically confirms his earlier notion, in the eighth chapter, that "*maybe happen is never once but like ripples maybe on water after the pebble sinks, the ripples moving on, spreading . . . maybe it took . . . Thomas Sutpen to make all of us*" (pp. 261–62). This final episode also makes of the novel an unending loop. What the initial five chapters foreshadowed, what in narrative time was only hours away at the fifth chapter's end, Quentin finds impossible to forget, more than four months later. He cannot stop remembering.

Several of Shreve's comments (pp. 373, 376) suggest that he has already heard about the trip from Quentin, or perhaps that he hears about it at the same moment the external narrator describes it. But directed narration ceases to be of much importance in this final chapter. The narrative focuses instead on what Quentin remembers and how it affects him. The chapter's major theme is the failure of understanding—Shreve's failure to understand a region he has never visited, Quentin's failure to understand the people and events with which he has grown up:

> "Gettysburg," Quentin said. "You cant understand it. You
> would have to be born there."
> "Would I then?" Quentin did not answer. "Do you understand
> it?"
> "I dont know," Quentin said. "Yes, of course I understand it."
> They breathed in the darkness. After a moment Quentin said: "I
> dont know."
> "Yes. You dont know. You dont even know about the old dame,
> the Aunt Rosa."
> "Miss Rosa," Quentin said. [Pp. 361–62]

Quentin's strangely brief answers, his shivering (like his shivering after he met Henry), his whole attitude intimates surrender, submission, despair, even preparedness for death: "He lay still and rigid on his back with the cold New England night on his face and the blood running warm in his rigid body and limbs, breathing hard but slow, his eyes wide open upon the window, thinking 'Nevermore of peace. Nevermore of peace. Nevermore Nevermore Nevermore'" (p. 373).[27] His depression and his awareness of his own mortality are reflected in this ironic exchange:

"I am older at twenty than a lot of people who have died,"
Quentin said.

"And more people have died than have been twenty-one,"
Shreve said. [P. 377]

The reliance on internal rather than directed narration allows a focus
which simultaneously emphasizes both the emotional distress of the
focal character and the events which helped to cause that distress.

Shreve deliberately makes several obtuse, sarcastic remarks which
cannot help but aggravate Quentin's despair at having failed to make
him understand the South or the Sutpen story: "'I didn't know there
were ten in Mississippi that went to school at one time,' Shreve said"
(p. 360); "'The South,' Shreve said. 'The South. Jesus. No wonder you
folks all outlive yourselves by years and years and years.'" (p. 377);
"Now I want you to tell me just one thing more. Why do you hate the
South?" (p. 378). Shreve's comments on what he sees as a Southern
obsession with history and tradition (p. 361), his analyses of Miss
Rosa (p. 362), Clytie's burning of the mansion (p. 374), Rosa's death
(p. 376), the demise of the Sutpen family (pp. 377–78), and the South's
racial future, though perhaps well intentioned and only mildly mali-
cious, also prove irritating. Repeatedly he forces Quentin to recognize
his failure of understanding, confronting him with problems more
profound than the story he has tried to tell: the nature of the past, the
constant flow of time, human mortality, the futility of human endeavor—be it his own efforts to uncover the past, Henry's efforts to
avoid killing Bon, or Thomas Sutpen's quest to achieve his design.

Because Quentin did not accompany Rosa on her second trip to
Sutpen's mansion (he evidently was at home when it occurred), his
knowledge of what happened comes indirectly from the ambulance
attendants who went with her. Yet his ability to "see" the second visit
is emphasized four times. He envisions it clearly. Having seen the
mansion, talked to the ambulance attendants, and met Clytie, Henry,
and Rosa, he probably imagines the episode with relative accuracy. A
few elements do seem the result of his compulsion to invest his vision
with a fitting dramatic intensity: the rapidity with which the house
burns, Rosa's collapse, and Jim Bond's howling, "the scion, the last of
his race, seeing it too now and howling with human reason now since
now even he could have known what he was howling about" (p.
376).[28] The last half of Mr. Compson's letter about Rosa's death links
the ninth chapter with the sixth, in which the letter's first half appeared, encapsulating the final four chapters, all of which occur well

after the last embers of the Sutpen house have grown cold. The letter's pompous verbosity contrasts with Quentin's vivid memory of his visit to the mansion, with his vision of the fire, and serves as another reminder of the impossibility of making sense of it all. Coming where it does, the letter's second half also indicates that since chapter 6 the narrative has progressed steadily toward a revelation of the events which culminate in Rosa's death, that Quentin has withheld until now the experience which most intensely affected him.

The climax of Quentin's involvement with the Sutpen story lies in his encounter with Henry. The italics which record their terse exchange indicate, as elsewhere, imagined or reconstructed speech. The dialogue's puzzling elliptical form reflects how it runs endlessly through Quentin's mind, how he cannot free himself of it. The dialogue likely represents the effect, though not the exact content, of what passed between Henry and Quentin. Several critics have speculated over what Henry might have told Quentin. Considering the circumstances, especially Henry's weak and sick condition, it seems unlikely that a long, probing talk could have occurred.[29] Yet previous chapters hinted tantalizingly that Quentin might have learned something important. In chapter 7, he reveals that he told his father Henry and Bon were brothers the day after his visit to Sutpen's Hundred (pp. 266–67). He never explains exactly how he came by this "fact" — whether he deduced or intuited it after seeing Henry or whether Henry simply told him. Moreover, he also suggests that General Compson knew of Henry and Bon's brotherhood but that he never bothered to tell his son of it. How Quentin learned what his grandfather knew but never told his own son is unclear. In chapter 8 the external narrator refers oddly to what Henry later remembered: "Henry would recall later" (p. 294); "*Nor did Henry ever say that he did not remember. . . . He remembers all of it*" (p. 355). This is the only place in the novel where the external narrator intrudes into the mind of a past-time character and reveals information which none of the narrating characters possess. Faulkner seems to have purposefully obscured what Quentin might have learned, encouraging the reader to wonder, making the meeting another part of an insoluble mystery. But there is a difference between the question of what transpired between Henry and Quentin and other questions in the novel. Elsewhere Quentin and the reader have been on an equal footing in their ignorance of the truth. The reader even comes to identify with Quentin's frustration. Here, however, Quentin knows what the reader does not. The reader's inability to discern the truth of the meeting proves one of the major barriers—perhaps the only barrier—to verifying much of the rest of the story. The consequence is simple but profound: to Quentin, Sutpen remains a mystery, as he does to the reader. But the reader must grapple with an additional mystery which Quentin never confronts at all: the novel itself, its structure, its contents, its meanings.

The important fact is that Quentin meets face to face a leading actor in the Sutpen drama. In Henry the past merges with the present. But the Henry whom Quentin meets differs radically from the character he and Shreve have imagined. Henry's illness and old age painfully bespeak how remote the past is. In him, Quentin confronts the reality that time moves ever forward, that he, like Henry Sutpen, is doomed by the biological fact of his existence to die and vanish. Quentin's final despairing and bitter "*I dont. I dont! I dont hate it. I dont hate it!*" (p. 378) may itself be an irrelevant response to Shreve's irrelevant question, but the novel suggests that the search for truth itself is irrelevant, that truth exists only in the mind of the truthseeker, in what he perceives, believes, and remembers. Correlations between truth and historical reality simply do not exist.

In *Absalom, Absalom!* two inextricably interwoven, inherently interdependent narratives exist within a single novelistic framework. Certainly Quentin's efforts to discern the meaning of the past would have no significance without his specific interest in the Sutpens, but much of the importance of Sutpen and his family results from how other characters talk and react to them—as they existed in fact and as they were envisioned. One critic has suggested, without much justification, that the Sutpen story alone is inadequate, full of "too many holes."[30] Another critic adds that the novel's basic interest lies in the perceivers of the story rather than in the story itself: "The tale was to be found more in belief than in action, its results to ensue more in the beholder or the hearer than in the participant." According to this view, the narrating characters give the Sutpens significance by mythicizing, finding meaning where none exists.[31]

Faulkner's comments at the University of Virginia, in his letters, and elsewhere clearly show his belief in the significance of Sutpen's life. Elements of the Sutpen tale occur frequently in his stories and other novels. "The Big Shot," with its account of a young boy turned away at the front door of a mansion, was written as early as January 1930, while "Evangeline" was written no later than July 1931.[32] The Old Frenchman's Place, setting for portions of *Sanctuary* (1931) and "Lizards in Jamshyd's Courtyard" (1930), is a prototype of the ruined mansion which Quentin visits in *Absalom*. In all three works the ruined mansion starkly symbolizes the past and the ravages of time. Sutpen is frequently alluded to as a symbol both of the vanished past and of ambition. In *The Unvanquished* (1938), Bayard Sartoris, referring to Sutpen's arrival in Jefferson "out of nowhere," describes his ambitious dream and its destruction by the Civil War from a perspective much like the community viewpoint in *Absalom*'s second chapter. *Requiem for a Nun* (1951) alludes to him several times, contrasting the failure of his dream with Jefferson's ambition to grow and prosper. Lucius Priest in *The Reivers* (1962) describes him as a man with a dream which "destroyed not only itself but Sutpen too." He is also mentioned twice in "The Bear" of *Go Down, Moses* (1942) and again in *The Town* (1957).[33] Sutpen belongs integrally to the history of Jefferson and Yoknapatawpha County, as legend and as citizen. If his story had no real value of its own, Quentin and his forebears would never have found reason to become interested in it, and there could never have been an *Absalom, Absalom!*

While the facts of Sutpen's life seem difficult to come by, the various narrators make a great deal of what they learn. The story they develop, some of it factual, some of it probable, some of it unlikely, is important for what it reveals about its creators and for what it reveals about Faulkner's attitudes towards American history—slavery, the Civil War, class distinctions—and towards human existence in general. General Compson's theory of Sutpen's innocence may indeed be nothing more than theory and may shed little light on Sutpen, but it shows a great deal about the community in which the old general lived. His narrative bears its own philosophical value, both related and unrelated to Thomas Sutpen. To suggest that his theories are interesting only insofar as they bear the marks of his personality, that they have no inherent value because they are largely speculative and poorly grounded in fact, is to suggest finally that narrative literature itself has no importance because it is, after all, a lie.

If anyone in the novel finds Sutpen's story full of holes, Quentin does. Although the narrative leads the reader to sympathize with him, the external narrator's descriptions, Shreve's proddings, numerous inconsistencies in thought and fact, along with Quentin's own emotions, oblige the reader to regard him as a character, not merely as an inert but reliable transmitter of narrative. Quentin becomes interested in the Sutpens because he senses in their lives a connection with his own. He searches the past in hopes of explaining the present. But his efforts to find coherent patterns and meanings only obscure the past further. He learns that he can learn nothing—that ultimately there are no explanations. As his father tells him, "It's just incredible. It just does not explain. Or perhaps that's it: they dont explain and we are not supposed to know. . . . Judith, Bon, Henry, Sutpen: all of them. They are there, yet something is missing" (pp. 100–101).

The final burden of interpretation and understanding falls on the reader, whose active involvement provides the only remedy for Quentin's despair. The reader must accept the obligation of believing facts which he also must disbelieve. Unlike Quentin, who searches for one central explanation and thus dooms himself to failure from the start, the reader can accept several explanations, recognizing that one of the great virtues of literature is its ability to explain life pluralistically. Two stories unfold simultaneously—the lives of the Sutpens and the exploits of the characters who try to explain them. Each story makes a mystery of the other. Together they make a coherent whole. Compounding levels of narrative, of irony, of belief and disbelief, of fact and speculation, of simple confusion make of this novel a highly intricate puzzle and a magnificently realized work of art. *Absalom, Absalom!* must be embraced in its entirety, with its rich, continually rewarding complexities, if it is to be understood and appreciated as its author surely meant it to be, as the great work of art which it surely is.

Chapter Five
Requiem for a Nun

Faulkner wrote *Requiem for a Nun* (1951) as a novel, not as a drama interrupted by prose prologues or as a play within a novel. He emphasized its novelistic form on several occasions: "It may be a novel as it is," he wrote to Robert Haas in May 1950; later the same month he explained to Bennett Cerf, "It is not a play, will have to be rewritten as a play. It is now some kind of novel, can be printed as such, rewritten into a play." To his editor Saxe Commins in June 1951, he wrote, "to me the prose is not at all a prologue, but is an integrated part of the act itself."[1] Finally, in a brief introduction to the dramatic version published in 1959, he stated: "This play was written not to be a play but as what seemed to me the best way to tell the story in a novel."[2]

Because they are inherently part of a novel, the dramatic sections of *Requiem for a Nun* must be regarded as narratives, not as drama. They can properly be termed "dramatic narratives." Their dramatic nature influences the reader's response to them, but only because of the general absence of narratorial commentary. A narrator does, however, work actively as a scene setter and characterizer. Various characters may seem to speak independently, interacting among themselves, assuming an existence of their own. But because the dramatic sections exist alongside prose narratives in a novelistic framework, these characters are fictional inhabitants of an external narrative in which the narrator does little more than report dialogue, intruding occasionally in the stage directions to characterize and describe.

A critical principle underlying the narrative structure of this novel is that the dramatic sections are narrated. A usually unseen, uninvolved narrator observes events, comments on them in the stage directions, identifies speakers, and relays dialogue directly to the reader. As a novel, *Requiem* creates a fictional illusion which utilizes drama as one of its methods. Within the dramatic framework, characters themselves occasionally function as narrators. One dramatic scene (act 2, scene 2) employs a focal character, whose thoughts and memories are represented in dramatic form by the external narrator.

The reader reacts to the dramatic sections almost as he does to the prose. This dramatic-narrative structure is founded upon principles demonstrably different from those at work in published editions of such purely dramatic plays as Arthur Miller's *Death of a Salesman* or Ibsen's *Hedda Gabler*, where the absence of long narratives or novelistic frames allows the reader to react almost as if he is viewing the characters on stage. Of course, reading dialogue, rather than listening to it, imposes at least a minor barrier between the reader and the printed page. Such a barrier does not affect performed plays which project the dramatic illusion in its purest form. *Requiem* is a far cry from a book of intermingled drama and fiction. It contains no drama per se. All of it—stage directions, characters, dialogue—is narrative fiction.

Thus, the novel can be divided into six equally important narrative units. A narrator relates the first, third, and fifth units in prose which ranges from external to internal to translated narrative. Individual citizens of Jefferson may emerge briefly as focal characters, but the narrator concentrates primarily upon the community as a whole. Each prose section assumes the form of a long sentence, internally divided into short, one-paragraph subsections, separated by line spaces and end-stopped by semicolons (except the last, end-stopped with a period). The subsections treat specific aspects of the story—a particular event, character, idea, or perspective. The initial paragraph of each section usually proposes a thesis or topic which the succeeding narrative then develops. Concluding paragraphs evaluate, always dramatically, the significance of what has been discussed: the courthouse symbolizes time, permanence, and order; Jackson, Mississippi, becomes nothing more than a list of guidebook statistics; Cecilia Farmer represents the universal human desire for immortality and identity.

Because the narrator relies on the knowledge and beliefs of the characters, of the town's communal memory, he usually speaks semi-omnisciently, a historian trying to discern the most likely sequence of, and explanation for, events. Conditional, speculative narrative is common. The narrator often describes the town's memory without comment, though in some cases (the Cecilia Farmer story, for example) he also notes the fallibility of the town's knowledge. Significantly, an early version of "The Courthouse" (entitled "A Name for the City") embodied these characteristics in Gavin Stevens, who as the story's unseen source consciously served this role. Noel Polk surmises that the narrator of this version was probably Charles Mallison, relating what he had been told by his uncle. When revising the story for the novel, Faulkner dropped the character narrator and eliminated the influence of the Stevens personality, thus creating a narrative voice which, according to Polk, "becomes the culture itself, relating its collective and imperfectly synthesized memories of its own beginnings, memories mystical in character, compounded of fact, legend, and hope, which have been transformed into myth by the workings of the numerous imaginations that have passed them down from generation to generation."[3]

In *Light in August, Pylon,* and *Absalom, Absalom!,* narrative structure emphasized the individual; in *Requiem* the prose sections, describing a great evolutionary sweep of natural and human history, deemphasize the individual. Characters emerge briefly and ephemerally—small actors in a historical pattern rather than independent, self-determinant entities. Dramatic narratives, alternating with the prose, so starkly emphasize the individual's free will and responsibility that other elements seem to disappear. Characters stand alone, seemingly cut off from the past, dependent only on their own resources. Accordingly, the dramatic characters do not appear in the prose sections, though Gavin Stevens is mentioned once, characterized merely as "the town lawyer and the county amateur Cincinnatus" (p. 214).* In fact, the novel's structure encourages the reader to recognize the absence of obvious connections between prose and drama. As historical themes in the prose become evident, however, the reader slowly realizes that the drama marks the accretive end-result of the historical events and processes which the prose chronicles. Juxtaposed against the immense panorama of history, individuals interact dramatically at a specific moment in time. Their lives may be unimportant from the historical perspective, but on the individual level, their experiences are clearly significant.

Requiem's narrative structure also emphasizes the transmission of knowledge through time, from one generation to the next, and its transformation into a general community heritage. The narrator, as a historian, focuses on the community. No one individual provides the major source of information. Moreover, transmitted knowledge is not a primary theme; rather, it indicates the community's awareness of history and its desire, at times, to create history which it has not itself made. The community's tendency to embellish, exaggerate, and even enshrine its heritage first becomes evident in "The Courthouse,"

---

*William Faulkner, *Requiem for a Nun* (New York: Random House, 1951).

where the town decides that escapees from its jail must have been a notorious gang of highwaymen: "twenty-five years later legend would begin to affirm, and a hundred years later would still be at it, that two of the bandits were the Harpes themselves" (p. 5). The town's desire to believe that it once harbored the Harpes exemplifies its concern with finding its own important historical niche. Even when the "old notched and mortised logs" of the original jail "which . . . had held someone who might have been Wiley Harpe" have been forgotten, the town remembers the jailbreak and its supposed perpetrators: "this, the town and county did remember; it was part of its legend" (p. 249).

Another instance of how the town molds history for its own aggrandizement is the account of Cecilia Farmer. Never viewing her directly, the narrator describes only the town's communally remembered image of her. In the final prose section the narrator explains several times that the Cecilia revered by the town bears little resemblance to the girl who actually existed. Although her hair is said to have been blonde, "without doubt in the town's remembering after a hundred years it has changed that many times from blonde to dark and back to blonde again: which doesn't matter, since in your own remembering that tender mist and vail will be forever blonde" (p. 256). Her scrawled name on a windowpane becomes for the community a symbol of history and tradition. She assumes significance because of what she represents: a community obsession, a legend and myth, emblematic of the town's attraction to a long dead past: "musing, not even waiting for anyone or anything, as far as the town knew . . . just musing amid her blonde hair in the window facing the country town street, day after day and month after month and—as the town remembered it—year after year" (p. 229). Embodied in a faintly scratched name, finally enshrined in a museum, Cecilia Farmer signifies a past time of which she was an unimportant part. But Jefferson's belief in her makes her important. The prose narratives reveal through other references that community knowledge of family origins, the Civil War, and the jail has accumulated in similar fashion.

The narrator serves two functions in the transmission of knowledge. First, he reports it, offering corrections when necessary. Second, he organizes the narrative around it, especially in "The Jail." "The Courthouse" account of the early days of Jefferson, for instance, contrasts emphatically with the town's memory of those days in "The Jail." Yet neither version proves historically less valid: one is history more or less as it occurred; the other is history as perceived in the present. At times the narrator serves as a spokesman for the community, evaluating and summarizing the community's attitudes and feelings. In this guise he remains constantly detached—while he seems to share the "dream" of the founding fathers in "The Courthouse," he also has the advantage of knowing what will transpire in the future, how Jefferson will both fail and live up to the dream, how it will corrupt and be corrupted. Even the dramatic narratives contain some evidence of the dream's compromise; Temple and Gowan Stevens belong to a social class interested in living "on the right street among other young couples who belong to the right church and the country club" (p. 53) and who are "usually concerned with money" (p. 54). Hence, in describing the ringing of the courthouse bell as a shattering of the "virgin pristine air with the first loud dingdong of time and doom" (p. 48), the narrator is indicating the town's attitude towards its self-created emblem, as well as symbolizing history's presence in Jefferson.

Although the dramatic sections intentionally avoid (on the surface) the prose narrative themes, they also acknowledge the importance of a communally transmitted heritage. Temple Drake's kidnapping by Popeye Vitelli eight years in the past, though vaguely understood, already belongs to the communal heritage and is alluded to a number of times. It has even already been embellished, as Gavin Stevens's art nouveau characterization of Popeye in "The Golden Dome" reveals:

> this *precieux*, this flower, this jewel. Vitelli. What a name for him.
> A hybrid, impotent. . . . He was a gourmet, a sybarite, centuries,
> perhaps hemispheres before his time; in spirit and glands he was
> of that age of princely despots to whom the ability even to read
> was vulgar and plebeian and, reclining on silk amid silken airs
> and scents, had eunuch slaves for that office, commanding death
> to the slave at the end of each reading, each evening, that none
> else alive, even a eunuch slave, shall have shared in, partaken of,
> remembered, the poem's evocation. [Pp. 145–46]

Readers familiar with Popeye in *Sanctuary* would find this characterization not merely inaccurate but absurd. Stevens describes a Popeye who simply never existed, just as he looks for a meaning in Temple's past which, perhaps, is simply not there. Nancy Mannigoe's past has also entered the heritage—the town's frequent use of the "nigger dope fiend whore" epithet typifies its attitude towards her. Temple recalls how Nancy's teeth were once kicked out on a city street by a Baptist deacon, Mr. Stovall (apparently an incident in "That Evening Sun"). Her query to Stevens reflects the town's memory of this event: "You remember, Gavin: what was his name? it was before my time in Jefferson, but you remember: the cashier in the bank, the pillar of the church" (p. 121). She also recalls one other incident from the town's history, the story of Rider in "Pantaloon in Black," of _Go Down, Moses_: "There was another one, a man this time, before my time in Jefferson but Uncle Gavin will remember this too" (pp. 198–99). Each historical allusion illustrates a particular meaning important to the speaker. Stevens finds in the past a sin in need of expiation, while Temple senses in Rider's story an apt analogy to her own state of mind. Each of them makes something different of the past. References to legends from Jefferson's past show the dramatic characters' participation in a community, their inevitable dependency on the history in the prose narratives. _Requiem_'s concern with transmitted knowledge, rather than casting doubt on facts, emphasizes the community's cohesiveness in the present, and continuously on back through time to its earliest origins.

Requiem's narrator speaks with one of the most versatile, powerful lyric voices in Faulkner's fiction. He also plays his role more purposefully than other Faulknerian narrators. A very tangible, self-conscious personality, he seems at times almost a character, as indeed he becomes in the third prose narrative, "Nor Even Yet Quite Relinquish," where he invites the reader to enter the novel as an outlander. Because of this novel's concern with history and the evolutionary development of civilization, the narrator's ability to range back and forth in time is important, yet it does not endow him with omniscience, even when he attends the events he describes, as he seems to do in the first prose narrative, "A Name for the City." Essentially a chronicler and observer, he objectively reports what he sees, speculating when facts are lacking. The beginning of the novel, with its allusions to the "minuscule of archive" (p. 3) that record the settlement's history, emphasizes his role as historian. The narrative itself comprises a historical record, the narrator's factual account.

One of the narrator's primary characteristics is his objective, occasionally clinical detachment from the story—an odd trait in a voice so vital and personal. Yet it is the key element in his personality, enabling him to offer his own interpretations of events after he describes them. Unlike the citizens of Jefferson, unlike Gavin Stevens, he does not warp history to suit his whims. Even in the Cecilia Farmer story, he carefully notes that he is reporting the town's beliefs, not necessarily the facts—which are lost and much less significant than what the town believes. In specific accounts of events and personalities, the narrator primarily uses external narrative, with some shallow intrusions into the thoughts of characters—information which could probably be deduced through simple observation and familiarity with the town. This external perspective varies from one section to the next. "The Courthouse" seems to be factual reporting; speculation is apparent only in the analyses of character motivations. In "The Golden Dome" the perspective remains wholly detached and withdrawn, an abstract, lyrical account which gradually changes to the dry, technical style of a state history or guidebook.[4] The history of Cecilia Farmer, which at first appears to be the most intimate characterization in the prose narratives, actually turns out to be a deeply poignant account of Jefferson's belief in a legend. This section also expresses the narrator's reaction to the girl and the town which enshrined her; his creation of the hypothetical outlander, whom he equates with the reader (with every individual), and who finally reacts to her in much the same manner as the town, gives her a universal significance.

At points in the novel the narrator finishes his specific historical reporting, withdraws from his subject, and holds forth, often in a highly lyrical manner. Alternated with factual paragraphs of history, this lyric extemporizing creates the tone of "The Golden Dome"; on a less intense level it works significantly in the last five sections of "The Courthouse" and throughout "The Jail," especially in the powerful final paragraph. Such passages give meaning, significance, and power to the dry facts of history. In them the narrator fuses his general knowledge of human and natural history with his specific familiarity with the townspeople. He alone can recognize the fifteen-pound padlock's significance while Pettigrew, Compson, and Ratcliffe perhaps cannot; he understands the dreams, illusions, and fears which the townspeople harbor. In this sense, Polk, referring to the town's attitude towards the federal government (p. 12) and the Civil War (pp. 239–40, 246–47), asserts that "it is primarily the Dream talking."[5] More specifically, the narrator talks *for the town* and for himself, informing the reader of the dream's glory and its danger, of what the townsmen hope for from the future and what the future holds. *Requiem's* voice thus results from total fidelity to the town's perspective, counterbalanced by a detached view which points out the fallibility of the town's memory. Fully withdrawn, the narrative forgets the town except as a concept, a small part in the panoramic sweep of history. Jefferson then assumes its proper place on the cosmic scale.

The tone and method of each prose narrative can be characterized briefly:

"THE COURTHOUSE (A Name for the City)." The narrative is generally external, especially in the subsections ending on page 38, after the naming of Jefferson. The first half of the section deals in leisurely fashion with the period immediately prior to the founding of the town: it includes an account of the settlement's "Damocles sword of dilemma" (p. 5) after the jailbreak (pp. 3–8); of Alex Holston's lock (pp. 8–14); and of the jailbreak and the lock's disappearance (pp. 14–16). The more fast-paced second half details the settlement's response to its dilemma.[6] Once the town has been founded, history begins to unfold. Focus then moves from the founding fathers to the symbol they have created—the courthouse. The narrative generally provides pure exposition, straightforward description with a minimum of dialogue. However, when Compson, Peabody, and Ratcliffe are debating a solution to the compound problem of the missing lock and Pettigrew, exposition is mixed with dialogue (pp. 18–35); when they inform Pettigrew about naming their settlement after him, dialogue almost entirely replaces the exposition (pp. 26–29). This brief but critical moment of dramatic interaction anticipates the dramatic section which follows, fixing the plight of the early Jeffersonians and the dilemma of Temple Drake in ironic counterpoint. It is also the pivotal moment in the town's history—a moment of humorous chicanery rather than noble resolve.

The narrator serves the important function of establishing the symbolism of the courthouse, whose construction becomes the first obligation of the founding fathers after they have named the town. The last part of the narrative directly concerns the courthouse's importance as a hub of order, commerce, law, and history. Although the town grows and changes around it, the courthouse stands unscathed (though "its doom is its longevity . . . its simple age is its own reproach" [p. 47]). The narrator eulogizes the ideal which it embodies: "the courthouse: the center, the focus, the hub; sitting looming in the center of the county's circumference like a single cloud in its ring of horizon, laying its vast shadow to the uttermost rim of horizon; musing, brooding, symbolic and ponderable, tall as cloud, solid as rock, dominating all: protector of the weak, judiciate and curb of the passions and lusts, repository and guardian of the aspirations and the hopes" (p. 40). Contrasted with this ideal are the circumstances and the less-than-ideal community which erected the courthouse.[7] The section's first half thus explains the dream's development, and the last half its compromise. In tone and subject, the narrative's two-part structure reflects the contradiction, the paradox, inherent in the symbol it explains.

"THE GOLDEN DOME (Beginning Was the Word)." External narrative, in a highly rhetorical mode, predominates. Moving swiftly through a brief list of vital statistics and the natural and human history of Jackson and Mississippi, the narrative consists of a long series of fragmentary noun and adjective clauses—strung together in one long sentence which terminates in the final guidebook information. The concern is a capitol dome, the center of a state rather than a town. The colon is the important mark of punctuation, symbolizing the inevitable succession of one event by another, the constancy of change. Various elements of the state's history appear and disappear as the narrative progresses: Indian, Spaniard, Frenchman, pioneer, citizen; wilderness, farmland, city; footpath, riverboat, railroad, airplane. The narrator serves more as a cataloguer than a historian, and in nine pages he briefly enumerates a chain of events leading toward the present-day city. His relatively cold, clinical tone contrasts with the first and third prose narratives; the lyrical representation of natural history is highly abstract and definitely not anthropomorphic: "the steamy chiaroscuro, untimed unseasoned winterless miasma" (p. 99); "the gilded pustule . . . soaring, hanging as one blinding spheroid above the center of the Commonwealth" (p. 110). Historical individuals become mere stages in an evolutionary pattern. "The Golden Dome" illustrates one of the novel's critical themes: history as an inevitable process not necessarily related to human concerns, the necessity of accepting as natural the changes which it causes. The capitol dome means for the state what the courthouse does for the town, and what Cecilia Farmer, in another context, means to the human condition.

The second prose narrative's rhetoric seems influenced by two different sources: the phrase "one nation, under God, with liberty and justice for all" in the pledge of allegiance to the United States flag, and these famous lines from Shakespeare's *Richard II*:

> This blessed plot, this earth, this realm, this England.
> This nurse, the teeming womb of royal kings
> Fear'd by their breed and famous by their birth.

[2. 1. 38–40]

The Shakespearean rhetoric applies ironically to the history of Mississippi. Yet Faulkner also intends that the comparison of Mississippi with England be taken quite seriously. Like other regions where people settled and civilization developed, Mississippi fostered dreams, ambitions, and beliefs microcosmically symbolic of the ideals expressed in the pledge of allegiance. In the beginning the state's potential was as great as the dream exemplified in the lines from *Richard II*. Irony surfaces when the realities of the present, embodied in the towns of Jackson and Jefferson, conflict with the visions of the past. The influence of these two sources also becomes occasionally evident in the rhetoric of the final prose narrative.

"*THE JAIL (Nor Even Yet Quite Relinquish——)*." The final prose section uses both internal and external narrative, and centers on the community heritage, the "mind" of Jefferson, as its focal character. Again the narrator observes from an uninvolved standpoint, but he obviously sympathizes to an extent with his subject. He also provides a lyric commentary on the community perspective. The section begins with what seems the second main clause of a compound sentence: "So, although in a sense the jail was both older and less old than the courthouse, in actuality, in time, in observation and memory, it was older even than the town itself" (p. 213). Since the jailbreak led directly to the town's birth in the first prose narrative, since the jail and courthouse were once closely related, the sentence structure establishes the first and third prose narratives as two independent clauses in a single compound sentence—metaphorically indicating the continuity of Jefferson's history.

Because "The Jail" concerns the community heritage, which often contains several distinct versions of the same story, it makes considerable use of speculative narrative. Yet speculation is not so important as in *Light in August* or *Absalom, Absalom!*, mainly because the nature of truth is not a major theme. The town believes its legends, which have a concrete effect. Their possible falsehood is unimportant except in suggesting how really remote is the past to which many Jeffersonians cling. To illustrate, the narrator creates in the chapter's third division a completely hypothetical, fictional scene; the reader enters into it as a stranger taken on a tour of the town by a hypothetical guide. The concrete palpability of this episode proves particularly haunting. The "hot cramped strange room already fierce with the sound and reek of frying pork-fat" becomes as real as "the old milky obsolete glass, and the scratches on it: that tender ownerless obsolete girl's name and the old dead date in April almost a century ago" (p. 254). The scene lends reality, tangibility, to the image of the girl who scrawled her name upon the windowpane. For the reader, as for

the citizen of Jefferson, the scratched name symbolizes human identity, the desire for immortality. The concluding exclamation—*"Listen,
stranger; this was myself: this was I!"* (p. 262)—represents the deepest
expression of how anyone, outlander or native, might react to Cecilia's name.

The Dramatic Sections. Although the narrator functions from an external perspective in the dramatic narratives, he can at points suggest
inner thoughts and emotions. Scenesetting compels the reader to react to the dramatic narratives as scenes from a play as well as episodes
from a novel, bringing into question the nature of their relationship to
the prose. At the beginning of each dramatic section the narrator
points out the setting's architectural symbolism. In "The Courthouse"
he notes the "symbolism of the elevated tribunal of justice of which
this, a county court, is only the intermediate, not the highest, stage"
(p. 49); in "The Golden Dome" he carefully describes the layout of the
Governor's office, "carrying still further the symbolism of the still
higher, the last, the ultimate seat of judgment" (p. 112). Each of the
prose sections discusses the architectural symbols which become central motifs in the drama, thus enforcing the novel's unity.

The narrator also comments on physical behavior and movement.
A staged play would provide such emphasis through detailed block-
ing instructions which a director might or might not follow. This
novel, however, uses behavior and movement as a narrative motif.
References to Gowan's drinking in "The Courthouse," scene 2, suggest that his immaturity from eight years earlier in *Sanctuary* persists,
while Temple's chain-smoking reflects her nervousness. The narrator
specifically emphasizes her assertive independence when she refuses
the assistance of other characters: Gavin's offer of the handkerchief
(p. 56) and the cigarette lighter (p. 92) in act 1; his effort to give her
physical support (p. 212) in act 2 and cigarettes in act 3 (p. 268), where
she also rejects the jailer's offer of comfort (pp. 284–85). Facial expressions and vocal intonations are also noted. Finally, at rare points the
narrator engages in subjective evaluative characterizations which are
the province of fiction, not drama. He describes the jailer's efforts to
avoid offending Temple, for example, with a simile: "it is getting out
of hand; he realises it, but there is nothing he can do now; he is like
someone walking a foot-log: all he can do is move as fast as he dares
until he can reach solid ground or at least pass another log to leap to"
(p. 265). He expresses a "quick concern, with that quality . . . almost
gentle, almost articulate" (p. 284). The narrator successfully maintains
a carefully controlled tone, a specific symbolic reverberation which

clarifies the meaning of the dramatic sections. Such a strategy insures Faulkner a degree of control over his readers' reactions; as a dramatist, he can hope only that good fortune, a skillful director, and a perceptive audience will give him the reaction he desires.

Requiem's unique structural element is the form of the three dramatic sections. Although they seem to be a wholly unheralded innovation, their roots lie in the earliest beginnings of Faulkner's career. One of the first things he wrote was a play, *Marionettes* (1920); later in his life he occasionally attempted to write drama in various forms. His intermittent stints in Hollywood during the 1930s and 1940s gave him some screenwriting experience—he was at least partially responsible for the lively dialogue between Lauren Bacall and Humphrey Bogart in the 1946 movie adaptation of Raymond Chandler's *The Big Sleep*. He tried casting early versions of *Intruder in the Dust* and *A Fable* in dramatic form before finally settling on conventional prose. And after *Requiem*'s publication he wrote occasional television scripts.[8]

Obviously, however, dramatic conventions in narrative fiction were not at all foreign to Faulkner. They had become a basic part of his novelistic technique as early as *The Sound and the Fury*. The dramatic sections in *Requiem* utilize a number of narrative conventions: character narratives, focal characters, and the hearer-teller relationship. Significantly, the drama functions no differently in the novel than the prose. The narrator's separation from character and scene is distinctly marked; at points he totally vacates the "stage," reappearing whenever necessary. Especially when juxtaposed with the wealth of descriptive detail in the prose sections, the dramatic narratives serve to isolate the characters. They exist, temporarily, solely in the context of their private emotions, thoughts, and dilemmas. Stylized, symbolic settings heighten the sense of their isolation. Only the Stevens apartment—in stark contrast to the courthouse, the Governor's office, and the jail—is described concretely, but the beginning of act 2 clearly indicates its symbolic character. Changes in lighting denote emotion, symbolism, and tone. Of course, in opposition to the emphasis on the individual in the dramatic sections, the prose narratives analyze social, historical, and cultural factors underlying character struggles, generally ignoring the individual. This bifurcated structure implies that while history and environment may wield a strong influence on the problems people face, finally the individual human will, conscience, and mind must shoulder the responsibility of solving them— the painful lesson which Temple has learned by the end of "The Jail."

Long character speeches delivered by Gavin and Temple are a major feature of scenes 1 and 3 in "The Golden Dome." Several are quite lengthy, especially for a play (they were shortened and broken up for the stage production); the stylized setting of the Governor's office (defined by the narrator as "the last, the ultimate seat of judgment") makes them resemble a confession (though not necessarily a Christian one). The longest speech, by Gavin, runs four pages at the end of scene 1 (pp. 167–72); Temple gives a three-and-a-half page monologue (pp. 156–60). These speeches are self-conscious and carefully plotted out; they employ symbols and imagery introduced previously in the prose narratives and are meant to explain clearly and emphatically the nature of Temple's dilemma, its causes, and possible consequences. Gavin, for instance, seeks to characterize the moral nature of the man who tries to blackmail her:

> a man so single, so hard and ruthless, so impeccable in amorality,
> as to have a kind of integrity, purity, who would not only never
> need nor intend to forgive anyone anything, he would never even
> realise that anyone expected him to forgive anyone anything; who
> wouldn't even bother to forgive her if it ever dawned on him that
> he had the opportunity, but instead would simply black her eyes
> and knock a few teeth out and fling her into the gutter: so that she
> could rest secure forever in the knowledge that, until she found
> herself with a black eye and or spitting teeth in the gutter, he
> would never even know he had anything to forgive her for.
> [P. 171]

Such speeches are hardly realistic, nor are they meant to be. Their effect is almost ritualistic, as in a morality play. Similar rhetorically stylized, self-conscious character narratives illuminate Temple's inner struggle and inform the reader of how Gavin perceives and tries to solve her problem.

Noel Polk suggests that Gavin Stevens based his accounts of Temple's past on what Nancy had told him about it,[9] remarking that the lawyer never thought to consult other sources before confronting her in act 2, scene 1. Stevens's theories and conclusions obviously determine his entire effort to force Temple's confession. They also bear the mark of his personality, just like his analyses of Lucas Beauchamp and the town of Jefferson in *Intruder in the Dust* and of Joe Christmas in *Light in August*. He is patently untrustworthy, despite his sincere intentions. Faulkner's character narrators always speak with independence and integrity, and also with fallibility—Stevens proves no exception. His prating self-righteousness, his seeming omniscience about Temple's motives and her past, his solicitude—these should incline the reader to view him skeptically. His previous important appearances in Faulkner's fiction, where he also expressed demonstrably incorrect opinions, provide additional evidence of his unreliability. In fact, the last chapter of *Go Down, Moses* makes him a symbol of racial misunderstanding. But even if he had spoken authoritatively in *Light in August, Go Down, Moses,* and *Intruder in the Dust,* he could still not be safely believed here. Faulkner never established his characters as spokesmen or as infallible ideals. Like V. K. Ratliff, Quentin Compson, Rosa Coldfield, and the Reporter, Gavin Stevens is human, unreliable, and often totally wrong in what he says.

Temple's own comments on her situation occasionally echo Stevens's, but she never completely accepts his views. She evidently considers several methods of dealing with her past, including escape to California. Stevens, a relative with intimate knowledge of her life, can influence her as others cannot. He persuades her to wonder whether his solution to her problems is a good one. In addition, his knowledge of her past, which he distorts into his own version of her story, may very well "blackmail" her into confessing the events dramatized in scene 2, a possibility which would place him in the same moral category as Pete. Only she can tell her story properly, if at all. Finally, the end of "The Jail" shows that she has accepted neither Stevens's nor Nancy's solutions to her dilemma. She expresses her essential agnosticism—opposed to Nancy's simplistic optimism and the lawyer's well-meant humanism—in her final comment to Stevens: "Anyone to save it. Anyone who wants it. If there is none, I'm sunk. We all are. Doomed. Damned" (p. 286).

The hearer-teller relationship works as an important element in the dramatic relationship of Gavin and Temple, and in the prose account of the outlander and guide in "The Jail." Gavin desires, evidently, to bring Temple to a state of "repentance" through a forced and painful "confession." A similar situation characterizes a play which Faulkner read and disliked, T. S. Eliot's *The Family Reunion* (1939), which explores some of the same themes as *Requiem.*[10] In the play Harry Monchensy returns home after a long absence, tormented by guilt over his supposed murder of his wife. To atone, he decides to follow a career "of care over lives of humble people, / The lessons of ignorance, of incurable diseases."[11] Both Harry and Eliot believe that the path to repentance is a painful one. In another Eliot play, *The Cocktail Party* (1950), a group of "guardians" instruct several characters on how to earn redemption. One of them, a young woman, enters a nursing order and ministers to a tribe of natives who eventually crucify her alive near a hill of ants, which devour her. Whether Faulkner knew this play is unclear (his lifelong interest in Eliot makes it possible he did), but Gavin seems extremely intent that Temple suffer pain for her sins before allowing her to live with them, or achieve redemption. Eliot's play may possibly have influenced Faulkner's decision to have Gavin appoint himself as Temple's "guide" and Nancy as the ideal of spiritual contrition. That Faulkner disliked *The Family Reunion* is interesting, and the relationship of Nancy, Gavin, and Temple may well mark his parodic rejection of Eliot's concept of redemption. Temple's ultimate refusal to accept Nancy's solution suggests that for Faulkner the path to redemption is internal rather than external—in strength of will and mind, in acceptance of responsibility and the worldly human condition—a path regarded in *Requiem* as too painful and demanding for most to follow.

The Gavin-Temple relationship strongly resembles other character relationships in Faulkner's fiction. In *Intruder*, for instance, Stevens served as a kind of instructor and counselor to Charles Mallison. The Shreve-Quentin relationship in *Absalom, Absalom!* provides a stronger analogue. Yet Stevens misunderstands Temple, and, if anything, her "Damocles dilemma" is worse at the novel's end than its beginning; he ironically succeeds only in bringing her to realize the absence of the external solution which he urges her to embrace. The "guide" in the prose section of "The Jail" leads his outlander towards another lesson—about Jefferson and its obsession with the past, about human identity. Because the narrator describes the guide's talk to the outlander, no conversation occurs. Yet the hearer-teller relationship is present: the guide shapes his description and analysis of Jefferson according to the outlander's (and the reader's) unfamiliarity with the town. The guide also tells the outlander a story which the community has passed down for generations as part of its heritage—a major aspect of the hearer-teller relationships in *Absalom, Absalom!* and other novels. Making the reader a listener, forcing him to identify with the town by imagining his presence there, the narrator leads the reader towards a participatory understanding of Cecilia Farmer and Jefferson, an understanding which more conventional narrative methods could not allow.

One dramatic scene also uses a focal character. The stage directions to act 2, scene 1, introduce the second scene as a "flashback" episode from Temple's past, with her memory as the narrative source. The scene provides a retrospective account of Temple's decision to run away with Pete and of Nancy's murder of the child: it immediately follows Stevens's long speech at the end of scene 1, where he presents his own version of Nancy's discovery that Pete was blackmailing Temple. Changes in stage lighting help prepare for the flashback: towards the beginning of Gavin's speech the lights flicker, dim, then steady (p. 165). Midway through his speech they dim again (p. 171), completely darkening the stage. Interruptions by the narrator carefully match the pace of Gavin's speech with the dimming of the lights. At the end of scene 1, Stevens says to Temple, "Now tell him" (p. 172). In the scene's last sentence the narrator announces that the stage is completely dark. Obviously, what Temple "tells" is dramatized in the second scene. Although the first scene prepares for a long confessional speech by Temple, scene 2 instead turns out to be straightforward drama, complete with dialogue and stage directions. It occurs six months in the past, at the Stevens apartment. If the transition between the two scenes were rendered as prose narrative, the source of the second scene would clearly be Temple's memory. The transition resembles the introduction to the two italicized narratives about Sutpen's meeting with Henry in chapter 8 of *Absalom, Absalom!* (pp. 346–58). There, as here, characters envision the scenes. Temple's memories, refined and objectified, then presented in dramatic form by the unseen narrator, provide the content of scene 2. The result is an accurate version of what really happened, one which strongly contradicts Gavin's account. Faulkner could have had Temple describe the events in scene 2 in her own character narrative. However, by dramatizing those events, permitting Temple's monologue to Gavin and the Governor to go unheard (that is, unread), he enables the reader to view the events directly and to understand their effects on Temple without the interference of another character's perspective, an advantage not possible in spoken character narrative, which is always to some degree subjective and unreliable. The scene's narrative structure thus provides the best possible perspective on Temple Drake's dilemma—her own.

A more ambitious and accomplished work than many readers have recognized, *Requiem for a Nun* is still far from perfect. Its intense, powerful prose narratives overshadow the dramatic sections for which they serve as prologues. In comparison the dramatic sections often seem lifeless and artificial, weakened by the characters' occasionally excessive posturing and histrionics. Dramatic character monologues are at times too stridently, unrelentingly moralistic, even if deceptively so. Because their prominent dramatic roles are not clearly enough defined or undercut by irony, these monologues have deceived too many readers into accepting Nancy Mannigoe and Gavin Stevens as the novel's ideals. The narrative presents sufficient evidence for Nancy's and Gavin's delusions, but it emphasizes both characters confusingly, obscuring Temple's place as the novel's moral center. Nancy herself proves decidedly ambiguous. Gavin seems to idolize her. Even the novel's title—*Requiem for a Nun*—appears to pay tribute to her, suggesting that she is the moral ideal. But her "nigger dopefiend whore" status, which would elicit the sympathy of most modern readers, is negated by her murder of Temple's child. Should the reader admire her killing of a helpless child to prevent Temple's adultery with Pete? Of course not. Nancy acts despicably and irresponsibly. But Gavin's insistence that Temple heed her example creates confusion. He appears as the foremost (practically the only) interpreter of Temple's dilemma. His opinions are generally unrefuted by other characters (except Temple), and the narrative structure fails to uncover his false, misperceiving attitudes convincingly. If the narrative seeks to exemplify through Temple a lesson about moral responsibility, it does not wholly succeed. The attitudes of *Requiem for a Nun* towards its characters remain uncertain. Thus also do its themes.

Though its narrative structure sometimes overburdens the reader's discriminatory abilities, *Requiem* still represents a noteworthy accomplishment, and it occupies a significant position among Faulkner's novels. Its prose narratives stand with the best of his writing. It also marks the final major structural innovation of his career, underscoring a last time his belief in narrative form as metaphor for meaning. Greater scrutiny of its structure, characters, and themes, of its probings into the complex relationship of history and the individual, will reward readers with a deeper, richer appreciation of William Faulkner's achievement.

Chapter Six
Narrative Perspective:
The Self and the World

Faulkner has often been characterized as an experimenter, a novelist searching in book after book for new, untested ways to tell his stories. The same term has also been applied to Joyce. That Faulkner considered himself an experimenter, however, is unlikely. "Style is a result of a need, of a necessity," he told an interviewer; "style is incidental."[1] An experiment seeks to prove a hypothesis, or to uncover a set of principles which allow a hypothesis to be made. The very word—*experiment*—suggests tentativeness, uncertainty of outcome. The experimenter never quite knows what his findings will be until he has completed his research. Faulkner was neither tentative nor uncertain about his writing. Though he often tried different narrative forms while composing his novels, the final methods he chose were ones he believed would work. He was a novelist, an artist. His characters may display tentativeness in thought and action, but the fiction they inhabit is concrete, certain, and absolute. Their strengths and weaknesses result from their creator's talent and personality, his conception of the novel, his ability to do what he set out to do—not from their failure to prove a literary hypothesis. Joseph Reed argues convincingly against considering Faulkner's work experimental: "in all these experiments, even the more extreme, experiment is not undertaken for the sake of experiment. Faulkner tries out this and that, but not so much to see how it works as to show that it *does* work. . . . He devises the narrative shape to fit the shape and demands of the substance; he does not endow a narrative shape with substance to demonstrate the flexibility of his art, or his ability at tour de force, or his fancy footwork."[2]

Faulkner was, however, an innovator. He saw novelistic form as a potential way of reflecting meaning, much as an Etruscan urn or Attic vase reflects the cultural sensibility which produced it. For Faulkner, narrative was more than a succession of semantically related words; it was a medium to be worked and molded, a means of saying something. Readers must rise to the challenge of Faulkner's structural innovations, recognizing that beneath the pastoral landscape and the frequently unsophisticated, self-tormented characters there works a strictly disciplined, sophisticated, deeply philosophical artistic intellect.

During the first half of his career, ending roughly in 1941, Faulkner used a startling variety of narrative forms, from the undirected character narratives of *The Sound and the Fury* to the community perspectives of *Light in August* and the disjunctively parallel chapters of *The Wild Palms*. Because each novel employs a different combination of structural elements, each works upon a unique set of narrative principles. What holds true in one book may not hold true at all in the next. The reader must approach such a work as *Absalom, Absalom!* on its own terms, divesting himself of all preconceptions, whether formed from reading Fielding, Flaubert, and Conrad, or *As I Lay Dying*, *Pylon*, and *The Unvanquished*. Faulkner seemed to do the same as he began each new book. But he also built upon what he had discovered, moving gradually but purposefully from isolated character perspectives, to the interaction of individual and community, to different ways of knowing, to different but parallel modes of experience, in *The Wild Palms* and *Go Down, Moses*.

In terms of pure enjoyment, Faulkner's narrative innovations reached full flower in *The Hamlet* (1940), which at first appears a rather conventional effort in comparison with the novels that came before it. In fact, it complexly synthesizes structural elements from each of its predecessors. An external narrator's framing presence, community perspectives, Ratliff's narratives and his focal perspective, his imagined vision of Flem Snopes in hell, the perspectives of Labove, Mink, Houston, and the men on the porch of Varner's store, the vast array of differing characters, the mystery of what Flem Snopes really wants— these and other elements fuse into a masterpiece of storytelling. Perfectly attuned to the content it shapes, structure is hardly evident. *The Hamlet* may be one of Faulkner's two or three greatest achievements, a position of eminence not often accorded it, perhaps because it seems too smooth, too easy and comfortable alongside *The Sound and the Fury* or *Absalom*.

After *Go Down, Moses*, structural innovation ceased to play a major role—with the notable exception of *Requiem for a Nun*. During the last fifteen or so years of his life, Faulkner seemed more interested in pure storytelling, or the exploration of philosophical issues (primarily in *Requiem* and *A Fable*). This shift does not mean that form loses its importance for Faulkner, or that his talent suffered a falling off; it simply means that striking new forms do not appear, that he employed variations of structures developed earlier, using them as he saw fit to shape his stories. Yet even the later novels possess their own structural integrity and demand careful, discriminating reading, especially *Requiem, A Fable,* and the last two volumes of the Snopes trilogy.

Despite the diversity in narrative structure—the dynamic intersection of external narrator with individual character perspective—when Faulkner's fiction is examined as a whole, certain cohesive patterns begin to emerge. These patterns reveal much more about what Faulkner believed, what he was "trying to say," than any single statement his characters ever made. In fact, the metaphoric potential of narrative structure remains perhaps the least understood aspect of Faulkner's fiction, one which critics are just beginning to explore. Taken together, the novels and stories elucidate several pervasive and fundamental themes. Foremost among them is the supremacy of the individual, who stands at the center of each of the novels. The predominance of narrating characters, focal perspectives, and the hearer-teller relationship keeps the reader's attention focused on individual characters. Moreover, the individual is nearly always pictured in conflict—with himself, his community and heritage, with evil, nature, and time. The external narrator places these conflicts in a context, allowing characters to speak for themselves and call attention to their own dilemmas. Only in the Compson Appendix and the prose sections of *Requiem for a Nun* does the external narrator overshadow character perspectives, and even then he does so to illustrate the individual's place in time and history.

Changes in narrative structure show a gradual evolution in Faulkner's treatment of the individual. In *The Sound and the Fury* and *As I Lay Dying* interior character narratives emphasize insulated selves, struggling to make connections with other selves, to understand the particular condition of their lives. In *Sanctuary* and especially in *Light in August*, Faulkner begins to examine the interaction of the self with its community, using both individual and community perspectives. The individual derives his identity from his participation in society, even if that society is hostile to him. Joe Christmas's quest for identity proves self-destructive because he seeks to live outside the community. In contrast with the misanthropic Christmas, who tries both to ignore and to flagrantly violate community values, is Byron Bunch, whose willing participation in the community, in the affairs of life, gives him his identity. *Absalom, Absalom!* views the individual from a different vantage point, adding to the individual's social dimensions his relationship to a region and history. Four present-time narrating characters try to understand a man who died more than forty years in the past. Each narrator sees and interprets him differently. *The Wild Palms* focuses in parallel narratives on the individual's conflict with nature—his own internal nature and his external environment. The tall convict struggles against a Mississippi River flood, his prison-bred passivity, and his innate distrust of the opposite sex to keep himself, a woman, and her newborn infant alive. Though he survives the flood, his fatalism and misogyny ultimately overwhelm him. Harry Wilbourne faces a different flood—a self-destructive woman's passion and his own moral cowardice. Both he and Charlotte Rittenmeyer seek to place themselves outside of nature and of time, of the everyday necessities of life—such as food and money. *The Wild Palms* depicts the need for a harmonious relationship between the individual and his natural environment, a relationship which each of the three main characters ignores.

The Hamlet returns to the subject of community. Like earlier novels, it narrates primarily through individual perspective, often that of V. K. Ratliff. Yet emphasis falls not on Ratliff's internal struggles, or his conflicts with other individuals, but rather on how his consciousness reflects a general community consciousness and its concern with the figure of Flem Snopes. Ratliff fits well in his society. Snopes, however, is an outsider. He does not belong. Yet he and Ratliff are much alike; both are financial wheeler-dealers whose transactions often exploit other people. That Ratliff openly talks about his business affairs does not lessen their occasional shadiness. What differentiates him from Snopes, aside from his congeniality, is the fact that he was born into his society and voluntarily participates in it. He also usually displays an awareness of the customs and ethics which regulate commerce among Jefferson citizens. Individuals in *The Hamlet* are bound to their community by a web of commerce. They fear Snopes because of the financial threat he represents—symbolized by the family barn-burning reputation which initially gives him a hold on Will Varner—rather than for his odd manner of dress, his unsociability, or his unsavory background.

Commerce, property, and ownership also lie at the core of community in *Go Down, Moses*. Though they unite the community financially, they divide it racially. Ike McCaslin seeks to expiate his guilt over his heritage of slavery by rejecting community responsibility and relinquishing ownership of his land. By doing so, he insures the preservation of his society's racism and dooms himself to a life of impotent, meaningless purity. In *Go Down, Moses*, the community's history and heritage impinge on each of its inhabitants. It is founded upon a system of moral and ethical values which determine how people behave towards one another. *Intruder in the Dust, Requiem for a Nun, A Fable*, and the last two volumes of the Snopes trilogy consider the dilemmas which these values can pose. How can an individual retain his membership in the community while trying to do what is right—even if what is right opposes the general communal will? How can the individual live with himself if he does not seek to do what is right—even if his refusal to do the right thing meets with community approval? What do individual and communal responsibility entail? The retrospective character narrative of *The Reivers* answers these questions by focusing on one individual's initiation into an imperfect world, his education in how to reconcile his moral and ethical ideals with his place in a flawed community of men and women who often do not measure up to those ideals. The Lucius Priest who narrates the story to his grandson enjoys a sense of peace with himself and his society, primarily because he has learned the necessity of accepting the past and the compromises of good and evil, Virtue and Non-Virtue, as innate conditions of his life. He achieves what no Faulkner character before him achieves. Emotionally, morally, and socially, he is a fully developed, fully self-fulfilled individual.

Despite their predominant focus, Faulkner's novels never establish the individual as an ideal. Though his voice is often heard, his beliefs, behavior, and thoughts always prove flawed and limited. Faulkner's characters are mortal human beings. Their perspectives reflect their fallen world, their imperfections. Many of them seek to act honorably, but they often fail in the attempt, or their good intentions have bad results. Others actively engage in the process of trying to understand—their fellow human beings, their society, their heritage, the nature of such absolutes as time or good and evil. Yet no character ever wholly measures up to the ideals he aspires to live by. The more obsessed he becomes with achieving an ideal, the more profound his failure.

Though narrative perspective constantly reveals the imperfections of speaking characters, the reader naturally tends to identify and sympathize with them. Yet he must never forget that they are *characters*—human beings with finite capabilities. Gavin Stevens, more than any other character, has frequently been identified as "Faulkner's spokesman." He is an amiable, gregarious, likeable figure. In *Intruder in the Dust*, worried over the harm which "*outlanders North East and*

West" might cause by forcing racial integration on the South, he expresses the hope that his region will grant the Negro equality without outside interference. In several essays and public letters, Faulkner expressed similar sentiments, though with more elegance and less bombast.[3] Still, Stevens was not his spokesman. He merely expressed, on one occasion, comparable views. And he often expressed other opinions, in *Intruder* and elsewhere, which definitely did not belong to his creator. Faulkner emphasized at the University of Virginia that he did not identify with any of his characters, and he also commented on Gavin's mistakes and imperfections.[4] Stevens is no more an ideal than Ratliff or Flem Snopes or Joe Christmas or Popeye Vitelli. He is simply another human being, more educated and articulate than most, perhaps, but still limited in what he knows, and rather out of touch with the reality of his world. He fails to achieve his goals, however low or lofty, for the same reasons all human beings fail—their own inadequacy, bad luck, inability to adapt to change or community standards, to confront oppressive conditions which require common sense, courage, and moderation to be overcome. Narrative structure emphasizes his individual sensibility while simultaneously stressing his imperfections. In this sense, character imperfections constitute a major element of Faulkner's narrative realism.

Composed of individual human beings, communities also are inherently flawed and imperfect. The community's aspiration to certain ideals and virtues gives meaning to its existence. Participation in the community is a requirement of the human condition. Yet social standards often conflict with individual ambitions, and characters frequently must struggle against the community whether they desire to live in it or not. Horace Benbow's effort to save Lee Goodwin in *Sanctuary* is a case in point, as is Chick Mallison's quest to prove Lucas Beauchamp's innocence in *Intruder*. Characters who try to withdraw from the community inevitably doom themselves. Joe Christmas, in no sense an ideal, struggles unconsciously and unwillingly against a prejudiced, conformist community which would reject him for his blackness and embrace him for his whiteness. The very fact of his misanthropy makes him the focus of community concern, reflected in the perspectives of the numerous people who talk about him. Other characters, such as Snopes and Sutpen, try to conform to the community but are rejected because of their methods or because they are outsiders. Gavin Stevens and the Reporter, on the other hand, seem socially well adjusted. They pride themselves on their knowledge of their societies and of human nature. Yet what they believe they know is often totally wrong. When they put their "knowledge" to work in relationships with other characters, the results are harmful. Stevens's desire to make Temple Drake face up to her sins in *Requiem for a Nun* only worsens her guilt and suffering. The Reporter helps cause a stunt flier's death. No individual can adjust fully. In one way or another he is always at odds with his community. The struggle between preserving one's integrity and trying to conform to social standards fosters a constant tension between community and individual which subtly underlies most of Faulkner's novels.

The inability to adjust completely—to one's own limitations, to an imperfect, ever-changing community and world—also creates a tension between human aspiration and human potential. The prose narratives of *Requiem for a Nun* brilliantly elucidate this theme in the contrast between the courthouse, whose construction marked the founding of Jefferson, and the town's failure to realize the ideals which the courthouse embodies. Quentin Compson, Thomas Sutpen, Gavin Stevens, and Isaac McCaslin, among many others, struggle in the grips of this tension.

Narrative structure keeps the intersection of individual and community, whether harmonious or not, constantly in view. It especially emphasizes the desire and need of characters to talk to one another, to pass back and forth information about themselves and others. Talking is a means of self-expression, a way of confirming one's identity and significance as a human being, his membership in the human community. Communication gives the community self-awareness and delineates its place in history, the foundation on which it is built; it enables the community to explore its environment. Similarly, directed narration portrays the individual in his natural setting—among the other individuals with whom he naturally belongs. A speaking character's narratives inevitably reflect not only the marks of his individual consciousness but of his social consciousness as well.

The individual's place in a social and historical context is another of the inescapable givens of his condition. Narratives usually evoke this context through character perspectives, the external narrator's scene-setting commentary, the hearer-teller relationship, the transmission of knowledge, and the problems which various characters confront. Faulkner's novels define certain laws which regulate the individual's role in the community. First, the individual must conform to a certain extent, restraining potentially destructive impulses in favor of the greater social good, at times even making personal sacrifices. Social responsibility itself is an ideal to which no character ever wholly measures up. Second, individuals who seek to dissociate themselves from society, in some way to ignore their social obligation, forfeit their identities and the possibility of a harmonious relationship with other people and even with nature. Joe Christmas again provides an example, along with Charlotte Rittenmeyer, Harry Wilbourne, and the tall convict of *The Wild Palms*. Third, an individual who tries too hard to understand his relationship with society imposes an unnatural barrier between himself and his environment. The social impulse is instinctive, unconscious, impervious to intellect or logic. To become too aware of it, to seek to manipulate it, is to disrupt it. Gavin Stevens and Isaac McCaslin ponder over their social obligation so intensely that, to a large degree, they destroy their effectiveness as community members. Faulkner's most satisfied, well-adjusted (and least ambitious) characters have no desire, and make no effort, to understand their society or world.

Though the community invests the individual with an identity and enforces rules and laws which protect as well as restrict his freedoms, it does not guarantee him satisfaction. In the end he must rely upon his own resources for support and sustenance, a necessity reflected in structural emphasis on individual character perspectives rather than general community viewpoints. Individual perception, emotion, and experience are the only ways of knowing the world. Reliance on ways of knowing which interfere with individual perceptions can be dangerous. The ideals they establish may so frustrate or oppress that the individual loses his humanity and grows alienated from himself and his neighbors. Such forms of knowing are formalized extensions of what began with one individual's genuine sensibility. But when they interfere with another individual's ability to perceive and respond humanely to the world, they become harmful. Simon McEachern's fundamentalist Protestantism gravely warps Joe Christmas's personality. Sam Fathers was born into his ritualistic worship of nature, the "big woods," but his mystical asceticism proves useless to the problems which Ike McCaslin tries to solve. Cora Tull's piety isolates her from Addie Bundren, whose basic problem is estrangement. Christianity is simply one means by which experience can be coherently organized and explained. For some characters it works quite well. But others use it to renounce individual responsibility, as does Nancy in *Requiem*. She accepts no responsibility for the murder of Temple's child, believing she was forced to commit it, and she expects salvation in heaven. Yet an individual sensibility can merge harmoniously with such a system of knowing as Christianity. Dilsey, of *The Sound and the Fury*, comes close to such a synthesis, though her religious faith leads her to accept suffering and servitude too blindly as a necessary condition.

Faulkner's emphasis on individual sensibility indicates his essential philosophical relativism. He embraces no belief and embraces all beliefs. Absolutes do not exist except as individual characters perceive them. Yet certain innately human values do seem to predominate: the "old universal truths" which he listed in his Nobel Prize acceptance speech, "love and honor and pride and compassion and sacrifice."[5] These qualities make the community vital, enable people to live together in relative harmony. Both major and minor characters embody them: Mrs. Armstid's gift of money to a pregnant stranger, Laverne Shumann's sacrifice of her child, Hagood's paternalistic toleration of the Reporter, the sheriff's kindness to Temple in *Requiem*, Uncle Parsham's simple goodness in *The Reivers*. Such virtues result from the individual's willingness to respond to the demands of living in an imperfect world, to accept the restraints which his society and his own physical existence impose upon him.

One limitation which Faulkner's characters must constantly confront is their inability to know—to discover truth whether it concerns the past, their lives, or simply what makes one of their neighbors tick. In most of the novels narrative structure precludes the possibility of omniscience, either among characters or external narrators. Speculative narrative, character perspectives, and a semi-omniscient external narrator limit knowledge to what characters themselves know, to what an observing individual without suprahuman powers can deduce. The reader must assume the burden of discovering truth, if such discoveries can be made. And Faulkner usually does not provide sufficient evidence to permit the reader to learn much more than the characters. *The Sound and the Fury* views the central figure of Caddy only through the perspectives of her three brothers; the reader knows her only as they know her. The reality of who she really is never emerges. *Absalom, Absalom!* leaves the truth of Bon's racial heritage, of his actual relationship with Sutpen and his real intentions towards Judith, permanently unclear. Even the end of *A Fable* never explains what happened to the corporal's missing body, suggesting only that it might have been interred among the Unknown Soldiers of France. The absence of absolute truth enriches the potential for pluralistic meanings. Narrative structure allows the reader to make what he will of the possible knowledge in each novel, yet it also continually reminds him that truth—whatever it may concern—cannot be known, that life itself is beyond explanation.

By limiting available knowledge to fallible, human perspectives, Faulkner establishes truth as an ideal which lies beyond the limits of human perception. Characters who believe they have discovered truth—Isaac McCaslin and Nancy Mannigoe, for example—invariably delude themselves, mistaking individual perceptions for universal law. They resemble the "grotesques" in Sherwood Anderson's *Winesburg, Ohio*: "It was the truths that made the people grotesques. . . . the moment one of the people took one of the truths to himself, called it his truth, and tried to live by it, he became a grotesque and the truth he embraced became a falsehood."[6] The individual's inability to discover truth drives him back to his own personal vision. Inevitably, characters who lead fulfilling lives rely upon their own sensibilities for sustenance. Strength, endurance, courage come from within. Characters who succeed because of their self-reliance may not always be admirable, nor may they stand among the most memorable inhabitants of Faulkner's world, but they have achieved a stable perspective, a stoic, fatalistic symbiosis with their environments which allows them to survive, to "endure and prevail."[7]

The burden of individuality is heavy. Many characters cannot shoulder it. Yet it is the basis of human identity. Faulkner viewed the individual as a responsible, sentient, and moral creature who must follow his own course in life, making his way as best he can. Characters strive for this ideal by trying to fulfill their community obligations, their responsibilities towards their fellow human beings. Some struggle to overcome their limitations. Others struggle to accept them. But rather than giving up when confronted with inevitable failure, they continue to aspire, realizing that aspiration itself makes life worthwhile. Faulkner defined the modern individual's condition more successfully than any other American writer. He portrayed contemporary men and women driven by a compulsion to find order and meaning in a world animated only by natural laws. Their desire for meaning— for knowledge and truth—is thus potentially tragic. Faulkner's exploitation of this tragic potential is the cornerstone of his success as a narrative artist.

The relativism of truth in the novels also poses a serious dilemma for the reader by presenting several contradictory levels of meaning, each equally significant in literary content and in its place in the overall narrative design. An episode describes a character's experience in a specific way, evoking specific themes and emotional responses. Yet as the reader moves beyond the episode and becomes aware of its place in a

Narrative Perspective: The Self and the World

larger narrative framework, he may feel compelled to reject its initial meanings, though such a rejection may deny the episode's integral worth as literature. Detective critics of *Absalom, Absalom!* tend to devalue the individual character narratives, identifying them as elements in a larger narrative about the illusory nature of truth and the people who try to discover it. Unfortunately, such a devaluation significantly reduces the potential for meaning. On one level *Absalom* presents numerous interpretations of experience; all are valid. On a second level *Absalom* explores the nature of truth. Accepting the meaning of General Compson's story of Sutpen's innocence, or Mr. Compson's tale of Wash Jones, or Quentin and Shreve's narrative of Bon and Henry during the last days of the Civil War in no way nullifies the novel's exploration of time, history, and truth. Embracing the meanings of both levels enriches the novel as a whole, opening up new areas for critical inquiry, new ways to appreciate a great work of literature.

Similar contradictory narrative levels occur in *Go Down, Moses*, especially in "The Old People" and "The Bear." Both chapters detail hunting experiences which profoundly affect Isaac McCaslin's attitude towards the wilderness and his heritage. Under the tutelage of Sam Fathers, he learns the ways of the big woods; for his efforts he is rewarded with a vision of a mystical buck and a primary role in the yearly hunt for Old Ben. The novel derives its unity from the common themes which seemingly unrelated episodes explore. As a result, the reader perceives each chapter as a separate unit. The narration of "The Old People" from Ike's perspective prompts the reader to believe in Ike's vision of the mystical buck. Even the chapter's conclusion, where Edmonds at first appears to doubt the vision and then reveals that he once saw the same buck himself, seems to authenticate the experience. "The Bear," less mystical but equally dramatic, chronicles Ike's education in the ritual of the hunt, the development of his reverence for nature. Both chapters present Ike sympathetically, though in "the Bear" he fails to achieve the goal Sam Fathers set for him—killing Old Ben—and the story's fourth section suggests the difficulties he will have in applying wilderness knowledge to the problems of a civilization. Not until "Delta Autumn," however, does the reader fully realize that the lessons of Ike's childhood and adolescence were essentially meaningless. Yet "Delta Autumn" leads some critics to overemphasize Ike's failure and to devalue the meaning of the hunting episodes. Again, such a view makes *Go Down, Moses* a rather two-dimensional work. On one level, Ike does see the mystical buck; he does learn important knowledge about nature and the woods; and the motives underlying his repudiation of his heritage are well intentioned. On the other level, his inability to respond effectively to the problems of his society, his reliance on anachronistic knowledge taught him by a man who himself was out of place and out of time, causes him to lead a completely ineffectual existence. His piety, his ascetic rejection of his heritage, only preserve the things he hated. In "Delta Autumn" he is a weak, old man, "uncle to half a county and father to no one," unable to give the granddaughter of Tennie's Turl the humanity and understanding she demands.[8] The intersection of these two levels of meaning permeates the novel as a whole, even those chapters where Ike plays no part. Both levels are important to the book's themes—the heritage of racism, the failure of communication between the races, the underlying social rigidity which for so long doomed one race to servitude and dissimulation, the other to inhumanity and guilt. The success of *Go Down, Moses* stems both from the integrity of its separate chapter units, and their place as elements in a larger narrative framework. Contradictory levels of meaning are another way in which Faulkner explores the relativity of truth and human experience, another challenge to which his readers must satisfactorily respond.

Many studies of an individual writer conclude with a tribute to his narrative talent, his philosophical insight, or his understanding of human character. Such a tribute is unnecessary here. I have examined a limited, though significant, aspect of William Faulkner's craft. No investigation of the complexly interwoven elements of his narrative structure, its implications in his fiction, can escape reflecting his genius. Faulkner's refusal to establish authoritative standards of behavior, knowledge, and truth (which he could have supplied through authorial intrusion) forces the reader constantly back to individual and unreliable character perspectives. The reader thus bears the considerable responsibility—one which Faulkner must have consciously intended—of evaluating individual perspectives and determining their thematic significance. What the reader realizes is that there is no discoverable ideal; that the world, along with human nature, is imperfect; that while aspects of it can be rationally explained, other aspects remain forever unknowable. This fact alone explains Faulkner's lifelong interest in time, which limits humankind to mortality and finitude, but which also remains indecipherable to those who try to explain it. Time is another of those ineluctable absolutes penetrating

Narrative Perspective: The Self and the World

Faulkner's fiction, underlying the tension between aspiration and potential. Narrative structure compels the reader to experience Faulkner's world from the same vantage point as his characters. The frustration, confusion, sympathy, and despair which so many readers feel at the end of such novels as *The Sound and the Fury, Light in August, Absalom, Absalom!*, and *The Hamlet* are emotions which characters themselves feel and through which Faulkner evoked the special textures of modern life. The key to his meanings resides in the minds of his characters, and the minds of his characters compose the foundation of his fiction.

Throughout his career Faulkner sought a high degree of privacy. In response to a request that he permit a magazine article on his life, he wrote, "It is my aim, and every effort bent, that the sum and history of my life, which in the same sentence is my obit and epitaph too, shall be them both: He made the books and he died."[9] His human personality, the authorial voice, goes unheard. His physical identity really matters little anyway. But his books do matter. His narrative strategies, consistently employed, demonstrate the desire to reflect not one individual's narrow, didactic views but instead the wealth and significance of human experience. Faulkner's fiction is his composite voice, transformed by art to a lasting, universal reflection of life and human history. He was one of a very few among his contemporaries to insure that his voice as a writer will continue to be heard, that his mortal existence will be remembered. To readers who never met him, who perhaps do not care who he was, the books are his final way of saying: *"Listen stranger; this was myself: this was I."*

Notes

Introduction

1. *Selected Letters of William Faulkner*, ed. Joseph Blotner (New York: Random House, 1978), p. 285.

2. Keats discusses negative capability and his admiration for Shakespeare in the famous letter to his brothers Tom and George, written in December 1817. See *The Letters of John Keats*, ed. Hyder Edward Rollins (Cambridge, Mass.: Harvard University Press, 1958), 1: 191–94.

3. Conrad Aiken, "William Faulkner: The Novel as Form," *Atlantic Monthly* 164 (November 1939): 650–54.

4. James B. Meriwether and Michael Millgate, eds., *Lion in the Garden: Interviews with William Faulkner, 1926–1962* (New York: Random House, 1968), pp. 61, 248, 252.

5. Ibid., pp. 106, 141, 203.

6. Ibid., p. 204.

7. E. M. Forster, *Aspects of the Novel* (1927; reprint ed., New York: Harcourt, Brace and World, 1955), p. 80.

8. Several chapters in *Go Down, Moses*, primarily "Pantaloon in Black" and the title story, have been attacked because they do not fit "traditional" patterns of the episodic novel; two critics who levy such attacks are Walter K. Everett, in *Faulkner's Art and Characters* (Woodbury, N.Y.: Barron's, 1969), p. 26, and Lionel Trilling, in "The McCaslins of Mississippi," review of *Go Down, Moses, Nation*, 30 May 1942, pp. 632–33. Objections to the coda story of Byron Snopes's Indian children in *The Town* employ similar arguments; see Andrew Lytle, "*The Town*: Helen's Last Stand," *Sewanee Review* 65 (Summer 1957): 484, and Edmund Volpe, *A Reader's Guide to William Faulkner* (New York: Farrar, Straus and Giroux, 1964), p. 321; even Cleanth Brooks expresses reservations in *William Faulkner: The Yoknapatawpha Country* (New Haven, Conn.: Yale University Press, 1963), pp. 215–16.

9. Joseph W. Reed, *Faulkner's Narrative* (New Haven, Conn.: Yale University Press, 1973); John T. Irwin, *Doubling and Incest / Repetition and Revenge: A Speculative Reading of Faulkner* (Baltimore: Johns Hopkins University Press, 1975); Arthur F. Kinney, *Faulkner's Narrative Poetics: Style as Vision* (Amherst: University of Massachusetts Press, 1978); Donald M. Kartiganer, *The Fragile Thread: The Meaning of Form in Faulkner's Novels* (Amherst: University of Massachusetts Press, 1979).

Notes

Chapter One

1. *Faulkner in the University: Class Conferences at the University of Virginia, 1957–1958*, ed. Joseph Blotner and Frederick L. Gwynn (1959; New York: Vintage Books, 1966), p. 257.

2. William Faulkner, *The Sound and the Fury* (1929; New York: Random House, 1966), p. 1.

3. Michael Millgate, "William Faulkner: The Problem of Point of View," in *Patterns of Commitment in American Literature*, ed. Marston La France (Toronto: University of Toronto Press, 1967), p. 182; Millgate has written another excellent essay on Faulkner's point of view, "Faulkner and History," in *The South and Faulkner's Yoknapatawpha*, ed. Evans Harrington and Ann J. Abadie (Jackson: University Press of Mississippi, 1977), pp. 23–39.

4. Cleanth Brooks and Robert Penn Warren, *Modern Rhetoric*, 2d ed., (New York: Harcourt, Brace, 1958), p. 259. The Brooks and Warren textbook definition is useful for its clarity, and important for its influence.

5. Wayne C. Booth, *The Rhetoric of Fiction* (Chicago: University of Chicago Press, 1961).

6. Brooks and Warren, *Modern Rhetoric*, p. 160; in *Faulkner's Narrative*, Joseph Reed inadvertently exemplifies the difficulties to which the third-person nomenclature leads. He refers to the source of third-person narrative as an "undesignated narrative presence" (p. 25) or as a "third person narrative presence" (p. 42) and often neglects the external narrator's importance. Nonetheless, his study provides useful insight into Faulkner's narrative structure.

7. Gérard Genette, *Narrative Discourse: An Essay in Method*, trans. Jane E. Lewin (Ithaca, N.Y.: Cornell University Press, 1980), pp. 244–45.

8. Ibid., p. 164. Percy Lubbock's influential *The Craft of Fiction* (1921; New York: Viking, 1957), was one of the first studies to suggest the innate superiority of third-person narrative. Lubbock, of course, was strongly influenced by the prefaces of Henry James to his novels.

9. Genette, *Narrative Discourse*, p. 164.

10. James Joyce, *A Portrait of the Artist as a Young Man* (1916; reprint ed., New York: Viking, 1964), pp. 214–15.

11. William Faulkner, *Mosquitoes* (1927; New York: Liveright, 1951), pp. 144–45; Patrick Samway, S. J., "New Material for Faulkner's *Intruder in the Dust*," in *A Faulkner Miscellany*, ed. James B. Meriwether (Jackson: University Press of Mississippi, 1974), pp. 107–9.

12. In "Faulkner's 'Mississippi,'" *Mississippi Quarterly* 25 (Spring supplement, 1972): 15–23, James B. Meriwether discusses significant differences between the fictional character and factual author of this essay.

13. Faulkner, *Selected Letters*, p. 206.

14. Thomas Wolfe, *Look Homeward, Angel* (1929; New York: Scribner's, 1957); the narrator's first-person references occur on pp. 4, 204, 522.

15. Kinney, *Faulkner's Narrative Poetics*, p. 5.

16. Characterizing Benjy's monologue as "the negation of narrative" and "stasis [rather than 'stream'] of consciousness," André Bleikasten calls Quentin's monologue the "most subtly modulated speech in the novel," with the greatest range in tone, style, and narrative form, "ranging as it does from clear and orderly narrative prose to opaque stream of consciousness, and from Benjy's 'reduced' syntax to Faulkner's rhetorical manner." See *The Most Splendid Failure: Faulkner's "The Sound and the Fury"* (Bloomington: Indiana University Press, 1976), pp. 69, 86, 93.

17. Ilse Dusoir Lind, "Faulkner's Uses of Poetic Drama," in *Faulkner, Modernism, and Film*, ed. Evans Harrington and Ann J. Abadie (Jackson: University Press of Mississippi, 1979), p. 73.

18. Booth (*Rhetoric of Fiction*, pp. 306–7) observes that neither narrator nor author need intrude with a corrective view; Jason's true character is utterly self-apparent.

19. Cf. Introduction, n. 4.

20. Warren Beck, "Faulkner's Point of View," *Faulkner: Essays by Warren Beck* (Madison: University of Wisconsin Press, 1976), p. 6; first published in *College English* 2 (May 1941): 736–49.

21. T. S. Eliot, "The Function of Criticism," in *Selected Essays* (New York: Harcourt, Brace, and World, 1950), pp. 12–22; first published in *Criterion* 2 (October 1923): 31–42.

Chapter Two

1. *Selected Letters*, p. 66.

2. In *William Faulkner: The Yoknapatawpha Country*, Cleanth Brooks provides the seminal discussion of community in this novel; see pp. 47–74, also pp. 10–28.

3. Olga Vickery, *The Novels of William Faulkner* (Baton Rouge: Louisiana State University Press, 1964), p. 66; see also Michael Millgate, *The Achievement of William Faulkner* (New York: Random House, 1966), p. 126.

4. Vickery, *The Novels of William Faulkner*, p. 66.

5. In his excellent dissertation on the novel, Carl Ficken makes a similar observation; see "A Critical and Textual Study of William Faulkner's *Light in August*" (Ph.D. diss., University of South Carolina, 1972), pp. 16–17. In *The Rhetoric of Fiction*, p. 186, Wayne C. Booth discusses conditional narrative in *Light in August*.

6. Sister Kristin Morrison, "Faulkner's Joe Christmas: Character through Voice," *Tennessee Studies in Language and Literature* 2 (Winter 1961): 423, 426; François Pitavy, *Faulkner's "Light in August*," trans. Gillian E. Cook and François Pitavy (Bloomington: Indiana University Press, 1973), p. 67.

7. Both Ficken ("Critical and Textual Study," p. 35) and Morrison ("Faulkner's Joe Christmas," pp. 436–38) note this characteristic pattern.

8. Lecture delivered at the University of South Carolina, October 1976. Bleikasten confirmed his comments in a letter, from which the quotation is taken.

9. Wolfgang Schlepper, in "Knowledge and Experience in Faulkner's *Light in August*," *Jahrbuch für Amerikastudien* (Heidelberg: Carl Winter-Universitatsverlag, 1973), pp. 182–94, analyzes the linguistic and thematic character of these lines and their implications for the novel. Joseph Reed, in *Faulkner's Narrative*, pp. 127–28, offers a translation of the chapter 6 introduction that is similar to my own, along with an excellent discussion of the importance of memory in the portrayal of Christmas.

10. Such a recent critic as Albert Guerard, in *The Triumph of the Novel: Dickens, Dostoevsky, and Faulkner* (New York: Oxford University Press, 1976), p. 55, views Stevens as Faulkner's spokesman, committing the same error as such an early critic as Irene C. Edmonds in "Faulkner and the Black Shadow," in *Southern Renascence: The Literature of the Modern South*, ed. Louis D. Rubin and Robert D. Jacobs (Baltimore: Johns Hopkins University Press, 1953), pp. 196–97. In "Knowledge and Experience" Wolfgang Schlepper employs a linguistic analysis to disprove that Stevens is Faulkner's spokesman. In *Faulkner's "Light in August": A Description and Interpretation of the Revisions* (Charlottesville: University of Virginia Press, 1975), pp. 57–60, Regina K. Fadiman observes that in early versions of the novel Stevens loudly echoed the omniscient narrator of chapter 5, who himself assumed that Christmas has black blood. Despite Stevens's credibility in early versions, the published novel shrouds Christmas's racial character in ambiguity and provides ample evidence to contradict Stevens's theory concerning his behavior on the day he died.

11. A similar case can be argued against stereotyping Lena Grove as a stupid, insensate farm girl. Supporting evidence occurs in chapter 17, section 2, where she weeps before Hightower; chapter 18, section 2, when Brown is brought to her cabin; and chapter 21. Donald Kartiganer's claim in *The Fragile Thread*, p. 59, that she is "barely conscious" is simply unsupportable.

12. Even the townspeople share Christmas's abstract view of Joanna Burden; the few times she is seen from their perspective, they regard her as a "nigger lover," an outlander—but not a woman.

13. The influential Leslie Fiedler mistakenly views Faulkner as a misogynist. In *Love and Death in the American Novel* (New York: Stein and Day, 1966), pp. 320–25, he accuses Faulkner of "dis-ease with sexuality," calling him a "village misogynist swapping yarns with the boys at the bar in order to reveal a truth about women which shocks even himself," a man who believes only in two types of women: earth mothers and whores.

14. Brooks, *William Faulkner: The Yoknapatawpha Country*, pp. 159–60.

15. Some critics have seen Grimm's murder of Christmas as a lynching, a symbolic act of communal revenge, which it is not. Joseph Reed, for instance, suggests that Grimm represents an "abstract ideal" which "everyone

can embrace . . . because of their automatism"; see *Faulkner's Narrative*, p. 134. Cleanth Brooks provides a corrective view in *William Faulkner: The Yoknapatawpha Country*, p. 377.

16. Does Hightower die? At the University of Virginia Faulkner said that "he didn't die" (*Faulkner in the University*, p. 75). Ficken agrees ("Critical and Textual Study," pp. 239–40), noting that Hightower's belief that he is dying cannot be trusted. Yet the narrative makes several significant references to his weak physical condition, especially in chapter 13, section 3, which contains evidence of a heart condition, and at the end of chapter 16, where he appears to faint. In chapter 20, perhaps the exhaustion and the slight head wound resulting from Grimm's pursuit of Christmas into his house cause him to suffer a fatal heart attack. Fadiman, *Faulkner's "Light in August*," pp. 170–71, shows that Faulkner changed Hightower's statement "Maybe I am dying" (on p. 83 of the manuscript) to "I am dying" in the published text (p. 466) to emphasize the certainty of the minister's belief. Narrative evidence for Hightower's death easily outweighs evidence for his survival. Whether he does die is impossible to know, and not really relevant to the novel. His spiritual death, of course, is not in question.

17. Millgate, *The Achievement of William Faulkner*, p. 125.

18. There has been some discussion about Christmas's place in the novel. Ficken sees him as one of four main characters ("Critical and Textual Study," p. 9); Millgate regards him as equal in importance with Lena and Hightower (*The Achievement of William Faulkner*, p. 126). Bruce McElderry, however, in "The Narrative Structure of *Light in August*," *College English* 19 (February 1958): 200–207, pronounces Christmas the main character, an opinion which he says does not deemphasize other characters but instead identifies the novel's structural center. More recently, Donald Kartiganer, *The Fragile Thread*, p. 38, has also identified Christmas as "the center of *Light in August*."

Chapter Three

1. *Faulkner in the University*, p. 36.

2. Richard Pearce, "'Pylon,' 'Awake and Sing!' and the Apocalyptic Imagination of the 30's," *Criticism* 13 (Spring 1971): 131–41.

3. Millgate, *The Achievement of William Faulkner*, pp. 144–45.

4. Irving Howe, *William Faulkner: A Critical Study*, 3d. ed. (Chicago: University of Chicago Press, 1975), p. 217; W. T. Lhamon, Jr., in "*Pylon*: The Ylimaf and New Valois," *Western Humanities Review* 24 (Summer 1970): 276, also comments on the absence of community and suggests that the city, unlike rural regions, lacks a pertinent history.

5. Brooks, *William Faulkner: The Yoknapatawpha Country*, p. 2. According to the *Oxford English Dictionary*, the word *community* derives from the medi-

eval Latin *communis*, "a body of fellows or fellow townsmen" with no implicit sense of the past required.

6. The hissing of wind through palm trees is a static image and a central motif in *The Wild Palms*, where it also symbolizes sterility and emotional numbness.

7. French critics have expressed special interest in communication images in *Pylon*, suggesting that Faulkner employs them to emphasize the role of language in the novel, the concern with characters who try to use and understand it. In this sense, they argue that Faulkner wrote the novel as a means of working out and expressing his frustration over problems he was having with the writing of *Absalom, Absalom!* Although they tend to underrate the integrity of *Pylon* by allying it too closely with *Absalom*, they have written the best criticism on it to date. The three best French essays on *Pylon* are André Bleikasten, "*Pylon:* Ou L'Enfer des signes," *Études anglaises* 24 (July–September 1976): 437–47; Michel Gresset, "Théorème," *Recherches anglaises et américaines* 9 (Summer 1976): 73–94; and François Pitavy, "Le Reporter: Tentation et derision de l'ecriture," *Recherches anglaises et américaines* 9 (Summer 1976): 95–108.

8. Bleikasten, "*Pylon*," p. 444.

9. Bleikasten, "*Pylon*"; Gresset, "Théorème"; Pitavy, "Le Reporter."

10. William Faulkner, *Absalom, Absalom!* (New York: Random House, 1936), p. 173.

11. Joseph McElrath, "*Pylon:* The Portrait of a Lady," *Mississippi Quarterly* 27 (Summer 1974): 277–90; on the other hand, Monique Paul considers Laverne a "lethal woman" whose glance brings death and whose change from male to female clothing in chapter 1 indicates bisexuality. Paul's reading takes little notice of the novel's narrative structure, or of the character perspectives from which Laverne is described; see "Laverne," *Recherches anglaises et américaines* 9 (Summer 1976): 109–23. See also Cleanth Brooks, "The Personality of Laverne," in *William Faulkner: Towards Yoknapatawpha and Beyond* (New Haven, Conn.: Yale University Press, 1978), p. 400.

12. Millgate, in *The Achievement of William Faulkner*, pp. 143–44, compares *Pylon's* chapters to short stories. In a letter to his publisher, Faulkner listed the order in which he submitted the chapters, indicating that he conceived and wrote each one separately from the others, a practice which would naturally lead to a short-story form; see *Selected Letters*, pp. 86–87.

13. In *Faulkner's Narrative Poetics*, pp. 100–101, Arthur Kinney suggests that the Reporter seeks an alter ego, a "secret sharer," among the fliers, but finally "it is Hagood, not Shumann, who we discover has . . . been the reporter's real secret sharer all along. . . . Hagood remains the living double who represents to the reporter his own guilt and short-comings."

14. Pitavy concedes the speculative nature of his theory ("Le Reporter," p. 107). Though Arthur Kinney (*Faulkner's Narrative Poetics*, p. 100) agrees that the Reporter has learned a "love of mankind," he does not suggest that the Reporter produces the Myron, Ohio, episode.

Chapter Four

1. Detective critics currently hold the upper hand in *Absalom* criticism. Two of the more successful Detectives are Elisabeth Muhlenfeld in " 'We have waited long enough': Judith Sutpen and Charles Bon," *Southern Review* 14 (January 1978): 66–80, and James H. Matlack, "The Voices of Time: Narrative Structure in *Absalom, Absalom!*," *Southern Review* NS 15 (Spring 1979): 333–54. Other Detectives are Virginia Hlavsa, "The Vision of the Advocate in *Absalom, Absalom!*," *Novel* 8 (Fall 1974): 51–70; Susan Resneck Parr, "The Fourteenth Image of the Blackbird: Another Look at Truth in *Absalom, Absalom!*," *Arizona Quarterly* 35 (Summer 1979): 153–64; Evan Watkins, "The Fiction of Interpretation: Faulkner's *Absalom, Absalom!*," in *The Critical Act: Criticism and Community* (New Haven, Conn.: Yale University Press, 1978), pp. 188–212; Joseph Reed in *Faulkner's Narrative*; John T. Irwin in *Doubling and Incest*. A successful Impressionist critic is Albert Guerard in *The Triumph of the Novel*. Less successful are Leslie Fiedler, *Love and Death*, pp. 412–14, 470–72; and Melvin Backman, *Faulkner: The Major Years* (Bloomington: Indiana University Press, 1966), pp. 88–112. Recently, an interesting blend of the Detective and Impressionist approaches has given rise to a critical stance which argues that the power of imagination compensates for the failure of the narrators to discover truth. Allan Chavkin suggests accordingly that "Faulkner's celebration of the imagination and its heightened moments of perception is at the heart of this affirmative work"; see "The Imagination as the Alternative to Sutpen's Design," *Arizona Quarterly* 37 (Summer 1981): 117. For a similar view see Thadious M. Davis, " 'Be Sutpen's Hundred': Imaginative Projection of Landscape in *Absalom, Absalom!*," *Southern Literary Journal* 13 (Spring 1981): 3–14.

2. *Faulkner in the University*, pp. 71, 77, 79, 93–94; 273–74; 274, 275.

3. Only a few critics—Cleanth Brooks, Michael Millgate, and Albert Guerard in particular—have been willing to accept both views of the novel. Millgate focuses upon the Sutpen story as well as on the various interpretations of it. He also expresses more interest in the impact of Sutpen's life on the characters than in how accurately they uncover it; see *The Achievement of William Faulkner*, pp. 150–64. Following a similar approach, Brooks considers the nature of Sutpen's ambition along with the narrators' fabrications. He regards both Sutpen and the characters as equally important. In a recent essay, he has even asserted that the basic facts of Sutpen's life do "come clear in the novel and . . . we never come up against a blank wall"; see *William Faulkner: Towards Yoknapatawpha and Beyond*, p. 302. Guerard, *Triumph of the Novel*, emphasizes the conjectural origins of much of the story but also argues that the narrative structure compels the reader to accept speculation as truth (pp. 302–39).

4. William Troy, "The Poetry of Doom," *Nation*, 31 October 1936, pp. 524–25.

5. Cleanth Brooks, "The Poetry of Miss Rosa Canfield [*sic*]," *Shenandoah*

21 (Spring 1970): 196–206. Warren Beck calls translated character narrative the "lyrical encompassment" of a story's meaning: "The justification of all such practices is empirical; imaginative writing must not be judged by its minute correspondences to fact but by its total effect"; see "William Faulkner's Style," in *Faulkner* (Madison: University of Wisconsin Press, 1976), pp. 43–44; first published in *American Prefaces* 6 (Spring 1941): 195–211.

6. Other critics have also noted Quentin's importance. Irwin incorrectly calls him a narrator, but defines him as a focal character: "Quentin is the central narrator, not just because he ends up knowing more of the story than do the other three, but because the other three only function as narrators in relation to Quentin." They talk "either actually or imaginatively, to Quentin," whose "consciousness is the fixed point of view from which the reader *overhears* the various narrators, Quentin included" (*Doubling and Incest*, p. 25). Millgate, Guerard, and Brooks also note Quentin's central role.

7. Hlavsa, "Vision of the Advocate," p. 54.

8. Estella Schoenberg, *Old Tales and Talking: Quentin Compson in William Faulkner's "Absalom, Absalom!" and Related Works* (Jackson: University Press of Mississippi, 1977), pp. 91–92.

9. Brooks, *William Faulkner: Towards Yoknapatawpha and Beyond*, p. 302.

10. *Uncollected Stories of William Faulkner*, ed. Joseph Blotner (New York: Random House, 1979), p. 583.

11. Joseph Blotner, *Faulkner: A Biography* (New York: Random House, 1974), pp. 828–30, 891.

12. *Selected Letters*, pp. 78–79, 84.

13. Guerard, *Triumph of the Novel*, p. 324.

14. Susan Parr, in "Fourteenth Image of the Blackbird," p. 163, supports this view of the external narrator: "The fifth narrator also distinguishes between fact and truth, noting that that which may be paradoxical and inconsistent—and thus not factual—may nevertheless reveal a truth, the truth which 'fit the preconceived.'"

15. Cf. Faulkner's comments on Quentin in a previously cited letter, *Selected Letters*, pp. 78–79.

16. Blotner, *Faulkner*, p. 889.

17. Millgate, *The Achievement of William Faulkner*, p. 164.

18. In "Imagination as Alternative" Allan Chavkin argues that the real theme of *Absalom* is "the renovating power of the imagination with its heightened moments of illumination in a world of suffering and death" (p. 116), and that the novel is thus structured around epiphanies, "*tableaux vivant*" or "spots of time": "meaning is conveyed through a series of timeless images that explode with intense illuminations" (p. 117). Unfortunately, Chavkin does not develop this intriguing idea beyond his demonstration of how epiphanies allow various characters to discover their own racism. Guerard (*Triumph of the Novel*, pp. 314–17) lists a number of tableaux in the novel.

19. John A. Hodgson, in "'Logical Sequence and Continuity': Some Observations on the Typographical and Structural Consistency of *Absalom, Absalom!*," *American Literature* 43 (March 1971): 97–107, proposes that Faulkner uses a system of punctuation and italics to "indicate discontinuities of time (past versus present), mode of expression (speech versus thought), and attention (to internal versus external phenomena; that is, to one's thoughts versus one's senses)" (p. 104). Unfortunately, his system does not work as consistently as he suggests, and it forces him to argue that the chapter 3 narrative occurs out of sequence, that Mr. Compson really gives it after Quentin's trip to Sutpen's Hundred—a contention he can barely support.

20. Muhlenfeld, "'We have waited long enough,'" pp. 73–76. This opinion contrasts markedly with the perceptions of other critics. M. E. Bradford, for instance, in "Brother, Son and Heir: The Structural Focus of *Absalom, Absalom!*," *Sewanee Review* 78 (Winter 1970): 77–78, argues that Bon "*is* his father's son . . . destructive in the extreme"; he "needs killing." Brooks's chapter on *Absalom* in *William Faulkner: The Yoknapatawpha Country* expresses less harshly a similar attitude.

21. William Faulkner, *As I Lay Dying* (1930; New York: Random House, 1964), p. 61.

22. Brooks, "The Poetry of Rosa Canfield [*sic*]," p. 204.

23. *Faulkner in the University*, p. 75.

24. Ibid., p. 77.

25. Brooks, *William Faulkner: The Yoknapatawpha Country*, p. 313.

26. Donald Kartiganer, in *The Fragile Thread*, p. 98, suggests that "Henry and Bon are . . . the incarnations of their creators": "These creations out of the past called 'Henry' and 'Bon,' are now being forced into a new arena, into an identification with Quentin and Shreve . . . , an identification of creator and created that must be the largest understanding of both. . . . Invention becomes a repetition, a reenactment of imagined acts that confers upon them reality." Bon's Negro blood is "the great imaginative leap of the novel." Thomas Daniel Young reflects a typical Detective sentiment when he states that "there is nowhere in the novel convincing evidence that Bon was part Negro"; see "Narration as Creative Act: The Role of Quentin Compson in *Absalom, Absalom!*," in *Faulkner, Modernism, and Film*, ed. Harrington and Abadie, p. 98.

27. An obvious allusion to Edgar Allan Poe's "The Raven" and its melancholic mood; Faulkner told Harold Ober that Quentin's suicide was a factor which influenced his use as the main character of *Absalom* (*Selected Letters*, p. 79). In *Old Tales and Talking,* p. vi, Estella Schoenberg cites a passage from the *Absalom* manuscript mentioning Quentin's suicide.

28. The rapidity with which the fire consumes the house bothers Guerard, but he notes that the whole novel has "prepared us to believe that Sutpen's Hundred is a place where strange, emblematic, mythical, 'impossible' things can happen" (*Triumph of the Novel*, pp. 317–18).

29. For comments on what Quentin might have learned during his meeting with Henry, see Millgate, *The Achievement of William Faulkner*, pp. 323–24n. Brooks has been especially interested in what Quentin might have learned, and how. See his *Absalom* chapter in *William Faulkner: The Yoknapatawpha Country*; pp. 320–25 of *William Faulkner: Towards Yoknapatawpha and Beyond*; and "The Secret of Bon's Parentage," in *The Novels of William Faulkner*, ed. R. G. Collins and Kenneth McRobbie (Winnipeg, Can.: University of Manitoba Press, 1973), pp. 159–83.

30. Schoenberg, *Old Tales and Talking*, p. 135.

31. Reed, *Faulkner's Narrative*, p. 156.

32. *Uncollected Stories*, pp. 707, 709; James B. Meriwether, *The Literary Career of William Faulkner* (Princeton, N.J.: Princeton University Press, 1961), pp. 170, 172.

33. William Faulkner, *The Unvanquished* (1938; New York: Vintage, 1966), pp. 255–56; *Requiem for a Nun* (New York: Random House, 1951), pp. 9, 37–45, 225, 227–28, 237–38, 244 ("The Jail" specifically describes Jefferson's history about the time of Sutpen's arrival there); *The Reivers* (New York: Random House, 1962), p. 20; *Go Down, Moses* (1942; New York: Modern Library, 1955), pp. 191, 255; *The Town* (New York: Random House, 1957), p. 316.

Chapter Five

1. *Selected Letters*, pp. 302–3, 304, 316.

2. Introduction to *Requiem for a Nun: A Play from the Novel by William Faulkner Adapted to the Stage by Ruth Ford* (New York: Random House, 1959), p. iii. Whether Faulkner began the book as a play or as fiction is unclear. Whatever his original intentions, however, what he succeeded in producing is indisputably a novel—narrative fiction which incorporates drama as a narrative method.

3. Noel Polk, *Faulkner's "Requiem for a Nun": A Critical Study* (Bloomington: Indiana University Press, 1981), pp. 19–20. "A Name for the City" was published in *Harper's* 201 (October 1950): pp. 200–14. Polk's study marks the culmination of a dissertation and a series of articles which have argued convincingly for the artistry of *Requiem*. The recent appearance of six essays on the novel in *Recherches anglaises et américaines* 13 (1980): 5–108, as well as the publication of a Vintage edition, attests to the attention which he and such other critics as Panthea Reid Broughton (in "*Requiem for a Nun*: No Part in Rationality," *Southern Review* NS 8 [October 1972]: 749–62), have helped bring to this once almost wholly neglected work.

4. According to Thomas McHaney, the American Guide Series volume on Mississippi was a major influence on this section; Faulkner even went so far as to quote from it: "Faulkner Borrows from the Mississippi Guide," *Mississippi Quarterly* 19 (Summer 1966): 116–20.

5. Noel Polk, "Alec Holston's Lock and the Founding of Jefferson," *Mississippi Quarterly* 24 (Summer 1971): 253.

6. Polk, in *Faulkner's "Requiem for a Nun,"* pp. 21–22, divides the chapter into two parts. The first, ending with the naming of the village, is leisurely paced, "whimsical and ironical, narrated with a gusto and humor, very much in the tall-tale tradition"; it covers the three days between the lock's disappearance and the building of the courthouse. The second part, considerably more serious in tone, moves quickly towards the present in its chronicle of the town's ensuing history.

7. Faulkner's description of the courthouse is reminiscent of Wallace Stevens's poem "Anecdote of the Jar," which describes how the placing of a mere jar, a symbol of civilization, on a hill in the wilderness immediately imposes order upon nature's chaos; see Wallace Stevens *Harmonium* (1931; New York: Knopf, 1947), p. 129.

8. Faulkner's use of drama within the framework of a novel might well have been influenced by chapters 37–40 of Herman Melville's *Moby-Dick*, and by the Nighttown chapter in James Joyce's *Ulysses*—two works with which he was familiar. Polk's *Faulkner's "Requiem for a Nun"* examines the novel's origins, dramatic and otherwise, especially in the appendix, "The Composition of *Requiem for a Nun*," pp. 237–45; Polk presents the same material in somewhat different form in "The Textual History of Faulkner's *Requiem for a Nun*," *Proof: The Yearbook of American Textual and Bibliographical Studies* 4 (1975): 109–28. Joseph Blotner describes Faulkner's movie-writing career in *Faulkner*; full-length treatments of this topic are George Sidney, "Faulkner in Hollywood: A Study of His Career as a Scenarist" (Ph.D. diss., University of New Mexico, 1959), and Bruce F. Kawin, *Faulkner and Film* (New York: Frederick Ungar, 1977).

9. Polk, *Faulkner's "Requiem for a Nun,"* pp. 130–31.

10. Blotner, *Faulkner*, p. 1506.

11. T. S. Eliot, *The Family Reunion* (1939), in *The Complete Plays of T. S. Eliot* (New York: Harcourt, Brace and World, 1967), p. 111. Nancy's definition of hope—"that would have been hoping: the hardest thing of all to break, get rid of, let go of, the last thing of all poor sinning man will turn aloose" (p. 272)—resembles Harry's: "You do not know what hope is, until you have lost it. / You only know what it is not to hope: / You do not know what it is to have hope taken away from you, / Or to fling it away, to join the legion of the hopeless" (p. 79). Similar parallels between the novel and play suggest that Faulkner might have had Eliot's work somewhere in mind while writing *Requiem*.

Chapter Six

1. Meriwether and Millgate, eds., *Lion in the Garden*, pp. 141, 203.

2. Reed, *Faulkner's Narrative*, p. 48.

3. *Intruder in the Dust* (New York: Random House, 1948), pp. 215–17; *William Faulkner: Essays, Speeches, and Public Letters*, ed. James B. Meriwether (New York: Random House, 1965), pp. 86–91, 92–106, 203–4, 221–22.

4. *Faulkner in the University*, pp. 25–26, 72, 40–41.

5. *William Faulkner: Essays, Speeches, and Public Letters*, p. 120.

6. Sherwood Anderson, *Winesburg, Ohio* (1919; New York: Modern Library, 1947), p. 5.

7. *William Faulkner: Essays, Speeches, and Public Letters*, p. 120.

8. *Go Down, Moses*, p. 3.

9. *Selected Letters*, p. 285.

Bibliography

The following is in no sense a comprehensive listing of works relevant to narrative perspective in William Faulkner's fiction, but it does include books and articles which proved specifically useful during the preparation of this study, and which students of Faulkner's methods would also find of value.

Adams, Richard P. *William Faulkner: Myth and Motion*. Princeton, N.J.: Princeton University Press, 1968.

Aiken, Conrad. "William Faulkner: The Novel as Form." *Atlantic Monthly* 164 (November 1939): 650–54.

Backman, Melvin. *Faulkner: The Major Years—A Critical Study*. Bloomington: Indiana University Press, 1966.

Baldanza, Frank. "The Structure of *Light in August*." *Modern Fiction Studies* 13 (Spring 1967): 67–78.

Beck, Warren. *Faulkner: Essays by Warren Beck*. Madison: University of Wisconsin Press, 1976.

———. "Faulkner's Point of View." *College English* 2 (May 1941): 736–49.

———. "William Faulkner's Style." *American Prefaces* 6 (Spring 1941): 195–211.

Bleikasten, André. *The Most Splendid Failure: Faulkner's "The Sound and the Fury."* Bloomington: Indiana University Press, 1976.

———. "*Pylon*: Ou L'Enfer des signes." *Études anglaises* 29 (July–September 1976): 437–47.

Blotner, Joseph. *Faulkner: A Biography*. 2 vols. New York: Random House, 1974.

Booth, Wayne C. *The Rhetoric of Fiction*. Chicago: University of Chicago Press, 1961.

Bradford, M. E. "Brother, Son and Heir: The Structural Focus of *Absalom, Absalom!*" *Sewanee Review* 78 (Winter 1970): 76–98.

Brooks, Cleanth. "Faulkner as Poet." *Southern Literary Journal* 1 (December 1968): 5–19.

———. "The Poetry of Miss Rosa Canfield [*sic*]." *Shenandoah* 21 (Spring 1970): 196–206.

———. "The Secret of Bon's Parentage." In *The Novels of William Faulkner*, edited by R. G. Collins and Kenneth McRobbie. Winnipeg, Can.: University of Manitoba Press, 1973.

———. *William Faulkner: Towards Yoknapatawpha and Beyond*. New Haven, Conn.: Yale University Press, 1978.

———. *William Faulkner: The Yoknapatawpha Country*. New Haven, Conn.: Yale University Press, 1963.

Brooks, Cleanth, and Warren, Robert Penn. *Modern Rhetoric*. 2d ed. New York: Harcourt, Brace, 1958.

Broughton, Panthea Reid. "*Requiem for a Nun*: No Part in Rationality." *Southern Review* NS 8 (October 1972): 749–62.

Chavkin, Allan. "The Imagination as the Alternative to Sutpen's Design." *Arizona Quarterly* 37 (Summer 1981): 116–26.

Davis, Thadious M. "'Be Sutpen's Hundred': Imaginative Projection of Landscape in *Absalom, Absalom!*" *Southern Literary Journal* 13 (Spring 1981): 3–14.

Edmonds, Irene C. "Faulkner and the Black Shadow." In *Southern Renascence: The Literature of the Modern South*, edited by Louis D. Rubin and Robert D. Jacobs. Baltimore: Johns Hopkins University Press, 1953.

Eliot, T. S. "The Function of Criticism." *Criterion* 2 (October 1923): 31–42. Reprinted in his *Selected Essays*. New York: Harcourt, Brace and World, 1960.

———. *The Complete Plays of T. S. Eliot*. New York: Harcourt, Brace and World, 1967.

Everett, Walter K. *Faulkner's Art and Characters*. Woodbury, N.Y.: Barron's, 1969.

Fadiman, Regina K. *Faulkner's "Light in August": A Description and Interpretation of the Revisions*. Charlottesville: University of Virginia Press, 1975.

Faulkner, William. *Absalom, Absalom!* New York: Random House, 1936.

———. *As I Lay Dying*. 1930. New York: Random House, 1964.

———. *Collected Stories of William Faulkner*. New York: Random House, 1950.

———. *A Fable*. New York: Random House, 1954.

———. *Faulkner in the University: Class Conferences at the University of Virginia, 1957–1959*. Edited by Joseph Blotner and Frederick L. Gwynn. New York: Vintage Books, 1966.

———. *Go Down, Moses*. 1942. New York: Modern Library, 1955.

———. *The Hamlet*. New York: Random House, 1940.

———. *Intruder in the Dust*. New York: Random House, 1948.

———. *Light in August*. 1932. New York: Random House, 1967.

———. *Mosquitoes*. 1927. New York: Liveright, 1951.

———. *Pylon*. 1935. New York: Random House, 1965.

———. *The Reivers*. New York: Random House, 1962.

———. *Requiem for a Nun*. New York: Random House, 1951.

———. *Sanctuary*. 1931. New York: Random House, 1962.

———. *Selected Letters of William Faulkner*. Edited by Joseph Blotner. New York: Random House, 1978.

———. *The Sound and the Fury*. 1929. New York: Random House, 1966.

———. *The Town*. New York: Random House, 1957.

———. *Uncollected Stories of William Faulkner*. Edited by Joseph Blotner. New York: Random House, 1979.

———. *The Unvanquished*. 1938. New York: Vintage Books, 1966.

———. *William Faulkner: Essays, Speeches, Public Letters*. Edited by James B. Meriwether. New York: Random House, 1965.

Ficken, Carl. "A Critical and Textual Study of William Faulkner's *Light in August*." Ph.D. dissertation, University of South Carolina, 1972.

Fiedler, Leslie A. *Love and Death in the American Novel*. New York: Stein and Day, 1966.

Forster, E. M. *Aspects of the Novel*. 1927. Reprint. New York: Harcourt, Brace and World, 1955.

Genette, Gérard. *Narrative Discourse: An Essay in Method*. Translated by Jane E. Lewin. Ithaca, N.Y.: Cornell University Press, 1980.

Gresset, Michel. "Théorème." *Recherches anglaises et américaines* 9 (Summer 1976): 73–94.

Guerard, Albert J. *The Triumph of the Novel: Dickens, Dostoevsky, Faulkner*. New York: Oxford University Press, 1976.

Harrington, Evans, and Abadie, Ann J., eds. *Faulkner, Modernism, and Film*. Jackson: University Press of Mississippi, 1979.

————, and Abadie, Ann J., eds. *The South and Faulkner's Yoknapatawpha*. Jackson: University Press of Mississippi, 1977.

Hlavsa, Virginia. "The Vision of the Advocate in *Absalom, Absalom!*" *Novel* 8 (Fall 1974): 51–70.

Hodgson, John A. "'Logical Sequence and Continuity': Some Observations on the Typographical and Structural Consistency of *Absalom, Absalom!*" *American Literature* 43 (March 1971): 97–107.

Howe, Irving. *William Faulkner: A Critical Study*. 3d ed. Chicago: University of Chicago Press, 1975.

Irwin, John T. *Doubling and Incest / Repetition and Revenge: A Speculative Reading of Faulkner*. Baltimore: Johns Hopkins University Press, 1975.

Kartiganer, Donald M. *The Fragile Thread: The Meaning of Form in Faulkner's Novels*. Amherst: University of Massachusetts Press, 1979.

Kawin, Bruce F. *Faulkner and Film*. New York: Frederick Ungar, 1977.

Keats, John. *The Letters of John Keats*. Edited by Hyder Edward Rollins. 2 vols. Cambridge, Mass.: Harvard University Press, 1958.

Kinney, Arthur F. *Faulkner's Narrative Poetics: Style as Vision*. Amherst: University of Massachusetts Press, 1978.

Lhamon, W. T., Jr. "Pylon: The Ylimaf and New Valois." *Western Humanities Review* 24 (Summer 1970): 274–78.

Lind, Ilse Dusoir. "Faulkner's Uses of Poetic Drama." In *Faulkner, Modernism, and Film*. Edited by Evans Harrington and Ann J. Abadie. Jackson: University Press of Mississippi, 1979.

————. "The Design and Meaning of *Abslaom, Absalom!*" *PMLA* 70 (December 1955): 887–912.

Lubbock, Percy. *The Craft of Fiction*. 1921. New York: Viking, 1957.

Lytle, Andrew. "*The Town*: Helen's Last Stand." *Sewanee Review* 65 (Summer 1957): 475–84.

McElderry, Bruce. "The Narrative Structure of *Light in August*." *College English* 19 (February 1958): 200–207.

McElrath, Joseph. "*Pylon*: The Portrait of a Lady." *Mississippi Quarterly* 27 (Summer 1974): 277–90.

McHaney, Thomas. "Faulkner Borrows from the Mississippi Guide." *Mississippi Quarterly* 19 (Summer 1966): 116–20.

Matlack, James H. "The Voices of Time: Narrative Structure in *Absalom, Absalom!*" *Southern Review* NS 15 (Spring 1979): 333–54.

Mayoux, Jean-Jacques. "The Creation of the Real in William Faulkner." *Études anglaises* 5 (February 1952): 25–39. Reprinted in *William Faulkner: Three Decades of Criticism*. Edited by Frederick J. Hoffman and Olga Vickery. Translated by Frederick J. Hoffman. New York: Harcourt, Brace and World, 1963.

Meriwether, James B. *A Faulkner Miscellany*. Jackson: University Press of Mississippi, 1974.

———. "Faulkner's Mississippi." *Mississippi Quarterly* 25 (Spring supplement 1972): 17–23.

———. *The Literary Career of William Faulkner*. Princeton, N.J.: Princeton University Press, 1961.

———, and Millgate, Michael, eds. *Lion in the Garden: Interviews with William Faulkner, 1926–1962*. New York: Random House, 1968.

Millgate, Michael. *The Achievement of William Faulkner*. New York: Random House, 1966.

———. "Faulkner and History." In *The South and Faulkner's Yoknapatawpha*. Edited by Evans Harrington and Ann J. Abadie. Jackson: University Press of Mississippi, 1977.

———. "William Faulkner: The Problem of Point of View." In *Patterns of Commitment in American Literature*. Edited by Marston La France. Toronto: University of Toronto Press, 1967.

Morrison, Sister Kristin. "Faulkner's Joe Christmas: Character through Voice." *Tennessee Studies in Language and Literature* 2 (Winter 1961): 419–43.

Muhlenfeld, Elisabeth. "'We have waited long enough': Judith Sutpen and Charles Bon." *Southern Review* 14 (January 1978): 66–80.

Parr, Susan Resneck. "The Fourteenth Image of the Blackbird: Another Look at Truth in *Absalom, Absalom!*" *Arizona Quarterly* 35 (Summer 1979): 153–64.

Paul, Monique. "Laverne." *Recherches anglaises et américaines* 9 (Summer 1976): 109–23.

Pearce, Richard. "'Pylon,' 'Awake and Sing!' and the Apocalyptic Imagination of the 30's." *Criticism* 13 (Spring 1971): 131–41.

Pitavy, François. *Faulkner's "Light in August."* Translated by Gillian E. Cook and François Pitavy. Bloomington: Indiana University Press, 1973.

———. "Le Reporter: Tentation et derision de l'écriture." *Recherches anglaises et américaines* 9 (Summer 1976): 95–108.

Polk, Noel. "Alec Holston's Lock and the Founding of Jefferson." *Mississippi Quarterly* 24 (Summer 1971): 247–69.

———. "A Critical and Textual Study of William Faulkner's *Requiem for a Nun*." Ph.D. dissertation, University of South Carolina, 1972.

———. *Faulkner's "Requiem for a Nun"; A Critical Study*. Bloomington: Indiana University Press, 1981.

————. "The Textual History of Faulkner's *Requiem for a Nun*." In *Proof: The Yearbook of American Textual and Bibliographical Studies* 4 (1975): 109–28.

Reed, Joseph. *Faulkner's Narrative*. New Haven, Conn.: Yale University Press, 1973.

Samway, Patrick, S. J. "New Material for Faulkner's *Intruder in the Dust*." In *A Faulkner Miscellany*. Edited by James B. Meriwether. Jackson: University Press of Mississippi, 1974.

Schlepper, Wolfgang. "Knowledge and Experience in Faulkner's *Light in August*." *Jahrbuch für Amerikastudien*. Heidelberg: Carl Winter-Universitatsverlag, 1973.

Schoenberg, Estella. *Old Tales and Talking: Quentin Compson in William Faulkner's "Absalom, Absalom!" and Related Works*. Jackson: University Press of Mississippi, 1977.

Sidney, George. "Faulkner in Hollywood: A Study of His Career as a Scenarist." Ph.D. dissertation, University of New Mexico, 1959.

Trilling, Lionel. "The McCaslins of Mississippi." Review of *Go Down, Moses*. *Nation*, 30 May 1942, pp. 632–33.

Troy, William. "The Poetry of Doom." Review of *Absalom, Absalom! Nation*, 31 October 1936, pp. 524–25.

Vickery, Olga. *The Novels of William Faulkner: An Interpretation*. Baton Rouge: Louisiana State University Press, 1964.

Volpe, Edmund. *A Reader's Guide to William Faulkner*. New York: Farrar, Straus and Giroux, 1964.

Waggoner, Hyatt H. *William Faulkner: From Jefferson to the World*. Lexington: University of Kentucky Press, 1966.

Watkins, Evan. "The Fiction of Interpretation: Faulkner's *Absalom, Absalom!*" In *The Critical Act: Criticism and Community*. New Haven: Yale University Press, 1978.

Wilde, Meta Carpenter, and Borsten, Orin. *A Loving Gentleman: The Love Story of William Faulkner and Meta Carpenter*. New York: Simon and Schuster, 1976.

Young, Thomas Daniel. "Narration as Creative Act: The Role of Quentin Compson in *Absalom, Absalom!*" In *Faulkner, Modernism, and Film*. Edited by Evans Harrington and Ann J. Abadie. Jackson: University Press of Mississippi, 1979.

Index